The Conservation Easement Handbook

PRINCIPAL AUTHORS

Janet Diehl, Trust for Public Land
Thomas S. Barrett, Public Resource Foundation

CONTRIBUTORS

Russell L. Brenneman, Murtha, Cullina, Richter & Pinney
Kingsbury Browne, Hill & Barlow
William R. Ginsberg, Hofstra University School of Law
William T. Hutton, University of California Hastings School of Law
Stefan Nagel, National Trust for Historic Preservation
Richard J. Roddewig and Cheryl A. Inghram, Pannell Kerr Forster
Edward Thompson, Jr., American Farmland Trust

COVER PHOTOS
(clockwise from upper left)

This 30,000-square-foot oasis in the heart of Manhattan—Tudor City Park—is doubly protected. The Trust for Public Land holds the easement protecting the park from development, and the underlying fee is held by a local land trust, Tudor City Greens. Photo by Ken Sherman.

The family that owns this 62-acre farm in Pennsylvania has ensured that the land can remain in production by donating an easement to the Lancaster County Agricultural Preserve Board. The board holds easements on 5,000 acres of farmland in the county. Photo by Joel Day.

The Trust for Public Land purchased and transferred to the U.S. Forest Service an easement to protect the scenic and historic values on this 1,781-acre ranch within the Sawtooth National Recreation Area in Idaho. To overcome opposition to the area's protection by owners of local ranches, Congress specified that scenic easements would be the predominant means of land protection in the Sawtooth.

The Conservation Easement Handbook

Managing Land Conservation and Historic Preservation Easement Programs

Janet Diehl
Thomas S. Barrett

Trust for Public Land
San Francisco, California

Land Trust Exchange
Alexandria, Virginia

Printed in the United States of America.

First printing.

For information, address the Land Trust Exchange, 1017 Duke St., Alexandria, Virginia 22314,
(703) 683-7778

Library of Congress Cataloging-in-Publication Data

Diehl, Janet, 1959-
    The conservation easement handbook.

    Bibliography: p. 257
    Includes index.
    1. Land trusts—United States.   2. Nature conservation
—United States.   I. Barrett, Thomas S., 1947-
II. Land Trust Exchange (U.S.)   III. Trust for
Public Land (U.S.)   IV. Title.
KF736.L3D54 1988   346.7304'35   88-11321
ISBN 0-943915-03-1 (pbk.)   347.306435

Editing and production coordination: Katherine Barton and Caroline Pryor
Text and cover design: Judith Barrett
Typography: Chronicle Type & Design
Printing: BookCrafters, Virginia

Contents

Foreword

For the 20 years that I have served as a legal advisor to landowners and nonprofit organizations in the land conservation field, one of the subjects of persistent interest has been the conservation easement. How can we prevent easement violations? Can we ever change the terms of an easement? And always: will this easement qualify as a tax-deductible gift? When several hundred participants at the first national meeting of land trusts in 1985 were asked what tools they needed to improve their land protection efforts, one of their answers was: a handbook on conservation easements.

The challenge was accepted by three nonprofit organizations well suited to the task: the Trust for Public Land, the Land Trust Exchange and the Public Resource Foundation. The Trust for Public Land provided one of their experienced field staff, Janet Diehl, to serve as principal author. The Land Trust Exchange provided overall project direction and served as publisher. The Public Resource Foundation provided the time and expertise of attorney Thomas S. Barrett, a published expert on drafting conservation easements. For special considerations relating to historic preservation easements, these organizations were assisted by the National Trust for Historic Preservation. With the able assistance of a host of expert reviewers and advisors, and contributions from some of the most experienced attorneys in the field, these organizations have provided a blueprint for conservation easement management. More than a how-to-do-it handbook, it is a declaration of land conservation values and what it takes to maintain them.

The handbook will serve many purposes. In addition to providing land trust and public agency personnel with detailed guidance for operating a successful easement program, it will help landowners to understand the technique, attorneys and appraisers to comply with the law, and government officials to perceive, understand, and accommodate competing land use opportunities.

The chapter on criteria for measuring the desirability of a proposed conservation easement should be particularly useful, for it presents in rich detail an overall picture of the many land values for which protection may be sought.

The discussion of the ethical responsibilities of land trusts reflects the author's sensitive awareness that public benefit—the essential underpinning of every easement program—is a broad concept that includes not only conservation values but others, such as the protection of tax revenues.

The handbook colorfully describes the essentially burdensome character of easements in the hands of grantee land trusts and public agencies: an easement extinguishes otherwise valuable development rights that thereafter "lose their golden value and turn into the grantee's muddy monitoring responsibility." An easement accords benefit to the public, but there is an open-ended, ongoing cost to the recipient. Monitoring realities reinforce the view that, for purposes of applying the public support test to determine tax-exempt status, easements have no monetary value.

Since monitoring easements is repetitive and costly, the handbook encourages land trusts to establish endowment funds with cash contributions from easement donors.

A deed of conservation easement is an important contribution of the handbook. Drafted by Mr. Barrett, the easement contains extensive annotations illustrating problems and options. Although boiler-plate language is essential to every conveyance, carefully crafted language also is necessary to reflect the unique circumstances of the particular land and people involved. Mr. Barrett, skilled in land protection law, has provided a wealth of drafting ideas. A historic preservation easement document provides similar assistance to drafters of easements of this type.

The handbook also addresses the difficult problems of amending and terminating easements and the intermediate problem of providing back-up enforcement in the event the original grantee goes out of business. Although rarely thought of as romantic, federal tax law calls for qualified conservation easements that last forever—a bold notion in this summer of 1987, when we celebrate the 200th birthday of the Constitution and the 96th of the oldest land trust in America. Notwithstanding geologists who predict the disappearance of Cape Cod by wave erosion within 2,000 years, local counsel on the Cape prepare easements that dutifully recite the impossible. Notwithstanding history abundant with examples of dramatic land use changes from overgrazing, rising and falling seas, industrial development, population shifts, and pollution, each of the easement documents in the handbook proclaim that the easement shall be "in perpetuity"—as indeed it must if the easement is a gift that is to qualify as a deductible charitable contribution.

Eventually conservationists and tax administrators will have to resolve some thorny issues. If an easement designed to protect the nesting habitat of a rare shore bird prohibits man-made alteration, would an amendment to modify the limitation to permit the construction of a dike to hold back rising seawaters be permissible under the amendatory language? The answer is by no means clear if *perpetual* really means *perpetual*. One suspects that future editions of the handbook will have a lot more to say on these subjects. In the meantime, the handbook takes this food for thought and adds it to the daily menu.

The Conservation Easement Handbook is a thoroughly useful resource— solid information presented in lively prose. The conservation community finally has the tool for which it has been asking.

Kingsbury Browne
Hill & Barlow

Panel of Reviewers

The following individuals generously contributed their time and expertise to review all or various portions of the draft handbook manuscripts. Their thoughtful comments and suggestions have been incorporated in the discussion and have greatly enhanced its accuracy and depth of analysis. Any inaccuracies are the responsibility of the authors.

Hugh Beattie
St. Croix National Scenic Riverway
Wisconsin (retired)

C. Richard Bierce, AIA
National Trust for Historic
Preservation, Washington, D.C.

Russell L. Brenneman
Murtha, Cullina, Richter & Pinney
Hartford

Kingsbury Browne
Hill & Barlow, Boston

Bruce A. Bugbee
Bruce A. Bugbee and Associates
Missoula, Montana

Paula K. Craighead
Preservation Consultant
Portland, Maine

Michael Dennis
The Nature Conservancy
Arlington, Virginia

Gary Everhardt
Blue Ridge Parkway
North Carolina

Ralph W. Benson
Trust for Public Land, San Francisco

William S. Blades
Philadelphia Historic Preservation
Corporation

Warren Lee Brown
National Park Service
Washington, D.C.

Gurdon Buck
Robinson & Cole, Hartford

Thomas A. Coughlin
Boasberg & Norton
Washington, D.C.

Polly Dean
The L'Enfant Trust
Washington, D.C.

Benjamin R. Emory
formerly with
Land Trust Exchange

Jennie Gerard
Trust for Public Land, San Francisco

William R. Ginsberg
Hofstra University School of Law
Hempstead, New York

William T. Hutton
University of California Hastings
School of Law, San Francisco

Tom Kovalicky
Nez Perce National Forest, Idaho

Walter Matia
formerly with
The Nature Conservancy
Arlington, Virginia

Stefan Nagel
National Trust for Historic
Preservation, Washington, D.C.

Art Reese
Wyoming Game and Fish
Department

Richard J. Roddewig
Pannell Kerr Forster, Chicago

Carroll J. Schell
Acadia National Park, Maine

H. William Sellers
Brandywine Conservancy
Chadds Ford, Pennsylvania

Stephen J. Small
Powers & Hall, Boston

Sarah Thorne
Society for the Protection of New
Hampshire Forests, Concord

A. Elizabeth Watson
Pennsylvania Department of
Environmental Resources

Jean Hocker
Land Trust Exchange
Alexandria, Virginia

Bruce Jacobson
Maine Coast Heritage Trust
Northeast Harbor

Nelson J. Lee
Trust for Public Land, San Francisco

Marilyn M. Montgomery
formerly with
Society for the Protection of New
England Antiquities, Boston

Sabin Phelps
The Nature Conservancy
San Francisco

Sandy Rives
Fredericksburg and Spotsylvania
National Military Park, Virginia

Jody Roesler
Maryland Environmental Trust
Annapolis

Thomas M. Schmidt
Western Pennsylvania Conservancy
Pittsburgh

William L. Sigafoos
St. Croix National Scenic Riverway
Wisconsin

Edward Thompson, Jr.
American Farmland Trust
Washington, D.C.

Richard E. Tustian
Montgomery County Planning
Department, Maryland

Acknowledgements

This handbook is a joint publication of the Trust for Public Land and the Land Trust Exchange. The Trust for Public Land developed the handbook outline, wrote Part 1, solicited reviewers' comments, and critiqued the model easement documents and commentaries. Janet Diehl, a project manager with the Trust for Public Land, was the author of Part 1. The Land Trust Exchange provided overall project coordination, critiqued and edited all chapters, and coordinated production of the handbook.

The handbook would not have been possible without the generous contributions of a third organization—the Public Resource Foundation. One of the original proponents of the project, the foundation contributed financial support and, more importantly, the time and expertise of Thomas S. Barrett, a lawyer and secretary of the foundation. Mr. Barrett, author of *The Conservation Easement in California*, researched the state of the art of drafting conservation easements to produce the superb model conservation easement and commentary in Part 3 of the handbook.

A fourth organization—the National Trust for Historic Preservation— also provided important assistance to the project through its assistant general counsel, Stefan Nagel. Mr. Nagel provided relevant sections related to the administration of historic preservation easements in Part 1 and edited and adapted the model historic preservation easement document and commentary, originally produced by Richard J. Roddewig and Cheryl A. Inghram.

Many other people gave generously of their time and experience. Other distinguished attorneys in the easement field contributed essential expertise to the handbook. William R. Ginsberg, a professor at Hofstra University School of Law, discusses the legal issues surrounding the term of conservation easements and their termination. William T. Hutton, an attorney with extensive practical experience with nonprofit organizations and easements, describes how nonprofit organizations can treat easements in calculating public support. Russell L. Brenneman, a pioneer in the land conservation movement in New England, provides a context for considering the model easement documents and commentaries in his introduction to Part 3. Edward Thompson, Jr., general counsel for the American Farmland Trust, details the ins and outs of qualifying farmland easements for income tax exemption.

We also received invaluable help from many other land conservation and historic preservation easement professionals across the country, including the panel of reviewers and, particularly, the many individuals who provided the basic underpinning data and information for much of the book by answering a detailed questionnaire on their easement practices. At the core, this is a handbook for users, by users.

Finally, we are especially grateful for the generous gifts that several individuals and institutions gave in support of this publication. Individuals we wish to thank include: Madelyn and Bruce Glickfeld, Joe and Beth Moore, Charles Page, and Betty Williams, as well as a donor who wishes to remain anonymous.

The California State Coastal Conservancy awarded the Trust for Public Land a grant to write a portion of this book, thereby furthering one of that agency's primary goals: empowering citizens to voluntarily protect coastal natural resources. Grants from the William and Flora Hewlett Foundation and The Pew Charitable Trusts to the Trust for Public Land's land trust program also have provided support to this publication. Also contributing to this project were general support grants to the Land Trust Exchange from the Hewlett Foundation, the David and Lucile Packard Foundation, the American Conservation Association, and the R.K. Mellon Foundation.

Our sincere thanks to all.

Trust for Public Land
Land Trust Exchange

Editor's Note

Throughout the handbook we use the term "grantor" to identify the property owner that is "granting" the easement, which could be accomplished by donation or sale. "Grantee" is the nonprofit organization or public agency that receives a granted easement. The terms "donor" and "donee" are used where the discussion is solely about easements that are charitable gifts and thus are eligible for various tax benefits.

Citations to the federal law governing the deductibility of conservation easement gifts are cited as "I.R.C. § _____ ," which refers to Title 26 of the U.S. Code. Citations to the relevant regulations are shown as "Treas. Reg. § _____ ," which refers to Title 26 of the Code of Federal Regulations.

Many of the sample documents in Part I have been condensed in format. Those wishing to adapt these forms for their own use should add space for filling in information where necessary.

Introduction

Across America, people are using conservation easements to protect natural, scenic, agricultural, and historic lands. Easements have been used in all but four states, by some 500 nonprofit organizations and public agencies.

For almost as long as people have been using easements, they have been saying that someone should write and distribute a comprehensive handbook on how to run a responsible easement program. This handbook, they said, should address the day-to-day questions that nonprofit organizations and government agencies face as they try to meet the special demands that easements put on the holder. A few existing publications tell part of the story, but no one resource describes the state of the art of easement management.

That's why the Trust for Public Land, the Land Trust Exchange, the Public Resource Foundation, and the National Trust for Historic Preservation joined forces to write this handbook. Our subject is easement program management—how to begin an easement program or improve the one you already have.

This handbook is not a history of easements, nor a guide to tax planning through easement donation, nor a menu of the other land-protection tools. Those topics already are ably covered in other publications (many of them listed at the end of this handbook). For a quick review of how easements work, see this handbook's first chapter, entitled "Answers to Common Questions About Easements."

The Best of What's Being Done

The information in this handbook does not come from dusty law tomes; it comes from the people who are making easements work, today. We asked more than 200 easement program administrators to tell us how they handle the demands of holding easements. Forty of the most experienced administrators served as reviewers of this text. They represent diverse experience in easement program administration—from national agencies to local land trusts. We also enlisted two top easement attorneys to draft the handbook's model land conservation and historic preservation easements.

Throughout the handbook, we have made every effort to avoid reinventing the wheel. You'll notice many quotes and direct reprints from various easement-holders' handouts. The point of this handbook is to collect the best of what's being done and make it available in one resource.

The Beauty of Conservation Easements

Conservation easements occupy an appealing niche in the array of land protection techniques—halfway between outright public or nonprofit ownership, at one extreme, and government land-use regulation at the other. Easements are more permanent and often more restrictive than land use regulations, which can shift with the political winds. At the same time, easements are tailored to the protection requirements of the particular property and to the desires of the individual landowner. Easements keep property in private hands and on the tax rolls, and also can carry a lower initial price tag than outright acquisition.

For lands and historic properties where long-term protection is important but where private ownership and management make sense, easements are the right tool. For a 500-acre ranch that's been in the family for generations and lies in the foreground of a national park. For a 200-year-old stone house in the middle of a city's financial district. For the strip of private property that borders a wild and scenic river used by thousands for recreation. For the half-acre community garden in the midst of a senior-citizen housing complex. Their flexibility and their applicability to a wide variety of situations—that is the beauty of conservation easements.

A Note on Nomenclature

For the sake of clarity, the term *conservation easement* is used generically throughout this handbook to include all essentially similar restrictions on land use—historic preservation easements, agricultural preservation easements, scenic easements, open space easements, forever-wild easements, conservation restrictions, restrictive covenants, etc. *Conservation easement,* as used here, should be understood to include all easements granted for a conservation purpose, however else they may be designated in legislation or popular parlance.

No Substitute for a Lawyer

This handbook is no substitute for legal counsel. Every landowner contemplating or engaging in decisions affecting the ownership and use of property should do so only under the guidance of the landowner's own legal counsel. Moreover, the rules of the game are changing and variable. New tax laws are passed, easement-enabling legislation varies from state to state, and a few states have no enabling legislation at all. Only an attorney can keep easement grantors and grantees up to date.

But do not let the legal mazes scare you. Remember, this handbook could not have been written if there weren't hundreds of successful easement programs operating today.

PART 1

Managing a Responsible Easement Program

Janet Diehl

GARY RANDORF

For my friends, Piér and Bill W.,
and for my TPL colleagues

The Adirondack Land Trust is working with New York state's Adirondack Park Agency to protect this 20,000-acre parcel containing scenic views, wetland habitat, productive farmland, a historic village, undeveloped river and lake shoreline, and more. Productive lands will be protected with conservation easements.

CHAPTER 1

Answers to Common Questions About Easements

Note to easement program administrators: You may use these pages to develop your own fact sheets by tailoring the questions and answers to fit your unique program, locale, and audience.

What is a Conservation Easement?

A conservation easement is a legal agreement a property owner makes to restrict the type and amount of development that may take place on his or her property. Each easement's restrictions are tailored to the particular property and to the interests of the individual owner.

To understand the easement concept, think of owning land as holding a bundle of rights. A landowner may sell or give away the whole bundle, or just one or two of those rights. These may include, for example, the right to construct buildings, to subdivide the land, to restrict access, or to harvest timber. To give away certain rights while retaining others, a property owner grants an easement to an appropriate third party.

The specific rights a property owner forgoes when granting a conservation easement are spelled out in each easement document. The owner and the prospective easement holder identify the rights and restrictions on use that are necessary to protect the property—what can and cannot be done to it. The owner then conveys the right to enforce those restrictions to a qualified conservation recipient, such as a public agency, a land trust, or a historic preservation organization.

What is a Historic Preservation Easement? An Agricultural Easement? A Scenic Easement? A Conservation Restriction?

Easements often are called by different names, according to the resource they protect. Easements used to preserve the facade and surroundings of historic structures or historic land areas are called historic preservation easements. When used to preserve an agricultural operation, they are termed agricultural or agricultural preservation easements. When the resources are primarily scenic, easements can bear that name. Another term for a conservation easement is conservation restriction. Whatever they are called, the concept is the same.

Why Grant a Conservation Easement?

People grant conservation easements to protect their land or historic buildings from inappropriate development *while retaining private ownership*. By granting an easement in perpetuity, the owner may be assured that the resource values of his or her property will be protected indefinitely, no matter who the future owners are. Granting an easement can also yield tax savings, as discussed below.

What Kind of Property Can Be Protected by an Easement?

Any property with significant conservation or historic preservation values can be protected by an easement. This includes forests, wetlands, farms and ranches, endangered species habitat, beaches, scenic areas, historic areas, and more. Land conservation and historic preservation professionals can help you evaluate the relative features of your property.

Who Can Grant an Easement? To Whom Can They Grant It?

Any owner of property with conservation or historic resources may grant an easement. If the property belongs to more than one person, all owners must consent to granting an easement. If the property is mortgaged, the owner must obtain an agreement from the lender to subordinate its interests to those of the easement holder so that the easement cannot be extinguished in the event of foreclosure.

If an easement donor wishes to claim tax benefits for the gift, he or she must donate it or sell it for less than fair market value to a public agency or to a conservation or historic preservation organization that qualifies as a public charity under Internal Revenue Code Section 501(c)(3). Most land trusts and historic preservation organizations meet this criterion.

Holding an easement, however, is a great responsibility. A property owner should make sure that the recipient organization has the time and resources to carry out that responsibility. An organization that accepts the donation of an easement typically will ask the owner to make a contribution toward the costs of monitoring the easement in perpetuity or will establish a monitoring fund from other sources.

How Restrictive is an Easement?

An easement restricts development to the degree that is necessary to protect the significant values of that particular property. Sometimes this totally prohibits construction, sometimes it doesn't.

If the goal is to preserve a pristine natural area, for example, an easement may prohibit all construction, as well as activities that would alter the land's present natural condition. If the goal is to protect farm or ranch land, however, an easement may restrict subdivision and development while allowing for structures and activities necessary for and compatible with the agricultural operation. Even the most restrictive easements typically permit landowners to continue traditional uses of the land.

How Long Does an Easement Last?

An easement can be written so that it lasts forever. This is known as a perpetual easement. Where state law allows, an easement may be written for a specified period of years, and this is known as a term easement. Only gifts of perpetual easements, however, can qualify a donor for income and estate tax benefits. Most recipient conservation and historic preservation organizations accept only perpetual easements.

An easement runs with the land—that is, the original owner and all subsequent owners are bound by the restrictions of the easement. The easement is recorded at the county or town records office so that all future owners and lenders will learn about the restrictions when they obtain title reports.

What Are the Grantee's Responsibilities?

The grantee organization or agency is responsible for enforcing the restrictions that the easement document spells out. To do this, the grantee monitors the property on a regular basis, typically once a year. Grantee representatives visit the restricted property, usually accompanied by the owner. They determine whether the property remains in the condition prescribed by the easement and documented at the time of the grant. The grantee maintains written records of the monitoring visits. The visits also keep the grantee and the property owner in touch.

If a monitoring visit reveals that the easement has been violated, the grantee has the legal right to require the owner to correct the violation and restore the property to its condition prior to the violation.

Must an Easement Allow Public Access?

Landowners who grant conservation easements make their own choice about whether to open their property to the public. Some landowners convey certain public access rights, such as allowing fishing or hiking in specified locations or permitting guided tours once a month. Others do not.

If an income tax deduction is to be claimed, however, some types of easements require access. If the easement is given for recreation or educational purposes, public access is required. For scenic easements, much of the property must be visible to the public, but physical access is not necessary. Access generally is not required for easements that protect wildlife or plant habitats or agricultural lands.

For historic preservation easements, either visual or physical access is required, depending on the nature of the property or building to be preserved.

How Can Donating an Easement Reduce a Property Owner's Income Tax?

The donation of a conservation easement is a tax-deductible charitable gift, provided that the easement is perpetual and is donated "exclusively for conservation purposes" to a qualified conservation organization or public agency. Internal Revenue Code Section 170(h) generally defines "conservation purposes" to include the following:

☐ the preservation of land areas for outdoor recreation by, or the education of, the general public

☐ the protection of relatively natural habitats of fish, wildlife, or plants, or similar ecosystems

☐ the preservation of open space—including farmland and forest land—for scenic enjoyment or pursuant to an adopted governmental conservation policy; in either case, such open space preservation must yield a significant public benefit

☐ the preservation of historically important land areas or buildings.

To determine the value of the easement donation, the owner has the property appraised both at its fair market value without the easement restrictions and at its fair market value with the easement restrictions. The difference between these two appraised values is the easement value. Detailed federal regulations govern these appraisals.

An example: A property has an appraised fair market value of $100,000. Mrs. Price, the landowner, donates a conservation easement to a local land trust. The easement restrictions reduce the property's market value to $64,000. Thus, the value of her gift of the easement is $36,000. Assuming the easement meets the conservation purposes test, Mrs. Price—like any donor of appreciated property—is eligible to deduct an amount equal to 30 percent of her adjusted gross income each year for a total of six years, or until the value of the gift has been used up. If Mrs. Price has an annual adjusted gross income of $60,000, she can deduct $18,000 a year (30% x $60,000) until she has used up the $36,000 value. In this case, she will use up the gift in two years (2 x $18,000 = $36,000), if her income does not change.

This is just a simple example. Easement donors may qualify for greater tax savings, especially when state income tax deductions are applicable. Potential easement donors should seek legal counsel.

How Can Granting an Easement Reduce a Property Owner's Estate Tax?

Many heirs to large historic estates and to large tracts of open space—farms and ranches in particular—face monumental estate taxes. Even if the heirs wish to keep their property in the existing condition, the federal estate tax is levied not on the value of the property for its existing use, but on its fair market value, usually the amount a developer or speculator would pay. The resulting estate tax can be so high that the heirs must sell the property to pay the taxes.

A conservation easement, however, often can reduce estate taxes. If the property owner has restricted the property by a perpetual conservation easement before his or her death, the property must be valued in the estate at its restricted value. To the extent that the restricted value is lower than the unrestricted value, the value of the estate will be less, and the estate will thus be subject to a lower estate tax. (Note that if the property owner donates the easement during his or her lifetime, he or she may also realize income tax savings.)

Even if a property owner does not want to restrict the property during his or her lifetime, the owner can still specify in his or her will that a charitable gift of a conservation easement be made to a qualifying organization upon the owner's death. Assuming that the easement is properly structured, the value of the easement gift will be deducted from the estate, reducing the value on which estate taxes are levied. Again, a lower tax results.

Can Granting an Easement Reduce an Owner's Property Tax?

Property tax assessment usually is based on the property's market value, which reflects the property's development potential. If a conservation easement reduces the development potential of the property, it may reduce the level of assessment and the amount of the owner's property taxes.

The actual amount of reduction, if any, depends on many factors. State law and the personal attitudes of local officials and assessors may influence or determine the decision to award property tax relief to easement grantors.

CHAPTER 2

Developing Criteria:

Defining Your Easement Program's Goals

I t's surprising how quickly easement program administrators can get hooked on "desperation acquisition"—that compulsion to acquire protective interests in this or that property the day it becomes available, regardless of whether it really fits into their protection goals. Such eagerness to act is certainly understandable. But if action is not thoroughly examined, it may prove to be irresponsible and end up hurting rather than helping an easement program and the community it serves.

The Importance of Criteria

To run a responsible conservation easement program, you should have written criteria for accepting easements. Both public agencies and private nonprofit organizations are obligated to see that their resource protection programs result in public benefits and that they can carry out their stewardship responsibilities in perpetuity. Public agencies exist to serve the people; by definition, their programs must meet a public need. Private nonprofits face the same standards of public accountability by virtue of their tax-exempt status. Carefully thought-out, written criteria that are based on providing public benefits will assure both public and private agencies that they are accepting only easements that serve the public good and that can be enforced over the long term.

Written criteria for accepting easements also saves time and money. Every easement costs the easement holder money. No organization or agency can afford to acquire protective interests in all of the attractive properties in its area. And certainly none can afford to manage all of these properties forever.

Every easement program administrator needs a relatively quick and reliable method of choosing which properties to protect. Design your criteria well and they should lead you away from those easements that add to your monitoring burden but do not protect a truly significant resource. As Art Reese, chief of

Habitat and Technical Services for the Wyoming Department of Game and Fish, warns:

> An agency always risks the possibility of becoming the overnight owner of the "Surprise Conservation Easement" (SCE). Most wildlife agencies and several private organizations own at least one SCE. SCE's come about as a result of political, legislative, or monetary processes wherein a special interest group, either inside or outside the agency, presses for an acquisition of a specific conservation easement and the agency without long-term objectives cannot with document-able credence say no!

A clearly defined program also will appeal to easement and financial donors. Wouldn't you be most generous if you knew that the recipient organization had planned for the most strategic use of its resources?

Criteria Spring from Goals

Writing a list of criteria may seem arduous. Here's a simple guideline: look to your goals.

Responsible organizations and agencies ask themselves dozens of questions before accepting an easement. This process boils down, however, to four basic questions:

1. Is this the type of property we were formed to protect?
2. Is this an excellent example of that type of property?
3. Is an easement the best protection tool for this property?
4. Can we handle the responsibility of protecting it forever?

A fifth question often comes into play when the easement is a gift: will it qualify for an income tax deduction? Because this question may be important to potential donors, a thorough understanding of the Internal Revenue Service (IRS) regulations governing the deductibility of conservation easements is essential.

But these regulations can also serve another purpose: they can provide a framework from which your program's criteria can be built, even where a tax deduction is not a factor. Both the IRS and easement program administrators invested many months of effort to develop these regulations. Those who have worked with the rules generally consider them workable. For these reasons, even those who buy easements at fair market value, where tax deductibility is irrelevant, may find the IRS regulatory criteria a useful and logical starting point for the development of their own program's criteria.

IRS Tax-Deductibility Criteria

To qualify for a federal income tax deduction, an easement first must be donated in perpetuity. Second, it must be given to a qualified organization such as a land trust or historic society or a public agency. Third, it must be given "exclusively for conservation purposes." Internal Revenue Code Section 170(h)(4)(A) defines conservation purposes as:

i) the preservation of land areas for outdoor recreation by, or the education of, the general public,

ii) the protection of a relatively natural habitat of fish, wildlife, or plants, or similar ecosystem,

iii) the preservation of open space (including farmland and forest land) where such preservation is—

(I) for the scenic enjoyment of the general public, or

(II) pursuant to a clearly delineated Federal, State, or local governmental conservation policy,

and will yield a significant public benefit, or

iv) the preservation of an historically important land area or a certified historic structure.

Thus, the Internal Revenue Code allows tax deductions for donations of easements in five resource categories:

1. public recreation and/or education

2. significant natural habitat

3. scenic enjoyment

4. pursuant to local governmental policy (includes farmland and forest land)

5. historic preservation

This chapter fleshes out the criteria in the Internal Revenue Code and IRS regulations for each of these five broad categories. In addition, it provides examples of the questions program administrators ask themselves in evaluating a potential easement. Finally, it lists resources that can help you judge whether a potential easement fits one of the conservation purposes. Examples of criteria used by several excellent organizations are reprinted at the end of this chapter.

Criteria for an easement program depend on the unique goals of an organization. The following factors drawn from public agency and private non-profit easement programs across the country are intended to serve only as a guide for you to use in developing or refining your specific criteria.

Additional information on the deductibility of easements is covered in chapter 4. For essential detail, including letter rulings and tax court decisions, consult *The Federal Tax Law of Conservation Easements*, by a former IRS attorney, Stephen J. Small, and published by the Land Trust Exchange. Also be sure to consult your attorney.

Resource Category 1
Public Recreation and/or Education

The IRS regulations suggest an easement must meet the following requirements for income tax deduction purposes (see regulations for exact language):

☐ The general public must have the regular opportunity for access to and use of the property. This does not necessarily mean every day, but rather for a substantial number of days per year

and

☐ There must be something about the property that makes the public want to use it: it must either be attractive or contain resources of educational value.

Organizations and agencies also consider:

☐ Does the land have potential to be a part of a community, regional, or state park, or a greenway system?

☐ Is the land valuable to a community as open space due to its proximity to developing areas?

☐ Do facilities such as parking lots and visitor centers exist, or is there potential to build them?

☐ Is the potential number of visitors great, due to service area and population characteristics?

☐ Is the prior use compatible with the resource protection level that the easement would require?

☐ Is most of the land in the area privately owned—thus affording little or no other public recreation?

☐ Is the owner able to make an appropriate contribution to the easement's monitoring fund? (Most grantees ask this question for all types of easements they consider, although few refuse an important easement because a property owner cannot or will not make an additional monetary donation. See chapter 8.)

Resources for determining whether a property fits this resource category include:

☐ Comprehensive outdoor recreation plans (local, regional, statewide, etc.)

☐ Tourism bureaus' visitor-use surveys

☐ Recreation elements of general plans adopted by government agencies

☐ Local comprehensive land-use plans and zoning ordinances.

Resource Category 2
Significant Natural Habitat

The IRS regulations suggest an easement must meet the following requirements for income tax deduction purposes (see regulations for exact language):

☐ The property must be in a relatively natural state

and

☐ Either rare, endangered, or threatened species must be present; or the property must contribute to the ecological viability of a park or other conservation area; or it must otherwise represent a high quality native terrestrial or aquatic ecosystem.

Note: The IRS has the latitude to interpret this broadly or narrowly, so you should document the resource values thoroughly.

Organizations and agencies also consider:

☐ Can the resource be sufficiently protected by an easement or is it necessary to own fee interest? This question must be asked of every easement but it is particularly important when the natural resource is fragile.

☐ Is the property large enough to adequately protect the resource?

☐ Is there potential for acquiring control over adjacent land uses that might otherwise adversely affect the property?

☐ Is the owner able to make an appropriate contribution to the easement's monitoring fund?

Resources for determining whether a property fits this resource category include:

☐ Natural heritage programs operated by the state or The Nature Conservancy

☐ Research prepared by local conservation organizations and educational facilities, especially colleges and universities

☐ Special research publications about rare and endangered species. A good contact is The Nature Conservancy, which is highly experienced in rare and endangered species protection.

☐ Field observations

☐ Professional reports, such as baseline data surveys and environmental impact reports and statements. A professionally prepared report analyzing the ecological characteristics of a property may be worthwhile for donors concerned about IRS evaluation of the easement.

Resource Category 3
Open Space for Scenic Enjoyment

The two open space resource categories derived from I.R.C. § 170(h)(iii)—the preservation of open space for scenic enjoyment (category 3) and pursuant to governmental policy (category 4)—provide the justification for the great majority of conservation easements. These two categories cover farm and forest lands, scenic landscapes, aquifers and floodplains, as well as other lands that local, state, or federal agencies have clearly delineated policies to protect.

Because this subsection is so broad, however, the path along it to IRS acceptance can be thorny. Easement program administrators should be intimately familiar with the IRS criteria for qualifying easements under these two resource categories. A lengthy portion of the regulations covering these categories is reprinted here.

For the purpose of preserving open space for scenic enjoyment, the IRS regulations suggest an easement must meet the following requirements for income tax deduction purposes (see regulations for exact language):

☐ The property must indeed be scenic, as well as easily seen by the public *and*

☐ Protection of the property must yield a significant public benefit.

The entire view across the Potomac River from the front steps of Mount Vernon has been protected against adverse development by scenic easements donated to the National Park Service. Under an agreement with NPS, the easements are monitored by the National Colonial Farm of the Accokeek Foundation.

Regarding what qualifies as "scenic," the regulations state:

> Preservation of land may be for the scenic enjoyment of the general public if development of the property would impair the scenic character of the local rural or urban landscape or would interfere with a scenic panorama that can be enjoyed from a park, nature preserve, road, waterbody, trail, or historic structure or land area, and such area or transportation way is open to, or utilized by, the public. *See* Treas. Reg. § 1.170A-14(d)(4)(ii)(A).

The regulations continue:

> "Scenic enjoyment" will be evaluated by considering all pertinent facts and circumstances germane to the contribution. Regional variations in topography, geology, biology, and cultural and economic conditions require flexibility in the application of this test, but do not lessen the burden on the taxpayer to demonstrate the scenic characteristics of a donation under this paragraph. *See* Treas. Reg. § 1.170A-14(d)(4)(ii)(A).

The regulations state that the following are among the factors to be considered:

  1. The compatibility of the land use with other land in the vicinity;

2. The degree of contrast and variety provided by the visual scene;

3. The openness of the land (which would be a more significant factor in an urban or densely populated setting or in a heavily wooded area);

4. Relief from urban closeness;

5. The harmonious variety of shapes and textures;

6. The degree to which the land use maintains the scale and character of the urban landscape to preserve open space, visual enjoyment, and sunlight for the surrounding area;

7. The consistency of the proposed scenic view with a methodical state scenic identification program, such as a state landscape inventory; and

8. The consistency of the proposed scenic view with a regional or local landscape inventory made pursuant to a sufficiently rigorous review process, especially if the donation is endorsed by an appropriate state or local governmental agency. *See* Treas. Reg. § 1.170A-14(d)(4)(ii)(A).

Regarding the ability of the public to see the easement, the regulations state:

[T]he entire property need not be visible to the public for a donation to qualify under this section, although the public benefit from the donation may be insufficient to qualify for a deduction if only a small portion of the property is visible to the public. *See* Treas. Reg. § 1.170A-14(d)(4)(ii)(B).

Regarding what constitutes a "significant public benefit," the regulations list these factors to consider:

1. The uniqueness of the property to the area;

2. The intensity of land development in the vicinity of the property (both existing development and foreseeable trends of development);

3. The consistency of the proposed open space use with public programs (whether Federal, state, or local) for conservation in the region, including programs for outdoor recreation, irrigation or water supply protection, water quality maintenance or enhancement, flood prevention and control, erosion control, shoreline protection, and protection of land areas included in, or related to, a government approved master plan or land management area;

4. The consistency of the proposed open space use with existing private conservation programs in the area, as evidenced by other land protected by easement or fee ownership by [nonprofit organizations] in close proximity to the property;

5. The likelihood that development of the property would lead to or contribute to degradation of the scenic, natural, or historic character of the area;

6. The opportunity for the general public to use the property or to appreciate its scenic values;

7. The importance of the property in preserving a local or regional landscape or resource that attracts tourism or commerce to the area;

8. The likelihood that the donee will acquire equally desirable and valuable substitute property or property rights;

9. The cost to the donee of enforcing the terms of the conservation restriction;

10. The population density in the area of the property; and

11. The consistency of the proposed open space use with a legislatively mandated program identifying particular parcels of land for future protection. *See* Treas. Reg. § 1.170A-14(d)(4)(iv)(A).

Organizations and agencies also consider:

☐ Does the land contain unique or outstanding physiographic characteristics—such as a large rock outcropping overlooking surrounding countryside?

☐ Is the property of sufficient size that its scenic attributes are likely to remain intact, even if adjacent properties are developed?

☐ Is the owner able to make an appropriate contribution to the easement's monitoring fund?

Resources for determining whether a property fits this resource category include:

☐ Local scenic assessment maps prepared by the National Park Service and Soil Conservation Service

☐ Travel bureau publications (regional, state, and local) and commercially published road maps that designate scenic routes

☐ Books written on the area

☐ Local landscape architects

☐ State departments of the environment or natural resources

☐ Scenic rivers inventories—check to see if your state has conducted an inventory or use the 1982 Nationwide Rivers Inventory conducted by the National Park Service, U.S. Department of the Interior

☐ Statewide landscape inventories (Massachusetts and Oregon are the pioneers in developing this resource)

Resource Category 4
Open Space Pursuant to Governmental Policy
(Includes Farmland and Forest Land)

This category reflects the federal government's recognition of the validity of governmental efforts at all levels to protect open space, as long as there is a clearly delineated policy that states it is in the public's interest to preserve a certain type of property. The question is, exactly how "clearly delineated" does the policy have to be? Like resource category 3, scenic enjoyment, the broadness of this category means that special care is needed to meet IRS requirements. (See the previous discussion.)

The IRS regulations suggest that the following requirements must be met for income tax deduction purposes (see regulations for exact language):

☐ Protection of the property is "pursuant to a clearly delineated federal, state or local governmental conservation policy"

   and

☐ Protection of the property must yield a "significant public benefit."

Regarding what qualifies as a "clearly delineated governmental policy," the regulations state:

> A general declaration of conservation goals by a single official or legislative body is not sufficient. However, a governmental conservation policy need not be a certification program that identifies particular lots or small parcels of individually owned property. This requirement will be met by donations that further a specific, identified conservation project, such as the preservation of land within a state or local landmark district that is locally recognized as being significant to that district; the preservation of a wild or scenic river; the preservation of farmland pursuant to a state program for flood prevention and control; or the protection of the scenic, ecological, or historic character of land that is contiguous to, or an integral part of, the surroundings of existing recreation or conservation sites. *See* Treas. Reg. § 1.170A-14(d)(4)(iii)(A).

The regulations continue:

> A [government] program need not be funded to satisfy this requirement, but the program must receive a significant commitment by the government with respect to the conservation project. For example, a governmental program according preferential tax assessment or preferential zoning for certain property deemed worthy of protection for conservation purposes would constitute a significant commitment by the government. *See* Treas. Reg. § 1.170A-14(d)(4)(iii)(A).

And further:

> Acceptance of an easement by [a public agency] tends to [meet this requirement], although such acceptance, without more, is not sufficient. The more rigorous the review process by the governmental agency, the more the acceptance of the easement tends to establish the requisite clearly delineated governmental policy. *See* Treas. Reg. § 1.170A-14(d)(4)(iii)(B).

Regarding what constitutes a "significant public benefit," see the discussion under resource category 3.

For easements protecting farmland, organizations and agencies also consider:

☐ Is the property in agricultural use, or is it of such productive capability that agricultural use is feasible?

☐ Is the property zoned for agricultural use? Is it within an agricultural district?

☐ Is the property "economically significant agricultural land?" This refers to the productivity of the property, including use, size, soil and water quality, capital investment, condition of improvements, and management.

☐ Is the property of sufficient size that its agricultural integrity is likely to remain intact even if adjacent properties are developed?

☐ Is the property situated such that its conversion to nonagricultural use would adversely affect adjacent or nearby properties in agricultural use?

☐ Is the property adjacent or contiguous to other open farmland or other preserved areas?

☐ Is the owner able to make an appropriate contribution to the easement's monitoring fund?

Resources for determining whether a property fits this resource category include:

To find supportive adopted governmental policies, check:

☐ Government-approved plans on the federal, state, and local levels, including master, comprehensive, conservation, recreation, and open-space plans, and plans for water supply protection, water quality maintenance, flood prevention and flood control, erosion control, and shoreline or riverbank protection.

For agricultural resources, check:

☐ Soil Conservation Service (SCS) county-by-county soil maps, as well as the SCS Land Evaluation and Site Assessment System

☐ State maps of significant lands

☐ American Farmland Trust field offices

☐ Agricultural extension services

☐ Regional conservation plans

Criteria for accepting farmland easements are described in more detail in an article by American Farmland Trust's general counsel, Edward Thompson, Jr., in appendix A at the end of this chapter.

Resource Category 5
Historic Value

Income tax deductions may be granted for two types of historic properties: a "historically important land area" or a "certified historic structure."

The IRS regulations suggest an easement must meet the following requirements for income tax deduction purposes (see regulations for exact language):

☐ A "historically important land area" must be either independently significant or deemed to contribute to a registered historic district or must be adjacent to a property listed individually in the National Register of Historic Places where the physical or environmental features of the land area contribute to the historic or cultural integrity of the National Register property.

☐ A "certified historic structure" must be either individually listed in the National Register of Historic Places or certified by the Secretary of the Interior as contributing to the historic character of the registered historic district in which it is located. A structure must either be certified at the time of the easement gift or become certified by the due date, including extensions, for filing the donor's income tax return for the taxable year in which the contribution was made.

Organizations and agencies also consider:

☐ Is the building and/or site in good condition? Is it capable of being maintained in perpetuity?

☐ Is the property owner willing to rehabilitate the building if it is in poor condition?

☐ Is the proposed renovation of high quality?

☐ Has the property been irreversibly altered? If altered, does it nonetheless contribute to the streetscape (e.g., an open-space courtyard, landscaped areas, shopfronts, unusual scale, materials, or period of construction site)?

☐ Is the owner able to make an appropriate contribution to the easement's monitoring fund?

Resources for determining whether a property fits this resource category include:

☐ The National Register of Historic Places—contact your State Historic Preservation Office

☐ The National Trust for Historic Preservation

☐ Municipal historical commission or department of planning

☐ National Alliance of Preservation Commissions

☐ Local libraries and archives—public and private

Two Special Considerations:
Third-Party Mineral Rights and Mortgaged Property

Responsible organizations and agencies always ask: is an easement the appropriate protection tool? Can an easement indeed protect the resource in perpetuity? These questions become even more significant when someone besides the landowner has a legal interest in the property. This situation arises most typically when the property is mortgaged or when a third party owns the mineral rights.

How can an easement holder be sure that it can protect the resource "in perpetuity" when a third party has the legal right to repossess and/or alter the property? The easement holder is not the only one concerned with this question. In order to preserve the perpetual nature of the conservation purposes of an easement, the IRS has published the following rules in connection with tax-deductible donations of easements.

Mortgaged Property

In order for a donated easement to qualify for an income tax deduction, IRS regulations require that when a landowner contributes mortgaged property to a qualified organization, the mortgagee must subordinate its rights in the property to the qualified organization's right to enforce the conservation purposes of the gift in perpetuity (see chapter 5, Step 6). This rule applies for contributions made after February 13, 1986. *See* Treas. Reg. § 1.170A-14(g)(2).

Third-Party Mineral Rights

Will a donated easement qualify for a tax deduction if a third party owns the mineral rights to the property? There is no simple answer. One complication is that a donor cannot ensure that a third-party owner of the mineral rights will not engage in surface mining on the property. Furthermore, in some areas of the country, particularly the West, mineral rights generally are not owned by the surface owner. Often the federal government owns the mineral rights. Consulting an attorney on this question is essential.

For easement donations made after July 18, 1984, the regulations specify that a deduction will be allowed if:

1. Ownership of the surface estate was separated from ownership of the mineral interests before June 13, 1976, and remains so separated up to and including the time of the gift;

   and

2. The probability of surface mining occurring on the property is "so remote as to be negligible."

The regulations list some factors that may be considered to determine what is "so remote as to be negligible," but they are ambiguous and complex. For an in-depth treatment of this issue, see *The Federal Tax Law of Conservation Easements*.

At least one agency has judged that accepting easements over land where the subsurface rights have been severed is too risky. The Maryland Department of Natural Resources' policy forbids acceptance of agricultural easements over land where a third party holds the rights to minerals, oil, or gas. "Unless the oil and gas lessee agrees to construct only one wellhead and nothing else on each approximately 600 acres, we totally disallow [the acceptance of easements over property subject to] oil and gas leases," says Michael Kenney, staff attorney for Maryland's Department of General Services.

On the other hand, adhering to such a policy would nearly eliminate easement programs in some parts of the West. Recent favorable letter rulings on the deductibility of easements with severed mineral rights prove that it is possible to accept easements on such land. (You can stay current on such letter rulings by subscribing to the "Conservation Tax Program" of the Land Trust Exchange. Back issues are also available.)

State Laws

Individual state statutes are likely to differ from federal regulations and from the laws of other states. Your criteria for accepting easements should reflect the requirements of applicable state statutes. Learn the particularities of your state's laws, so that you can pass them on to potential donors and their counsel—reducing the counsel's workload and the donor's costs.

Purchased vs. Donated Easements: Cost as a Criterion

Although agencies and organizations that buy easements at fair market value rather than accept donations do not have to comply with IRS regulations, their criteria should be similar to those for donated easements, since their programs must still result in a public benefit. The criteria for purchased easements will differ, however, in that cost will also be a factor.

In fact, the criterion that tends to receive the most scrutiny in the case of purchased easements is cost, especially the difference in cost between acquiring the land in fee simple or acquiring an easement. But an easement's lower initial price tag is not necessarily a good reason for favoring an easement over fee acquisition. Warren Brown, an experienced public administrator of easements with the Office of Park Planning and Special Studies of the National Park Service, offers the following line of reasoning:

> Observers of the [National] Park Service's land protection program often want to know at what point is it more "cost-effective" to buy land in fee instead of an easement. This simple question has only one simple answer: it depends.... For both fee and easement acquisitions, there are direct and indirect expenses: costs of purchase, administrative expenses, maintenance of improvements and access, monitoring and enforcement, and payments in lieu of taxes to local governments. ... One clear conclusion is that there is no simple formula to decide if fee or easement is preferable. An easement costing 10% of the estimated fee value may not be a good deal if it fails to protect the resource, or provide for needed public use. An easement that costs 90% of the estimated fee value may be an excellent deal if it protects a historic structure without burdening the government with maintenance responsibilities, keeps the building in use and on the tax rolls, and avoids the need for condemnation.

Several easement program administrators assert that, when long-term costs of monitoring easements are factored in, the acquisition price difference between easement and fee does not amount to much. Wyoming Game and Fish Department's Art Reese says:

Some agencies ignore the reality that easement and land acquisitions have inbred constant and long-term costs and obligations associated with them. . . . The Wyoming Game and Fish Department philosophy is that the acquisition cost is considered to be a one-time "cost of doing business," while the maintenance and monitoring costs are a long-time commitment to the goals and objectives precipitating the acquisition. It is the long-term annual monitoring and maintenance costs that can erode an agency budget.

Easements and Agricultural Preservation

Edward Thompson, Jr.

Farmland is many things to many people. And so it is under the tax code. A farm may be scenic and include relatively natural wildlife habitat. Don't miss any opportunities to qualify farmland easements for tax deductions under these two tests.

First and foremost, however, a farm consists of open land that is particularly well-suited for producing crops or livestock. Regardless of any other conservation purposes it may serve, the principal objective of an agricultural preservation easement is to safeguard the most fundamental characteristic of farmland, its productivity. Where it is not particularly scenic and has no natural wildlife habitat, an easement over farmland must qualify under the tax code's open space test for "clearly delineated governmental policy" and "significant public benefit."

Types of Farmland Preservation Policies

In the past 10 years, many states and local jurisdictions have adopted policies and programs to preserve farmland exclusively because of its importance to food production and the local economy. These are the policies to cite to qualify an agricultural easement under this section of the tax code.

State Policies

State farmland preservation policies may include:

Preferential ad valorem taxation of farmland. This reflects a policy of keeping farms in agricultural use by reducing local property taxes, in order to counter their tendency to promote the "improvement" of farmland for residential and commercial uses.

Agricultural district legislation. Such legislation authorizes agreements between farmland owners and state government, under which land may not be developed for a period of years. In exchange, farmers receive certain benefits, such as preferential taxation and protection against condemnation.

Located between Vancouver and Seattle, Whatcom County—one of the most productive dairy counties in the country—is susceptible to development pressures. The Whatcom County Land Trust is protecting this valuable agricultural land through conservation easements.

Policy legislation or governors' executive orders. These establish a farmland preservation policy that binds state governmental agencies in planning and financing public works projects. The federal government has similar legislation, the Farmland Protection Policy Act of 1981. *See* 7 U.S.C. 4201, *et seq*.

Purchase of development rights legislation. Such legislation authorizes and funds the purchase of conservation easements or "development rights" to keep farmland in agricultural use.

Local Policies

Local farmland preservation policy typically is embodied in planning and zoning. Consult county and town master plans for farmland preservation as a policy objective. Zoning implements the local land use policy. The most common types of true agricultural zoning are:

Large minimum lot size. This restricts residential development by limiting it to parcels of 20 or more acres. Acreage varies with location.

Density-based allocation. This works like large-lot zoning to limit residential development to a low density—one house per 20 acres, for example—but minimum lot size may be as small as one-half acre.

Exclusive agricultural zoning. This excludes all nonagricultural uses in a designated agriculture zone. Nonagricultural uses are encouraged elsewhere in the community.

Conditional use or performance zoning. Residential development permitted only when the land accumulates enough "points" by virtue of availability of public services, such as water and sewerage systems.

Remember that easement contributions on farmland must be "pursuant to" the conservation policy. This means that the farmland in question must be the specific kind of land that the state or local program is aimed at preserving. For example, it is not enough that a county has adopted agricultural zoning if the farmland in question is not located within the agricultural zone designated on the zoning map of the community.

What "Significant Public Benefit" Does Farmland Yield?

Many factors may contribute to a finding that a conservation easement will yield a significant public benefit. In the context of an easement designed to preserve farmland as farmland, the four most relevant factors, discussed below, are:

1. land "capability;"
2. relative size of parcel;
3. stable agricultural infrastructure; and
4. absence of conflict with adjacent nonfarm uses.

Land "Capability"

"Capability" is a term of art among agriculturalists, referring to how well-suited the land is for producing crops or livestock. The most important elements of land capability are the soil—its fertility, depth, slope, and composition—and, especially in semi-arid regions, the availability of water. The Soil Conservation Service has prepared detailed soil maps of most counties that can help you to determine the "capability class" of the soils on a particular farm. Briefly, the classes are defined as follows:

☐ Classes I-II generally are considered "prime farmland," the best in the nation.

☐ Class III generally is very productive and worthy of saving. (Watch for Class IIIe land, however. The suffix "e" stands for erosion-prone, and this kind of land requires special conservation practices to retain its fertility.)

☐ Class IV usually is more steeply sloped, and includes lands particularly well-suited to orchards. Some land in this category is called "unique farmland."

☐ Class V is wetlands, which generally should not be cultivated.

☐ Classes VI-VII are found mostly in the West and are good only for livestock grazing, unless irrigated. They can be considered worthy of saving when cattle production is the major local agricultural enterprise. Irrigable lands in the West are, like prime and unique farmland, at a premium, and should be considered top conservation targets.

Your local SCS conservationist can help interpret soil maps. The SCS also has published maps designating "farmland of statewide and local importance" for some counties; these weigh many factors in addition to capability to pinpoint the most critical farmland in a given area.

The capability of land can be improved through the use of good conservation practices. The presence of terraces, grassed waterways, cultivation on the contour, and other conservation improvements should enhance the public benefit associated with preserving a parcel of farmland. The SCS prepares "conservation plans" for landowners, which can help document improvements.

Relative Size of Parcel

A tract of land must be large enough to be farmed using the methods common in a locality. This does not mean that it must be capable by itself of supporting a self-contained farming operation, but rather that it must be capable of being incorporated into a larger operation. Generally, a parcel should be of at least average size for agricultural holdings in the community, as documented on the local tax map.

Stable Agricultural Infrastructure

Regardless of its fertility or size, a tract of farmland may not be worth preserving for agriculture unless the farmer has convenient access to suppliers of seed, fertilizer, and other inputs necessary to grow crops. Where an adequate infrastructure of businesses catering to farmers does not exist, an easement will in all likelihood preserve open space but not agriculture.

The adequacy of the infrastructure will depend, of course, on the type of farming practiced in a locality. The existence of a good many commercial farms in an area will tend to demonstrate that the infrastructure is stable. If their numbers are rapidly declining, however, suppliers probably will not find it profitable to continue in business for long.

Absence of Conflict with Adjacent Nonfarm Uses

Commercial farming requires a lot of open space, not only to plant crops, but also to mitigate against potential conflict with residential land uses (manure odors, for one). Quite simply, farming is not likely to survive as an enterprise—although it may as a hobby—when hemmed in by subdivisions. There is little public benefit, at least from an agricultural standpoint, in preserving farmland that abuts too many backyards. The land may, however, qualify as scenic or wildlife habitat.

There is confusion about the role of farmland as open space. In an agricultural context, the more open space around a farm, the better are the chances that it will survive as land capable of producing food for the benefit of the public. The IRS implies just the opposite, however. The regulations state that the "intensity of development" in an area is one factor that indicates that preserving farmland serves a public benefit. The implication is that the benefit in preserving farmland as open space becomes greater as open space itself disappears.

A balance must be struck. The public benefit associated with an easement over farmland is maximized when there is sufficient residential or resort development in the general area to make the conversion of the farm a realistic possibility, but not enough in its immediate vicinity to doom farming as a going concern.

As the IRS regulations say, all relevant factors must be weighed in determining "significant public benefit." If a farm is particularly strong in one of the above categories, it could compensate for its weakness in another. This can get complicated. Preserving farmland for agricultural purposes involves careful judgment based on a sophisticated knowledge of farming. Fortunately, this judgment has been exercised in many cases by government officials who have adopted solid farmland preservation policies and have established sensible qualification criteria.

Policy as Indicative of Public Benefit

The IRS regulations governing easement deductibility recognize that adoption of a governmental conservation policy tends to show that a significant public benefit will result from the preservation of a parcel of land that serves that policy. Why else would officials adopt a policy of any kind? "The more specific the governmental policy with respect to the particular site to be protected, the more likely the governmental decision, by itself, will tend to establish the significant public benefit associated with the donation." *See* Treas. Reg. § 1.170A-14(d)(4)(vi).

In the context of agricultural preservation, the policies adopted by state and local governments are often quite specific about the kind of farmland that is intended to be preserved. Criteria for eligibility, whether for state agricultural districts or local agricultural zoning, tend to reflect a careful weighing of the same kind of factors that the IRS lists as indicative of significant public benefit. If the farmland you want to preserve meets state or local criteria, by all means cite these policies as evidence of public benefit.

JACKSON HOLE LAND TRUST

CRITERIA FOR EVALUATING
LAND PROTECTION PROPOSALS

The Jackson Hole Land Trust is organized to "protect the wildlife, scenery and traditional way of life of the extraordinary Jackson Hole Valley through the preservation and wise use of open land."

Because the Trust has been granted appropriate federal tax status, we can offer tax incentives to many people who protect open land. At the same time, we also have a legal and ethical obligation to be sure that our land protection programs result in real public benefits, and that the land protection obligations which the Trust assumes in perpetuity can be carried out. We therefore evaluate every potential project with great care.

Generally, protecting scenic values in Jackson Hole means maintaining the haymeadows, pasture land and undeveloped relatively natural lands that form the foreground for the peaks of the Tetons and other mountain ranges, and that are visible from adjacent federally protected lands. Wildlife conservation requires protection of the habitat and migration routes for Jackson Hole and the Greater Yellowstone Region. Continuation of the ranching way of life involves protecting productive hay and grazing land in sufficiently large blocks to encourage continued agricultural use. Finally, assuring the ability to carry out our obligations means that it must be reasonably likely that the restrictions on future land use will not be unduly difficult to enforce.

A.   Considerations that contribute to significant public benefit of land protection.

Conditions that tend to establish the significant public benefit of protecting a property include those listed below. Sometimes one factor alone is adequate, sometimes a combination is considered. Each proposal is evaluated on its own merits after careful investigation of the property and its resources.

1.   The Property includes important wildlife habitat and/or known wildlife migration routes.

2.   The Property buffers wildlife habitat, so that its protection from dense development would diminish impacts on wildlife from dogs, cars, and concentrations of human activities.

3.   The Property is in active ranching or other agricultural use.

4.   Much of the Property is visible from major highways, from rivers used by the public for recreation, or from public use areas within Grand Teton National Park of the National Forest.

5.   Much of the Property remains in a relatively natural, undisturbed condition.

POST OFFICE BOX 2897   JACKSON   WYOMING   83001   PHONE 307-733-4707

6. The Property shares a boundary with, or is in close proximity to, the Bridger-Teton National Forest, the National Elk Refuge, Grand Teton National Park, a Wyoming Game and Fish elk feedground, or other public preserve.

7. The Property is adjacent to or in close proximity to private land that is already permanently protected or that is likely to be protected in the foreseeable future.

8. The Property is situated such that its development would obstruct or diminish scenic views or would interfere with views across already protected open space.

9. The Property borders or affects the integrity of a significant river, stream, or creek, including those designated as Class I waters by the Wyoming Environmental Quality Council.

10. The Property is of sufficient size that its conservation resources are likely to remain intact, even if adjacent properties are developed.

B. Considerations that may preclude Land Trust involvement.

The following circumstances may lead to the Board's decision not to pursue a proposed project. Such a decision is not a criticism of the proposal, since the Trust believes that almost all open space in Jackson Hole is valuable. Rather, it reflects the Board's conclusion that the proposal does not fall within the specific purposes of the Jackson Hole Land Trust.

1. The Property's values are primarily scenic, but the Property cannot be readily viewed by the general public.

2. The Property is small, and there is little likelihood of adjacent properties being protected.

3. Adjacent properties are being developed in a way that is likely to significantly diminish the conservation values of the Property in question.

4. The landowner insists on provisions in a conservation easement that the Trust believes would seriously diminish the Property's primary conservation values.

5. There is reason to believe that an easement would be unusually difficult to enforce, for example, because of multiple or fractured ownerships, dog control problems, fencing restrictions, irregular configuration, etc.

6. The proposed open space is part of a development proposal which, overall, is likely to have significant adverse impacts on conservation resources and which the Trust cannot therefore endorse.

Triangle Land Conservancy

PO Box 13031 Research Triangle Park, NC 27709

CRITERIA FOR LAND ACQUISITION

To qualify for consideration for acquisition by purchase or donation, a site must be able to be justified as having value in one or more of the following nine (9) categories:

1. Lands that contain endangered, threatened, or rare species or natural communities.

2. Lands that contain, or have the potential to contain, ecosystems of educational or scientific value.

3. Lands of agricultural or forestry significance.

4. Wetlands, floodplains, or other lands necessary for the protection of water quality.

5. Lands of historical value, or adjacent to lands of historical value, and that are necessary for the protection of the items of historical interest.

6. Lands that have potential to be a part of community, regional, or state park or greenway systems.

7. Lands that contain unique or outstanding physiographic characteristics. (Example: A large rock outcropping overlooking surrounding countryside.)

8. Lands that contain exemplary ecosystems or natural features. (Example: Old-growth hardwood forest, migratory waterfowl wintering area.)

9. Land that is valuable to a community as open space due to its proximity to developing areas or its prominent position in how people perceive their community. (Example: Open fields on a major thoroughfare at the entrance to a town.)

Whether a site falls into one or more of the above categories is only the first state of the process in deciding whether the Triangle Land Conservancy will acquire the land. Once it has been determined that the site does qualify in one or more of the above categories, then the Board of Directors must consider the following items:

1. DOES THE SITE HAVE THE POTENTIAL FOR HAVING A SOUND MANAGEMENT PLAN?

Before TLC can accept any piece of property, it must be satisfied that it can properly manage the property. What will be the cost involved? Will there be access problems? What will the land be used for? These are all questions that must be answered and provided for before TLC can accept a piece of property. Each site is different and each site will have different problems. The Board of Directors must make a determination for each site on an individual basis.

2. IS THE SITE LARGE ENOUGH TO BE SIGNIFICANT FOR ITS PURPOSE?

There is no minimum size required for TLC to acquire a site. However, it must be large enough to have a significant impact on the reason it was selected. For example, suppose the site has been qualified as farmland. If it were only one acre in size, it might not be deemed large enough to really make a significant impact. Of course, in considering size, thought must be given as to whether there is potential for adding additional acreage in the future.

3. CAN THE LAND BE ACQUIRED WITH REASONABLE EFFORT IN RELATION TO ITS VALUE OR PURPOSE?

Triangle Land Conservancy has limited resources. While one site may be "more valuable," we cannot spend all our time and effort trying to acquire that site at the expense of other sites that may be more easily obtainable. What ramifications, if any, will it pose for the TLC if acquired? This, of course, is a decision to be made by the Board of Directors on a case-by-case basis.

ADIRONDACK LAND TRUST

PRELIMINARY PROTECTION PRIORITY CRITERIA

CRITERION	PRIORITY
1. Productive Agricultural Soils	
a. 75-100% "prime" soil	critical
b. 25-74% "prime" soil	high
c. over 25% farmland of statewide importance, with less than 25% "prime" soil	moderate
2. Productive Forest Soils	
a. 51-100% "good" soil	high
b. 25-50% "good" soil	moderate
c. all "fair" productivity soil	moderate
3. Key Tracts	
a. critical to wilderness, primitive or canoe areas	critical
b. small tracts surrounded by Forest Preserve (state land)	high
4. Scenic Vistas	
a. fore and middle ground (0-2 miles)	critical
b. background (2-3 miles)	high
5. Travel Corridors Within Adirondack Park	
a. within resource management zone	high
b. within rural use zone	moderate
6. Significant Natural Resource Areas	
a. major wetlands or important habitats	critical
b. undeveloped shoreline	critical
c. deer wintering areas	moderate
7. Agricultural Districts	moderate
8. Wild, Scenic, and Recreational Rivers System	
a. wild or scenic river corridors	critical
b. recreational river or study river corridors	high
c. National inventory rivers	moderate
9. Adirondack Park Legislatively Designated Open Space	
a. rural use	moderate
b. resource management	moderate

[These criteria are described in detail in a handbook published by the Adirondack Land Trust, <u>Developing a Land Conservation Strategy: A Handbook for Land Trusts</u>. Available from the Adirondack Land Trust or the Land Trust Exchange.]

**Society
for the Preservation
of New England
Antiquities**

Harrison Gray Otis House
141 Cambridge Street
Boston, Massachusetts 02114
617 227-3956

GUIDELINES FOR ASSESSING
SIGNIFICANCE OF COMMERCIAL STRUCTURES

Types of Impact

Architectural

1. Remaining example of particular style or period
2. Unique example of particular style or period
3. Work of nationally famous architect
4. Work of major local architect or master builder
5. Building of particular artistic merit
6. Important use of original materials or workmanship
7. Integrity of original design
8. Example of important technological development
9. Designated historic structure (local, state, or national)

Historic

1. Associated with life/activities of major historic person
2. Associated with major group or organization in national, state, or local history
3. Associated with major historic event (cultural, political, economic, social, or military)
4. Associated with past or continuing institution that has contributed substantially to the life of surrounding area

Setting

1. Level of visibility to the public
2. Important element in the character of a city or neighborhood (alone or in conjunction with other structures)
3. Contributes to architectural continuity of streetscape
4. Building(s) located on original site
5. Structure and site subject to encroachment

Economic

1. Existing development pressure on site/environs
2. Projected development pressure on site/environs
3. Building condition
4. Use of investment tax credit for historic buildings
5. Local economic revitalization policies
6. Neighborhood/district use profile

7. Current use/potential changes in use
8. Availability of similar space
9. Form of ownership
10. Imminent change in ownership
11. Sensitivity of building's fabric to environmental conditions
12. Projected means of owner to meet maintenance costs
13. Availability of alternate preservation restriction holder(s)

Level of Impact

Local
State
Regional
National
International

CHAPTER 3

Marketing an Easement Program:

Building Property-Owner and Community Support

The key to selling is simplicity. Easements, however, are extremely complex products. They involve too many conditions and consequences for an administrator to represent granting an easement as simple. Still, there are ways to market an easement program without smothering the public in intimidating detail.

Think About the Landowner's Interests

Whether you are selling easements or encyclopedias, you won't get anywhere unless you remember that people do things for *their* reasons, not yours. The fact that you are charged to protect natural and historic resources may not mean a thing to anyone except you. To make landowners pay attention, you have to tell them what your work can do for them.

The closer you pinpoint the specific benefit your product offers to the individual recipient, the more effective your presentation will be. This handbook gives you a starting point by laying out the main points used to sell easements. But only you can fine-tune your sales pitch to fit your community. Without that fine-tuning, the time and money spent on marketing your easement program will be wasted.

Four Key Selling Points
Easements Provide Permanent Protection

Program administrators can get so involved in describing the technicalities of easements that they forget to emphasize the main reason why people grant them: to protect their property forever. Whether they are moved by altruism, stewardship, a sense of heritage, or a love of the land, property owners who want to hear about easements are people who want to hear about protection. In your easement presentation, be sure to describe the thorough and permanent protection that easements can provide.

Property Remains in Private Ownership

Americans cherish their right to own and control property, and they frequently fight efforts by the government to take that right away. Conservation easements allow landowners to guarantee their property's permanent protection and still hold on to it. The private, voluntary aspect of an easement is a strong selling point. It is, after all, what makes an easement different from any other method of resource protection.

How do various programs market the private aspect of easements? Here are a few examples of clear and concise wording. From a New Hampshire publication:

> If you wish to provide long-term protection for your land *and* retain ownership and control, the conservation easement may be for you. . . . Typically, an easement does not change the way you use your property. You continue to use and enjoy it in ways you always have as long as those uses do not conflict with the terms of the easement.[1]

From a Maine booklet:

> An owner can still use the land and can still sell it. But if the land is sold, it remains subject to the terms of the easement.[2]

And from the Jackson Hole Land Trust's brochure:

> Easements are especially suitable for Jackson Hole, where it is usually desirable to leave protected open land in private ownership and to ensure that agriculture or other active and productive uses can continue.

One of the most popular ways to explain the private ownership aspect of easements is the bundle of sticks analogy:

> A landowner has many rights. Think of these rights as a bundle of sticks. One stick may represent the right to farm the land, another may represent the right to subdivide, a third, the right to hunt wild game.

---

1. Jan W. McClure, *Land Protection & the Tax Advantages for New Hampshire Landowners* (NH Office of State Planning and the Society for the Protection of New Hampshire Forests, 1984).

2. Janet E. Milne, *The Landowner's Options: A Guide to the Voluntary Protection of Land in Maine,* 3rd edition (Maine State Planning Office, The Nature Conservancy, Maine Chapter, Maine Coast Heritage Trust, 1985).

Any of these sticks may be selected individually and sold or given to someone else. A conservation easement identifies those sticks that threaten the long-term protection of the significant resources of the property (rare plant species, water quality, scenic views, etc.). The landowner sells or gives those sticks to a conservation group or government agency that is bound *never* to exercise the rights that they represent. In effect, then, the threatening sticks are removed, and the rest of the sticks stay with the landowner.

When face-to-face with a prospective client, this analogy can be especially effective because you can grab a bunch of pencils and physically act it out.

Easements are Tailored to the Circumstances

After you've described how easements allow landowners to protect their property and still own it, make the point that easements can be tailored to fit their particular needs. Here are some sample explanations. From a Jackson Hole Land Trust brochure:

Each easement is different, tailored to the property in question, the resources to be protected, and the desires of the landowner. The bottom line is that the restrictions must be adequate to protect something of public benefit—a scenic view which the public can enjoy, for example, or significant wildlife habitat.

From a Marin Agricultural Land Trust brochure:

The [land trust's] easement is tailored for the agricultural land uses in Marin County. It describes the permitted uses very broadly to take into account not only the variety of current agricultural uses and practices, but also future changes in economic conditions, agricultural technologies, and in farm and ranch management practices. . . . To the extent that a property or situation is unusual or unique, the easement can be tailored to take that into account.

And from a Lancaster County, Pennsylvania, Agricultural Preservation Board booklet:

[A conservation easement] can be structured to satisfy a landowner's needs and desires; for example, it can allow for the construction of a home when a farmer retires.

Easements Can Yield Tax Benefits

The donation of an easement can yield significant tax benefits for the donor, although how much this factors into a landowner's decision to make the donation is hard to quantify. In a 1985 survey of easement holders by the Land Trust Exchange, easement program administrators ranked tax benefits as the primary incentive for about one-fifth of all conservation easement donors, and the secondary incentive for about half. Donors of historic preservation easements, however, are likely to feel a much stronger draw to tax benefits, probably because the dollar figures are likely to be much higher. (For answers to specific questions that landowners might ask about the tax consequences of granting an easement, see chapter 4.)

In marketing the tax benefits of donated easements, the first rule is to promise nothing. Remember:

Caveat 1: There are no sure bets with the IRS.

Caveat 2: In tax law, as in everything else, change is the only constant.

Do not promise results, just describe the possibilities. Here is a concise example from The L'Enfant Trust of Washington, D.C.:

> A property owner who makes a conservation easement donation to the Trust receives valuable, tangible thanks for that generous act. Thanks to current tax laws, an easement donation may qualify as a charitable contribution, deductible for federal, estate, and gift tax purposes. In addition, there may be local tax benefits. All are government incentives designed to encourage private participation in preservation.

LU RAY PARKER PHOTO, COURTESY OF JACKSON HOLE LAND TRUST

Development pressures in spectacular Jackson Hole threaten the scenic quality of adjacent Grand Teton National Park and have raised property values, making it difficult for families to hold onto their working ranches. More than 3,200 acres of easements held by the Jackson Hole Land Trust protect the scenic and wildlife qualities, while often providing estate tax reductions that allow landowners to keep their ranches in the family.

THE DONEE'S RESPONSIBILITY

How responsible is the donee for seeing that the donor's appraisal and subsequent claim for an income tax deduction are valid? Like all recipients of noncash charitable contributions, easement donees face the temptation to encourage donations by implying that they will cast a blind eye on the appraisal the donor submits to the IRS. "After all," donee representatives could say to themselves, "it's none of our business what they tell the IRS."

Responsible nonprofits and agencies deplore this attitude. It should go without saying that the donee has an ethical obligation to make an honest transaction. That obligation must come across in all of your marketing efforts. Donees might give potential donors a statement similar to this:

> As the recipient, we play no role in determining the value of the easement a landowner donates. It is up to the landowner to justify that value to the IRS for tax purposes. Donors should be aware that their appraisals must meet strict federal standards. We would be happy to discuss these requirements.

Ethics aside, the practical consideration is that donors whose deductions are disallowed by the IRS may get angry at the donee for misrepresenting the ease with which they could expect to claim a deduction for any amount they like. Frustrated donors can get so angry, in fact, that they threaten to sue the donee for misrepresentation. This actually happened to one California land trust—twice. Nothing came of the threatened suits, but the land trust since has made it a policy to attempt to check each appraisal for adherence to federal appraisal standards—and to make it clear that the land trust cannot guarantee that the donor's claimed value will be upheld.

Presentation:
How to Sell the Selling Points

Chances are there is an experienced sales professional on your board of directors or in your community who would be flattered to be asked to help teach you how to promote your easement program. If you can find such help, use it. In the meantime, this chapter will give you the essentials of sales techniques.

There are three basic ways to promote an idea: talk about it, write about it, or show it. Effective marketing combines all three. Given the complex and personal issues that granting an easement involves, however, the most effective marketing technique is the most personal one: talking.

Talk About It

Brochures, newsletters, flyers, newspaper articles, slide shows, and videos are all important parts of an easement program's marketing approach. But the glossiest brochure counts for nothing if the people who put it together can't back it up. It is critical that each person involved in an easement program know how to make each individual landowner comfortable with the idea of an easement over his or her property.

The key is to remember how you felt when you first heard about easements. Before you talk to each new potential easement grantor, remember how foreign the concept once sounded to you. Remember the doubts you had. Are these easements legitimate? If they're so great, why have I never heard of them? Why aren't my neighbors talking about easements? Reviewing your initial questions about easements will help you focus your talk on what your listeners want to hear. Keep the following tips in mind:

Simplify, simplify. Before you start to sell, you should master a two-sentence definition of what an easement is. Write those two sentences down and review them to make sure they're not too technical. Then memorize them, so they flow effortlessly.

Use specific examples. The easement concept is very abstract. To make it as concrete as possible, use names of specific places where easement programs are working. Describe how widespread the use of easements is. (Use the 1985 easement survey by the Land Trust Exchange or contact the Exchange for more current information.)

Sell your program's accomplishments. Mentioning other successful easement programs may be useful, but what counts is what *your* program has done and what people who have participated in it have to say about it. Quote your satisfied customers—after obtaining their permission. If your record is not yet impressive, outline your strategy and its chance for success.

Tailor your approach. Use the circumstances of the people you are addressing to describe how easements might work for them. Discuss the selling points that are most likely to interest those particular people. Mention places and people familiar to them. When using dollar figures to illustrate tax benefits, choose figures that will seem neither intimidating nor insignificant to them.

Encourage questions. Stop often to make sure you are being understood. If you are making a formal address, leave plenty of time for questions.

Listen. Don't ignore potential donors' need to talk one-on-one, even if it's at great length. Remember, you are asking landowners to trust you with one of their most precious assets. They need to know that you are interested in their concerns.

Leave written material. Always have brochures or other public relations pieces on hand—in your briefcase, your car, etc. As you hand a listener a brochure, point out the contact name, address, and phone number.

Seek out and seize speaking opportunities; they're everywhere and they're free. Easements lend themselves to a surprising array of audiences. Agriculturalists, appraisers, architects, attorneys, developers, environmentalists, financial advisors, historians, land-use planners, even broadly focused civic groups such as the Junior League and the Chamber of Commerce—each of these groups could benefit from learning about easements. Find the person in your easement program who has the closest contact with people in these groups and have that person ask to speak at their next regular meeting or at an informal gathering called for the occasion.

Also free, although the competition can be fierce, are public service announcements on local radio and TV stations. This air time is contributed to an organization free of charge as a public service. While the FCC no longer requires stations to provide this free air time, most still do. A good rapport with local radio or TV representatives is essential to gain access to the limited time available. If you are chosen to submit a message, remember that the average listener hears 30 to 40 such messages a day. Make yours different, informative, and directly related to the lives of your audience.

Talk also to your state and federal legislators. Invite them—one at a time—to see your most impressive easement-protected properties. In addition to educating your legislators, such a tour may give you great free publicity and may open channels for future communication.

The one-on-one approach is the most effective. Take advantage of spontaneous opportunities to talk easements with a friend. Follow it up. Seize the opportunity to introduce past donors to potential donors. If you feel uncomfortable discussing "business" such as easements in social situations, remember that easements are not most people's idea of business. Professional marketers strive to attain a peer relationship with their prospective clients. Since you already have that relationship with your friends, you are one step ahead of the game.

Write About It

The first task a new nonprofit typically sets for itself is to print and distribute a brochure or a newsletter. Government agencies, too, try to quickly print handouts to describe a newly launched program. The urgency, of course, is to get the word out.

But more is at stake than written words. Any brochure or newsletter conveys not only the facts, but an image. The image your printed material creates will either attract people to what appears to be a solid program or will leave them with a bad impression that will be difficult to erase.

It is crucial, then, to be aware of the values that your printed promotional pieces communicate. Target your brochures and newsletters to reach the people you want to attract. Resist the temptation to just print anything and get it out. Without careful planning, proofreading, and test-marketing, your printed pieces have little chance of working in a world glutted with advertisements.

Before you draw up your own printed sales piece, take the time to dissect others. Ask several agencies or nonprofits that run easement programs to send you their promotional materials. You can also borrow collections of land trust brochures, newsletters, or annual reports from the Land Trust Exchange.

Take three minutes to look at each brochure or newsletter. Put it down and see what you remember about it. Does it leave you with the answer to the five w's: who, what, where, when, and why, and especially, why you should care?

Then try to analyze what elements in the piece made you feel the way you did. Say, for example, that you got the impression that this was an inexperienced group of people who failed to understand the complexities of property ownership and financial planning. What made you feel that way? Was it because the brochure was photocopied onto flimsy paper? Did the text contain misspellings and grammatical errors? Or did it sound like it was quoting a law textbook, with no understanding of what the words actually mean? Did it fail to give specific examples of what the group aims to do and what it already has accomplished? Were names and figures omitted? Or did the names and figures confuse rather than clarify?

Questions like these can help you isolate what to copy and what to avoid. Look at all advertising you encounter in this light—the subject doesn't have to be easements. Then write a working draft.

Next, proofread and edit. Good spelling and grammar still matter. So does style. Ask a local newspaper reporter to review your draft. If you approach reporters with sensitivity to their time pressures, this strategy can yield two rewards. First, reporters sift through piles of written materials each day. If your brochure looks just as boring as the next, a reporter will tell you so. A reporter can tell you if it's confusing, overwhelming, or poorly written. Second, reporters who are asked for help may develop a personal interest in your cause that could lead to favorable press coverage.

Finally, test-market. The best way to find out if you're getting your message across is to ask—before you print up hundreds of brochures, newsletters, or posters.

Ask people who know nothing about easements to look at the piece you've prepared. Ask a representative of each type of person you want to draw into your easement program—a farmer, developer, financial planner, or whatever. Ask members of your board of directors for appropriate contacts. (If no one on your board of directors knows them, perhaps you should rethink the composition of your board.)

Ask these people what impression they got from the piece about the organization it describes. Ask them:

☐ Who are these people and what are they doing? Why?

☐ Is what they are doing legitimate?

☐ Could it make your community a better place to live?

☐ What kind of people do you think work for this program?

☐ Could they understand you? Do they speak your language?

☐ Would you trust them?

☐ Do they have anything to offer that you want?

☐ Does it look easy to get in touch with them?

☐ What might happen if you called them or went to see them?

☐ Would you be doing something that other people have done?

The more specific answers you can get to these questions, the better you can adjust your words and pictures to attract your target.

Once you have zeroed in on your readers' values, go ahead and print. Use as high quality material as you can possibly afford. This does not necessarily mean glossy. Consider the tastes of your audience.

Producing Effective Brochures and Newsletters

Effective brochures and newsletters contain certain standard ingredients. They include:

Plenty of pictures. Whether they are glossy color photographs or pen-and-ink line drawings, pictures are crucial for keeping your readers awake. Choose scenes your readers will recognize.

Questions and answers. This is a good technique for conveying many rather dry facts in a lively format. Here are some good questions from a brochure published by the San Luis Obispo Land Conservancy in California when it was just a few months old:

Q. Who is the San Luis Obispo Land Conservancy?
Q. Why is it being organized now?
Q. What will it do for me? For my family? For my community?
Q. Where can I find out more about this organization?

Directors and advisors. One of a private nonprofit's top selling points is that its board of directors and/or advisory council includes some of the most respected names in town. List those names on your brochures, newsletters, program stationery, anything appropriate. If space allows and if it will reflect your board's diversity to your advantage, list the directors' occupations and home towns.

People, people, people. People do not want to read about organizations; they want to read about themselves. As second choice, they'll read about their neighbors. A newsletter is the ideal place to relate what your easement program does for the people who participate in it.

Write donor profiles on the intriguing aspects of your donors' lives. Include photographs. Take extra caution with articles about people, however. Some people do not want publicity. Be sure to secure their permission in advance. In addition, have someone outside of the program, or the subjects themselves, review those articles to make sure the tone is not offensive. If you publish an article that rubs its subject the wrong way, you will lose the support you were hoping to cement.

Also include photos and profiles of the program's staff or directors. Putting faces behind the work you're doing with easements makes you more approachable.

Many nonprofits solicit donated services from local designers and printers. Such financial savings, of course, are welcome. Be aware, however, that donated work can be put at the bottom of a printer's pile, and sometimes is done in haste. You may, indeed, get what you pay for.

One way that a Washington state land trust on a very low budget put some gloss into its newsletter was by inserting the Land Trust Exchange's four-page color spread on easements. You also could use these brochures as a folder for an easement fact sheet. They are available from the Exchange at a low cost.

Easement holders publish more than general brochures and newsletters. The more closely the piece focuses on the particular target audience, the more effective it is. Here are some ways that easement promoters have focused their printed materials:

Specialized brochures. Besides a general brochure that gives an overview of the easement program, many easement program promoters publish specialized brochures. Particular audiences for these pieces include: landowners considering donating easements; farmers and ranchers who have the opportunity to sell easements as part of a state or local program; attorneys, financial advisors, and estate planners; real estate appraisers; and architects and architectural historians.

Technical reports. Several easement promoters give people news about what they're already interested in, and incidentally mention how easements relate to these interests. The Maine Coast Heritage Trust, for example, printed a technical report on island forestry; the Marin Agricultural Land Trust sends technical reports on various agricultural issues to all of the county's ranchers and farmers.

Annual reports. Properly designed and written, annual reports can lend an easement program great solidity. The report shows that, year after year, this program accomplishes things. Annual reports usually start with a general message from the program's president or director on the program's accomplishments over the past year and goals for the next year. Then they include a description of each significant accomplishment, as well as highlights on volunteer and staff contributions and on major benefactors: individuals, corporations, and foundations. At the end, they include a summary of the program's audit or some other report on its financial status.

Letters to the editor. Don't ignore this free space. Don't abuse it, either. Occasional, articulate letters to the editor about issues that relate to land conservation and historic preservation (and, therefore, to easements) are a good way to establish your easement program's reputation as being in touch with community concerns.

News releases. Like letters to the editor, news releases can be invaluable sources of free public relations. Nothing gives an easement program more legitimacy than a favorable news article about its accomplishments. Remember, though, that an easement program's news release must really contain news—it must cover a concrete and significant event. Again, make sure that

News Release Pointers

1. Prepare the release so it is easily usable: type triple-spaced and use wide margins; list a contact person and phone number at the top of each page.

2. Work with local media to determine their format and timing preferences. Phone the newspaper or radio station ahead of time and ask who will handle the story. Talk to that person, and follow-up by sending him or her a press release.

3. Send the release to the particular reporter you've been working with, not to "Editor."

4. Present briefly all crucial information in the release—who, what, where, when, and why.

5. Quote prominent supporters, local government officials, and/or your directors in the text of the release.

6. Time a release far enough in advance of an event so there is time for follow-up questions, but not so early that the event is forgotten.

the people described in your news release do not object to publicity. (See box for additional pointers.)

Self-guided tour books. Organizations holding easements over several properties that allow either physical or visual access often print maps and self-guided tours so that the public can see the program's accomplishments. This works especially well in cities, where the properties often are within walking distance of each other.

The L'Enfant Trust, for example, publishes an inexpensive booklet entitled "Walker's Tour of Dupont Circle." The trust promotes this self-guided tour as allowing the walker to discover the architectural history of "many prominent historic buildings . . . peek into the lives of their original owners . . . and uncover fascinating tidbits about the buildings' survival over the years." You may want to distribute inexpensive maps showing your program's accomplishments at local tourism centers, chambers of commerce or city halls, libraries, bookstores, or even popular cafes and coffee shops.

Quizzes. People like to test their knowledge about things they think they know. The Napa County Land Trust distributes a flyer inviting the reader to "Test your knowledge about protected scenic, wildlife, historical, and watershed places in Napa County." The answers to the 10 test questions, of course, point to the land trust's work. At the bottom of the sheet, the land trust lists a report card recommending certain actions for certain test scores. For 10 correct, "You must be a long-time contributor and supporter of the Napa County Land Trust. This is our request for your membership renewal." For four or fewer correct, "You are a person who values special places, but hasn't heard about how to protect them. Join us today. . . ."

Handwritten notes. Don't forget the power of a handwritten note. Your program's supporters deserve to be individually thanked. Use personal letters, perhaps written by hand.

Winding down San Francisco's renowned Telegraph Hill, the Grace Marchant Garden harbors more than 100 species of plants, many of them exotic. Local citizens and the Trust for Public Land raised the funds to purchase an easement to protect the garden in response to threatened development. The city of San Francisco now holds the easement.

D. HOFFMAN

Show it in Pictures

Suddenly the whole world seems available on video. Why not easements?

The Sonoma Land Trust produced a "Land Trust in a Box" video show that depicts landowner-donors talking about what they have given and how much it means to them. The 12-minute show cost $6,000 to produce, and a subsequent foundation donation covered most of the expense. Land trust board members take this show to local meetings and into their friends' living rooms. Donors of more than $100 to the land trust are offered copies of the videos so that they, too, can promote the land trust's work.

Those who do not want to make their own videos can rent or buy one from the Land Trust Exchange. "For the Common Good: Preserving Private Lands with Conservation Easements," a 16-minute documentary on the public benefits being achieved with conservation easements, is available in 16mm film and on videocassettes in VHS, Beta, and ¾" formats. "For the Common Good" tells several easement success stories, and makes good viewing for public officials and landowners interested in land conservation.

Slide shows, with taped or live narration, are still an excellent way to get a message across visually. Photography exhibits, too, are extremely effective ways to sell people on the urgency of protecting the landscape. A gorgeous photograph of a trumpeter swan gliding on a glass-still lake is indeed worth a thousand exhortatory words about the need to protect that lake.

Local banks, libraries, cafes, and other public places seek interesting photos to put on their walls. Include a paragraph under each photo about how easements protect that resource and how the viewer can learn more. Or sponsor a photo contest with a subject that relates to your work with easements, and publicize and display the results.

Actions Speak Louder than Words

This chapter just touches on the many ways to market an easement program. Marking easement donors' doorways with bronze plaques, sponsoring a fishing contest in an easement-protected pond, holding an "open-space race" through easement-protected lands—the ideas are as varied as the people behind each program.

When all is said and done, however, actions speak louder than words. The best way to get noticed is to do something worth noticing!

CHAPTER
4

Tax Benefits:
Discussing Deductions with Property Owners

Mention tax benefits and most donors will think of income taxes. On reflection, their interest also may be piqued by the chance to reduce their estate, property, and gift taxes. Certain farmers, ranchers, and other land-rich-but-cash-poor property owners may be especially drawn to the chance of reducing estate taxes. Easement program administrators should be able to discuss all types of potential tax benefits with a familiarity that makes their listeners comfortable.

Explaining Income Tax Deductions

When telling property owners how donating an easement might lower their federal, and often state, income tax, here are essential points to convey:

Less than Fair Market Value. The easement must be donated or sold for less than fair market value.

Perpetuity. It must be granted in perpetuity.

Qualified Conservation Organization. The easement must be granted to a qualified conservation organization—such as a land trust or historic preservation organization—or a public agency charged with overseeing land conservation or historic programs.

Conservation Purposes. It must be granted exclusively for conservation purposes, as described in chapter 2.

Amount of Deduction. The amount a property owner can deduct for a donated easement generally equals the reduction in the property's value due to the easement—the difference between the property's value before the easement is granted and after the easement's restrictions take effect.

Appraisals. The appraisal that determines the easement value must meet strict standards set by the IRS.

Limits on Deductions. Taxpayers cannot eliminate all of their taxable income by making charitable donations, no matter how big the donation. In general, the deduction for charitable donations of appreciated property cannot exceed 30 percent of the taxpayer's adjusted gross income, although any excess amount may be carried forward and deducted over the five succeeding years.

The taxpayer can elect to deduct 50 percent of adjusted gross income, but in that case, the value of the gift must be reduced.

Alternative Minimum Tax. Under some circumstances, the donor may be subject to the alternative minimum tax (AMT), an alternate income tax required of taxpayers whose deductions and tax shelters might otherwise eliminate or vastly reduce their tax obligation. Under the alternative minimum tax, the allowable deduction for a donation of appreciated property may be limited to the taxpayer's cost basis in the property, rather than its full fair market value. For an easement, the deduction would be a proportional share of the cost basis— that is, the same proportion that the easement value bears to the unrestricted property value. Advise potential donors to consult an accountant or tax lawyer to determine whether the alternative minimum tax will apply.

These two Maryland landowners donated a perpetual conservation easement on their property in Garrett County to the quasi-governmental Maryland Environmental Trust. The entire property is bequeathed to the trust in the landowners' wills.

Need for Professional Counsel. Each donor's tax situation is unique. *Donees should never say that a donation will be deductible.* Instead, insist that each donor seek professional counsel, particularly if they may fall under the Alternative Minimum Tax.

Tax issues require a much more thorough treatment than this chapter can give. For a detailed treatment of easements and taxes, refer to Stephen J. Small's *The Federal Tax Law of Conservation Easements*, available from the Land Trust Exchange. What follows is the bare minimum that all representatives of easement programs should know in order to discuss easements effectively.

How Much of a Deduction Can Donors Expect?

Easement donees must be frank with potential donors about this question. You simply cannot know the answer for sure, and you must not suggest otherwise. You can, however, present a range of values that past donors have derived.

Each easement donation is different. In general, the biggest tax deductions arise from historic preservation easements donated over historic commercial property and from conservation easements donated over large tracts of open space in areas where development pressures are intense. The deduction depends on how much potential value the easement precludes. For example, the donor of an easement over a two-story historic landmark building surrounded by high-rise office complexes forgoes the huge potential profit of building another high-rise. As a result, that easement is worth a great deal of money and may qualify the donor for significant income tax deductions. The donor of an easement over 50 acres of remote farmland may not forgo so much potential value; therefore that income tax deduction may be relatively small.

What Requirements Must an Easement Appraisal Meet?

A book could be written about the complex art of easement appraisals—and it has. The best written source on the appraisal process is *Appraising Easements: Guidelines for the Valuation of Historic Preservation and Land Conservation Easements*, by the National Trust for Historic Preservation and the Land Trust Exchange.

The most important thing to tell potential easement donors about appraisals is that the donor of an easement who claims a value in excess of $5,000 must be absolutely certain to comply with all federal substantiation requirements. The donor's appraisal most likely will be scrutinized. It must be able to hold up under examination.

An excellent guide to the maze of appraisal substantiation requirements is *The Federal Tax Law of Conservation Easements*. Because this detail is important, the key information is reprinted here:

> The [appraisal] substantiation requirements fall into three categories. First, a donor must obtain a "qualified appraisal." Second, a "fully completed appraisal summary" must be attached to the donor's tax return. [*Author's note: Some organizations recommend sending the full appraisal report.*] Third, the donor must maintain certain specified records concerning the gift.
>
> A "qualified appraisal" must be done by a "qualified appraiser." A qualified appraiser must be "qualified to make appraisals of the type of property being valued" and cannot be a person whose relationship to the taxpayer or the donee organization "would cause a reasonable person to question the independence of such an appraiser."
>
> For example, the . . . Regulation notes that an appraiser who is regularly used by the donee organization "*and who does not perform a*

substantial number of appraisals for other persons" [emphasis added] cannot be a qualified appraiser with respect to the property contributed.

A "qualified appraisal" must include, among other things, a description of the property, the method of valuation used to determine the fair market value of the property, certain information about the appraiser and his or her qualifications, and a description of the fee arrangement between the donor and the appraiser.

The "appraisal summary" must be on IRS Form 8283 and must include information identifying the donee, the appraiser, and the property. The summary must be signed by the appraiser and by the donee organization, although the . . . Regulation notes that the donee's signature "does not represent concurrence in the appraised value of the contributed property. Rather, it represents acknowledgment of receipt of the property . . . and that the donee understands the information reporting requirements imposed by section 6050L" [which] requires the donee to file an information return (Form 8282) with the Service if the donee sells or otherwise disposes of the subject donated property within two years after the gift (pp. 19-2, 19-3).

The final category of substantiation requirements outlined by Small is the variety of other records an easement donor must keep. See his book for details.

Although the donee has no legal responsibility for the valuation claimed by the donor, the degree of ethical responsibility is an individual decision each donee must make. (Refer to chapter 3, specifically the subsection entitled "The Donee's Responsibility.")

What is the Penalty for a "Bad" Appraisal?

Donors who overvalue their easements can face penalties. If the valuation claimed on the taxpayer's return is 150 percent or more of the valuation determined by the IRS, the taxpayer must pay the additional tax due, plus a penalty equalling 30 percent of that additional liability. The appraiser also may be penalized.

Here's an example from *The Federal Tax Law of Conservation Easements*. A taxpayer claims that the fair market value of a donated conservation easement is $100,000. Upon audit, the IRS determines the value to be $50,000. As a result of the lower deduction, the taxpayer owes the government an additional tax. Further, because the valuation claimed on the return ($100,000) is more than 150 percent of the correct valuation (150 percent of $50,000 is $75,000), the penalty applies. The penalty is 30 percent of $20,000 (the additional tax due), or $6,000. Had the correct valuation been $70,000, the penalty would not apply, because the claimed valuation ($100,000) was not more than 150 percent of the correct valuation (150 percent of $70,000 is $105,000).

The IRS may waive the penalty if conditions prove that a real effort was made to arrive at a valid value. For details and examples, see *The Federal Tax Law of Conservation Easements*.

Don't Easement Donations Trigger IRS Audits?

"I've heard horror stories," a potential donor might say to you, "about people giving easements and writing off the donation. Five years later, the IRS audits them, disallows the donation, and slaps on a penalty. I don't want to risk that!" What can a responsible donee say to counter that fear?

Donees certainly cannot deny that the IRS has not always agreed with the claimed charitable gift deductions for easement donations. In the past, some IRS regional offices, especially in the Mid-Atlantic and Southeast regions, have taken a very hard-line position, reducing or disallowing many claimed preservation and conservation easements donations. However, recent Tax Court rulings, while not always fully agreeing with the taxpayers' claimed value, have favored the methods and conclusions of the donors' appraisers over the methods and conclusions of the IRS appraisers. (The best resource for keeping abreast of such significant tax developments affecting land conservation is the "Conservation Tax Program," a subscription service of the Land Trust Exchange.)

The only way for donors to be certain that their easement donation is tax deductible is to seek a private letter ruling from the IRS before granting the easement. To get a private letter ruling, the easement donor and his or her attorney submit to the IRS, in writing, the facts of a proposed transaction and what the writer believes to be controlling law (e.g., "Under Section 170(h) of the Internal Revenue Code, a deduction is allowed for the donation of. . ."). The taxpayer asks the IRS to rule, in writing, that the proposed transaction will indeed meet the requirements of the law and that the tax treatment suggested by the taxpayer will apply. A private letter ruling tells easement donors whether or not their contributions will qualify for an income tax deduction. The IRS will *not*, however, issue a private letter ruling on the *amount* of deduction.

The Land Trust Exchange's 1985 easement survey found that all 21 of the easement program administrators who reported that their donees had sought private letter rulings had received favorable decisions. The process, however, is quite expensive and time-consuming, sometimes taking longer than a year.

Private letter rulings are optional, not mandatory. Potential donors should not feel that they must undergo this expense. In fact, most easement donations are not challenged by the IRS.

Explaining Estate Tax Savings

Estate taxes reflect the value of property's "highest and best use"—the most profitable use at the time of the owner's death. For example, although a rancher simply may want to continue ranching on his or her 500 acres of mountain pasture, the estate taxes due on that pasture may reflect the value of the 50 ten-acre ranchettes that could be constructed on the property. Heirs may have no choice but to sell the property to cover estate (inheritance) taxes.

Easements can sometimes dramatically reduce estate taxes. As such, they can be significant estate planning tools and should be approached as such.

Different types of benefits may be realized, depending on whether an easement is donated during the property owner's lifetime or is included in the owner's will to be donated after his or her death.

If a property owner donates a perpetual easement during his or her lifetime, the uses to which the property can be put are limited forever. Thus the "highest and best use" for which the property can be valued in an estate is limited. This usually reduces the estate's value and thus reduces estate taxes. By donating an easement during his or her lifetime, the owner may realize the income tax savings of a charitable gift as well as lower estate taxes for the heirs.

Alternatively, a property owner may choose to donate an easement upon his or her death by specifying in his or her will that an easement gift be made. (The general terms of the easement and the designated recipient are spelled out in the will.) The full value of the easement donation is deducted from the value of the estate, reducing estate taxes accordingly. After the owner's death, the executor of an estate cannot make additional gifts to avoid estate taxes; the owner must make the decision before his or her death. Because the easement was not donated until after the owner's death, of course, the owner reaps no income tax benefits.

Explaining Property Tax Reductions

In most states, property tax assessment is based on the concept of "highest and best" use, which usually is development. Because an easement may remove most, if not all, of a property's development potential, it seems logical that—in states following the "highest and best use" approach—donating an easement should reduce the donor's property taxes. However, it is not that simple.

Reductions in property taxes are unpopular with local government officials. Especially since the flow of federal and state funds to the local level has been so sharply curtailed in recent years, local officials and assessors may well fear the further loss of tax revenue that easements represent. Assessors, who are paid to make assessments that will generate enough revenue to meet budgeted quotas, may see an easement program as frustrating their revenue collection efforts, or at least as an added complication.

Although state statutes are controlling, the personal attitudes of local officials and assessors influence or determine the decision to grant property tax relief to easement grantors. Organizations and agencies with easement programs must cultivate the enthusiasm of these local officials and assessors.

Applying for a reduction is the taxpayer's responsibility. Easement program administrators often can help, though, by guiding donees through the process and by explaining any precedents they know of. Here are some tips—taken from *Building an Ark,* by Phillip M. Hoose—to give donees:

☐ Don't assume that the assessment will be reduced automatically. You'll have to apply, probably in person.

☐ It helps greatly if the assessor's obligation to consider the value of rights surrendered is clearly a matter of law. Some state easement statutes are very clear in this matter. If such a law exists, take a copy with you.

☐ Take a copy of the appraisal of the easement with you. Make sure the appraisal clearly states the value of each right surrendered.

☐ Be prepared to appeal.[1]

Some donors hold back from seeking a property tax reduction out of concern that asking the assessor to consider the effect of an easement on property taxes may cause the property to be reassessed in its entirety. Where a property has greatly increased in value since its last assessment, the result *may* be a higher assessment, even after the easement is taken into account. Easement donors also may wish to forgo a reassessment to keep the transaction confidential or simply to avoid the hassle.

All in all, property tax reduction is rarely a strong motivation for easement donors. The Land Trust Exchange's 1985 easement survey found reduction of property tax near the bottom of donors' incentives. Because it may not strongly appeal to potential donors, and because it actually may harm relations with local public officials, easement administrators should decide whether the advantages of promoting easements as a way to reduce local property taxes outweigh the opposition that may be created.

Explaining Gift Tax Savings

Finally, easements also can reduce or eliminate gift tax on gifts of property made during a property owner's lifetime. For example, a farmer who wants to give land to his or her children will likely be faced with a gift tax on the transfer. By granting an easement to a qualified organization before giving the land, the value of the farm may be reduced so that the gift tax is substantially less or even eliminated.

Determining If an Easement Qualifies as a Tax-Deductible Gift

Most easement donors want to know whether the value of their easement will be deductible for federal income tax purposes. They should have an attorney review the question.

Many good attorneys, however, are not well versed in easement tax law. They do not know exactly which sections of the law embodied in the Internal Revenue Code and its resulting regulations will help them determine whether

---

1. Phillip M. Hoose, *Building an Ark: Tools for the Preservation of Natural Diversity through Land Protection* (Covelo, Calif.: Island Press, 1981).

their client's gift will qualify. The time it takes attorneys to research unfamiliar matters may increase legal costs.

Donees can do two things to help lower a donor's cost of legal review. First, they can refer attorneys to this handbook—particularly to the model easement documents and commentaries—and to *The Federal Tax Law of Conservation Easements*. Second, donees can research the facts and give that information to the donor's counsel, thus saving the attorney time and the client money.

The following checklist can help donees assemble information on a proposed easement's relation to the conservation purposes on which the deduction depends. The schematic overview outlines for an attorney the mental process to follow in order to make a tax evaluation. It can give an attorney the facts on which to rely. With this sheet in hand, an attorney may be able to say: "Assuming the facts presented by the donee are true, I conclude that the easement is deductible for income, gift, and estate tax purposes."

This is simply a starting point. As with all legal questions, bring the particulars of each case to an attorney. Donee organizations should never say that a donation will be deductible. Leave this to the donor's attorney and, ultimately, the IRS.

An Attorney's Checklist

In general, to qualify as a tax-deductible gift, an easement must meet three requirements outlined in Internal Revenue Code Section 170(h)(1):

(A) It must be a qualified real property interest;

(B) It must be given to a qualified organization; *and*

(C) It must be donated exclusively for conservation purposes.

An easement meets these requirements if it passes the four tests below.

TEST 1: QUALIFIED REAL PROPERTY INTEREST

The easement gift is a *qualified real property interest* because it is:

☐ a restriction (granted in perpetuity) on the use which may be made of the real property (i.e., a conservation easement). *See* I.R.C. § 170(h)(2)(C).

To support this fact you will need:

☐ a copy of the easement deed (cite page/paragraph numbers of "Prohibited Uses and Practices").

TEST 2: QUALIFIED ORGANIZATION

The gift is given to a *qualified organization* because the donee is: (*check one item under A; you must also check B and C*)

A. ☐ a governmental unit. *See* I.R.C. § 170(h)(3)(A) and I.R.C. § 170(b)(1)(A)(v) or (vi).

☐ a publicly supported charitable organization described in I.R.C. § 501(c)(3). *See* I.R.C. § 170(h)(3)(B)(i).

☐ an organization controlled by one of the two above (a closely held satellite). *See* I.R.C. § 170(h)(3)(B)(ii); Treas. Reg. § 1.170A-14(c) for all of the above.

and

B. ☐ the donee has the commitment and the resources to enforce the easement's restrictions. *See* Treas. Reg. § 1.170A-14(c)(1).

and

C. ☐ the easement is transferable only to other qualified organizations. *See* Treas. Reg. § 1.170A-14(c)(2).

To support your claim to meet these tests you will need:

For governmental units:

☐ a description of the governmental unit; *and*

☐ a copy of the agency's resolution to accept the easement.

For private nonprofit organizations:

☐ a copy of the charitable organization's letter of determination from the IRS of tax-exempt status;

☐ a copy of the organization's resolution to accept the easement; *and*

☐ a copy of the organization's articles of incorporation indicating that it is primarily organized for conservation purposes.

For controlled organizations (satellites):

☐ the satellite's resolution to accept the easement; *and*

☐ a copy of its IRS tax-exemption determination letter.

For all organization types, some indication must be provided of the donee's overall stability and commitment to enforce the terms of the easement. This could include:

☐ an annual report describing its track record of easement stewardship; *and/or*

☐ a financial statement indicating availability of funds to defend easement (although the regulations state that a separate enforcement fund is not necessary, it certainly helps); *and/or*

☐ availability of a back-up grantee; *and/or*

☐ a list of the nonprofit donee's directors and their occupations and organizational connections.

TEST 3: CONSERVATION PURPOSES

The gift is given for *conservation purposes* because it will: *(check all those that apply)*

☐ preserve land areas for outdoor recreation by the general public. *See* I.R.C. § 170(h)(4)(A)(i) and Treas. Reg. § 1.170A-14(d)(2).

☐ preserve land areas for the education of the general public. *See* I.R.C. § 170(h)(4)(A)(i) and Treas. Reg. § 1.170A-14(d)(2).

☐ protect a relatively natural habitat of fish, wildlife, or plants, or similar ecosystem. *See* I.R.C. § 170(h)(4)(A)(ii) and Treas. Reg. § 1.170A-14(d)(3).

☐ preserve open space (including farmland or forest land) for the scenic enjoyment of the general public, and which will yield a significant public benefit. *See* I.R.C. § 170(h)(4)(A)(iii)(I) and Treas. Reg. §§ 1.170.A-14(d)(4)(i), (ii), (iv), and (v).

☐ preserve open space (including farmland or forest land) that is pursuant to a clearly delineated federal, state, or local governmental conservation policy, and that will yield a significant public benefit. *See* I.R.C. § 170(h)(4)(A)(iii)(II) and Treas. Reg. §§ 1.170A-14(d)(4)(i), (iii), (iv), and (v).

☐ preserve a historically important land area. *See* I.R.C. § 170(h)(4)(A)(iv) and Treas. Reg. § 1.170A-14(d)(5).

☐ preserve a certified historic structure. *See* I.R.C. § 170(h)(4)(A)(iv) and Treas. Reg. § 1.170A-14(d)(5).

To support these facts you will need detailed evidence, as this is the meat of the qualification question. See chapters 2 and 6.

TEST 4: *EXCLUSIVELY* FOR CONSERVATION PURPOSES

The gift is given *exclusively* for conservation purposes because: *(both must be checked)*

☐ the conservation purpose is protected in perpetuity. *See* I.R.C. § 170(h)(5)(A) and Treas Reg. § 1.170A-14(e).

and

☐ surface mining is not permitted or (if surface and subsurface rights were separated before June 13, 1976) the possibility is so remote as to be negligible. *See* I.R.C. § 170(h)(5)(B) and Treas. Reg. § 1.170A-14(g)(4).

To support these facts you will need:

☐ a copy of the easement deed, citing the page/paragraph numbers that state that:

☐ the easement is given in perpetuity; *and*

☐ surface mining is prohibited *or* (if surface and subsurface rights were separated before June 13, 1976) the possibility is so remote as to be negligible (evidence for the latter will be needed);

and

☐ a copy of the title certificate (indicating mortgage subordination, if the property is mortgaged).

CHAPTER 5

The Acquisition Process:

A Step-by-Step Guide

Here is a plan of action to take you from a property owner's first curious inquiry to the post-closing thank-you letter of an easement acquisition. These steps are just a starting point; state and local laws may call for additional action. Be sure to factor in such requirements.

One fact you can count on is that acquiring an easement takes time. This is especially true when the easement is a donation and the landowner must take care to meet IRS requirements for a tax deduction. Easements donated at the end of the year can be particularly stressful. William S. Blades, executive director of the Philadelphia Historic Preservation Corporation, points out:

> Organizational authorities, chain of command, and review responsibilities require time in order to accept an easement. The grantor needs to realize that granting an easement for tax purposes at the eleventh hour can be quite perplexing and disruptive, not to mention the very real fact that the easement may not be accepted on time.

So leave plenty of time. Fit the following steps to the demands of your locality and to each owner. Put them in the order that suits your program's needs. Keep the owner's perspective in mind, and make the easement acquisition process as easy for them as possible.

To standardize the acquisition process and make it as equitable among property owners as possible, some easement programs ask potential grantors to fill out an application. Private historic preservation organizations operating in large cities as well as government agricultural protection programs typically use application forms to sift through the many easement offers they attract. See sample at the end of this chapter.

Using a form to collect pertinent information about potential grantors can streamline the acquisition process. Where the easement program is large and the public is relatively well informed and interested in participating, application forms are all but a necessity. Smaller easement programs, however, often prefer the personal touch. Having to fill out forms can put off potential easement grantors, and many easement programs cannot afford that risk.

Whether or not you use application forms, these are the basic steps to take when acquiring an easement.

Step 1. Tour the Property with the Owner to Determine If an Easement Is Appropriate

Arrange an informal tour of the property with the owner. If there is more than one owner, try to set a time when all can be there. Such a tour will allow you to begin to answer two crucial questions:

1. Does this property meet your organization's or agency's criteria for accepting easements?

2. Is this owner willing to accept the easement restrictions necessary to protect the significant resources of the property?

The answer to the second question will become clear when you and the landowners hammer out the exact restrictions of the easement. But that first guided tour should help you to discover how the potential grantor feels about the property, how strongly he or she cares about its special resources, and what concerns the property owner has about granting an easement.

Discussing money at the first meeting may not feel comfortable, but most easement program administrators strongly advise being up-front about the subject. If you are planning to buy the easement, the question will be straightforward; the property owner will want to know how much you can pay. If it's a donation, the issues are different. In most cases, you will want to solicit a cash donation to cover the costs of accepting the easement and to insure your financial ability to defend it. The sooner you plant the seed or request such a donation, the better (see chapter 8).

You might promote the concept of granting an easement at this time by providing a list of satisfied easement grantors. Encourage potential grantors to discuss their concerns with neighbors who have granted easements to your program, if they have agreed to talk about it. No one can make the case for granting an easement better than your satisfied customers.

Step 2. Decide as an Organization Whether or Not to Pursue the Acquisition

After you have toured the property with the owner, report back to the other decision makers in your easement program. Because the next steps will take time and cost money, the decision to further pursue the easement should be made at the group level. This is only a decision to pursue the acquisition, however, not a formal resolution to accept the easement.

Step 3. Advise the Owner to Consult Legal and Tax Advisors

As soon as you have committed to pursuing the easement acquisition, advise the property owner to consult with legal and tax advisors. This is particularly important if the easement is a donation. Note that reasonable expenses related to the easement donation may be tax deductible. These expenses may include legal and accounting assistance, survey cost, and recording and appraisal fees.

There is a good chance that the property owner's advisors will not be well versed in easement law. As a service, you might keep a file of local tax and property lawyers, accountants, appraisers, and other specialists familiar with easements to help the owner obtain skilled guidance.

Which party actually writes the easement document is decided case by case, depending on the preference and the resources of both the grantor and the grantee. Since your program almost certainly will have more experience with easements than your potential grantors, you and your attorney are the logical parties to do the writing. By doing the drafting, you also can keep your program fairly uniform. In any case, grantors and their advisors typically like to see other easement documents. Provide them with copies of easements over similar properties—with proper names deleted if the grantors prefer—and with a copy of this handbook's model easements and commentaries.

Step 4. Compile a Baseline Data Inventory of the Property

Study and record the condition of the property early in the easement acquisition process. Such baseline data will give your program decision makers hard evidence of the value of the easement. In addition, by defining the property's important resources, the study will show the easement drafter what restrictions must be written into the document. Finally, compiling baseline data is an IRS requirement for those easement donors who want to deduct their gift.

IRS regulations state that when an easement donor retains rights in a property that, if exercised, could impair the conservation values of that property, sufficient baseline data must be provided "to establish the condition of the property *at the time of the gift* (emphasis added)" *See* Treas. Reg. § 1.170A-14(g)(5). Both the donor and the donee must acknowledge the accuracy of this documentation.

Although the regulations place the responsibility for preparing baseline data on the donor, the donee typically performs this task, simply because it knows how. When the easement is not a donation, of course, the IRS rules do not apply. In that case, the task of preparing the baseline data falls to the party that wants the easement—the buyer. (For details on the importance and preparation of baseline data, see chapter 6).

Step 5. Obtain Title Information

Obtaining title information accomplishes several essential tasks. It identifies the legal owner or owners of the property. It furnishes the legal property description that must be included in both the easement document and baseline data. (If the property to be placed under easement is not a separate legal parcel, a survey may have to be commissioned.) And it identifies any liens and encumbrances on the property, such as mortgages.

Title practices vary from state to state. In most states, you can order a preliminary title report from a licensed land title company. A title search is not always necessary.

Step 6. Obtain Mortgage Subordination

Accepting an easement on a property subject to a pre-existing mortgage is a special problem. If the lender ever forecloses on the mortgage and takes title to the property, the easement may be extinguished. The only solution is to have the lender subordinate its rights in the property to the rights of the easement holder. That means that in the event of a foreclosure, the easement will not be extinguished. Responsible land conservation programs will not accept an easement on mortgaged property unless the holder of the mortgage agrees to subordinate.

Conservation easements held by the Sunnyside Foundation protect the common open space in historic Sunnyside Gardens in Queens, N.Y., the country's first planned community.

RICHARD BARR

Subordination is a *requirement* when the easement is a donation and the donor wishes to deduct the gift. The IRS regulations state that "no deduction will be permitted . . . for an interest in property which is subject to a mortgage unless the mortgagee subordinates its rights in the property to the right of the qualified organization to enforce the conservation purposes of the gift in perpetuity." *See* Treas. Reg. § 1.170A-14(g)(2). Failure to provide subordination on gifts made after February 13, 1986, will result in denial of the deduction.

The regulations, however, are binding on the donor, not the mortgagee (the lender). Since there is no legal or financial incentive for the lender to agree to yield its position and become junior to the easement, easement donors and donees have their work cut out for them.

Even when the easement is donated and it is the donor's responsibility to obtain the mortgage subordination, the donee should be involved in this process—simply to ease the donor's task. The process demands more expertise than donors can be expected to have. Some easement programs, such as the Maryland Environmental Trust, provide easement donors with a mortgage subordination form. Here are some things that you, as grantee, can do to make the subordination process flow more smoothly:

☐ Clearly explain to the lender the purpose of the easement. Describe how the easement benefits the community at large. If it's a donation, emphasize the charitable aspect.

☐ If the easement is a donation, explain that the IRS requires mortgage subordination. If it's a purchase, explain your desire to secure the easement's terms in perpetuity.

☐ Cite local subordination precedents whenever possible. Talk with other easement program administrators in your region or state; where you may be having difficulty getting a lender to agree to subordination, they already may have succeeded. Once there is a precedent, the second subordination often is routine.

☐ If the mortgage on the property is secured by the improvements alone and the easement is over the property's open space (not the improvements), point out that the mortgage is not imperiled by the easement.

☐ Send copies of publications that help explain easements. The Land Trust Exchange's *Report on 1985 National Survey of Government and Non-Profit Conservation Easement Programs* might be useful.

When dealing with a lending institution, be prepared to pay a processing fee (or prepare your donors to pay the fee). You may have luck citing your charitable purpose and requesting a waiver, but don't count on it.

Be patient, but persistent! As Elizabeth Weichec, executive director of the Malibu, California, Mountains Restoration Trust, notes:

> The process of gaining subordinations is noteworthy because of its arduousness. The request isn't a standard one, and the task of educating the decision-makers rests on the easement program. Each [subordination] has taken months, and the need to follow up is continual.[1]

---

1. Elizabeth Weichec, "Subordinating Mortgages to Conservation Easements," *Land Trusts' Exchange,* Fall 1986, 14-15.

Step 7. Negotiate the Restrictions and Draft the Document

This is the heart of the easement acquisition process. In most cases, you will start these negotiations the first time you talk to a prospective easement grantor. As conversations grow more serious, you will call in the attorneys and put it in legal language.

Throughout this process, you will work to establish the degree of protection you will need as grantee to protect the resource values of the property. At the same time, the grantors will seek assurances that they can go on using the property as they always have. Your challenge is to anticipate potential future points of conflict, being as specific as possible without alienating the grantor or creating a rigid monster of detailed regulations you cannot hope to enforce. (See the model easement commentaries.)

Legal help in drafting the easement is essential. The rules of the game are always changing. New tax laws are passed and state easement statutes are amended. Only an attorney can keep you up to date.

Your program's attorney may draft the easement, but a lawyer representing the owner's interests should review and approve the document as well. Provide both attorneys with this handbook's model easements and commentaries, as well as other specific easement documents you have developed to address the unique protection issues important to your organization or agency.

Step 8. Obtain a Qualified Appraisal

Whether you are buying an easement or accepting a donation, an accurate appraisal is essential. If you are buying, you want to be sure you are paying what it's worth. If it's a donation and the donor wants to claim a deduction, the IRS requires the donor to obtain a qualified appraisal to justify the value of the gift if the value claimed is more than $5,000. *See* Treas. Reg. § 1.170A-13T(c)(2)(i)(A).

Make sure you and your donors know what the IRS means by a qualified appraisal. (The subject is touched upon in chapter 4.) Someone in your easement program, however, should have a thorough understanding of this subject. The best resource is *Appraising Easements: Guidelines for Valuation of Historic Preservation and Land Conservation Easements* by the National Trust for Historic Preservation and the Land Trust Exchange.

When an easement is donated, it is strictly the donor's responsibility to obtain an appraisal. The value is a matter between the donor and the IRS. This does not mean that the donee should turn a blind eye to the appraisal process. Every donee has an ethical obligation to make an honest transaction and, therefore, must discourage inflated appraisals. If one easement donee's practices are perceived as questionable, the reputations of easement programs across the country will suffer.

There's another reason why a donee might want to obtain a well-documented appraisal. Public agency donees may be able to use the value of a donated easement to match a grant from government funding programs such as the federal Land and Water Conservation Fund[2] or similar state funds. Such easements generally involve some type of physical public access, such as hiking or skiing trails, although it may be possible to use the easement value as a match when the easement protects a public view.

The science of easement appraisals is still relatively young, and they take time. Begin the process—or advise your donors to begin the process—as soon as you have developed a working draft of the easement document that makes clear the restrictions and rights retained. The donor may want to consult an appraiser, at least informally, even earlier in the process so that he or she will have a realistic idea from the beginning of the value of restrictions under discussion.

Optional Step 9. Enlist a Back-Up Grantee

To ensure that easements will be enforced in perpetuity, many young or small easement programs rely on larger organizations or agencies to act as partners in holding the easement—most often as a back-up grantee. A back-up grantee is empowered to enforce an easement if the original grantee fails to do so, or to take over an easement if the original grantee can no longer manage it. The validity of using a back-up grantee varies from state to state and should be checked carefully.

You may find other organizations and agencies quite willing to serve as back-up grantees. After all, providing back-up services strengthens conservation in their own back yards. By serving as a back-up, an easement program stretches the good it can do. With easement negotiations well underway, now is the time to ask. (For further discussion, see chapter 9.)

Step 10. Obtain a Formal Acceptance from Your Program's Authorities

Once the final easement document has been drafted and the grantor has approved it, take it to your program's officials for approval to acquire. Government agency programs may require several levels of review and approval. Private organizations typically require a resolution by the board of directors.

Step 11. Sign and Record the Easement

When all of the parties have agreed to all of the terms and the wording of the easement, it is time for both parties to sign. Make sure you get each owner's signature, and have an authorized person sign for your easement program.

---

2. For information about the Land and Water Conservation Fund, contact your state liaison officer or write: Recreation Grants Division (775), National Park Service, U.S. Department of the Interior, Washington, D.C. 20013-7127.

If you're buying the easement, you may want to go through escrow. You also may want to obtain title insurance, depending on the risk.

Once the deed is signed, record it in the office of the local recorder of deeds and any other repositories required by state and local law. Both you and the landowners should keep copies of the document and countersigned copies of the baseline data. Any back-up grantee also must keep copies.

State law also may require you to notify local government agencies, such as the local planning commission. Even when not required, such notification is a good idea—the more people and governing bodies that know about the easement restrictions, the less chance that a violation will go unnoticed. The Brandywine Conservancy, for example, notifies a local township by letter when it has accepted an easement within the township's jurisdiction. The conservancy encloses a map locating the easement, briefly describes its provisions, and offers to send a staff member to answer any questions the township administrators might have.

Step 12. Express Your Appreciation and Publicize Your Results

Getting this far required cooperation, generosity, or both from the property owner. Express your appreciation in a letter. Remember that the property owner's good will is critical to the continuing success of the easement. Cultivate that good will throughout the acquisition process and afterward.

Finally, publicize your program's success in acquiring the easement—if the property owner does not object—and describe the ways that the community will benefit from it. With luck, your efforts to publicize the completion of one easement will lead you back to Step 1: negotiating the *next* easement.

APPENDIX C   Sample Easement Application Form

THE FOUNDATION FOR SAN FRANCISCO'S ARCHITECTURAL HERITAGE

FACT SHEET FOR HISTORIC PRESERVATION EASEMENT

Street Address of Property _____

Cross Streets _____

Block and Lot Number (from City Assessor's records) _____

Owner _____

Mailing Address _____

_____ Zip _____

Telephone: Days _____ Evenings _____

PHYSICAL DESCRIPTION

1. Architectural style

2. Date of construction

3. Architect/builder (if known)

4. Present use (and original use, if known)

5. Number of stories

6. Building material

7. Condition of exterior

8. Exterior color(s)

Architectural/historic significance (including bibliographical references):

Description of surrounding neighborhood:

Present zoning of parcel and adjacent properties:

Attachments: 1. Photographs of exterior of structure and architectural drawings

2. Legal description (photocopy of ownership deed)

3. Copy of block map (from Assessor's office)

Prepared by _____

Address/Phone _____

Date _____

2007 FRANKLIN STREET • SAN FRANCISCO, CALIFORNIA 94109 • (415) 441-3000

CHAPTER
6

Baseline Data:

Compiling a Thorough Inventory

For the same reason that an heiress files photographs of her antique emerald jewelry with an insurance company, responsible easement-holding organizations insist on having a baseline data file on each easement that they acquire. If a thief steals the heiress's jewelry, she needs proof of the value of the jewelry; with that proof, she is entitled to restitution. If a violation occurs on a property over which an easement is granted, the grantee needs proof of the resource value of that property; with that proof, the grantee is in a good position to win restitution.

If the condition of the property at the time of the grant has been fully recorded in the baseline data file, the grantee has an accurate record on which to rely if controversy arises about any future damage to the property's resources. The baseline data file contains the facts that could support allegations of violations in a court of law.

Good baseline data, then, is absolutely essential to the easement holder. For landowners claiming income tax deductions for easement donations, baseline data is an IRS requirement (if the donor reserves rights that, if exercised, could impair the property's conservation values).

Who, then, is responsible for compiling the baseline data: the grantor or the grantee? When must they do it? How much information must they assemble? And where can they find it?

Whose Responsibility— Grantor's or Grantee's?

If the easement is a tax-deductible gift, and if the donor retains rights in the property that, once exercised, could impair the conservation values of that property, the IRS holds the *donor* responsible for providing sufficient baseline data "to establish the condition of the property at the time of the gift." *See* Treas. Reg. § 1.170A-14(g)(5)(i). If the easement is purchased at fair market value, it is the *grantee's* responsibility to document the property's condition.

Either way, the grantee is almost certain to be involved in the job. Sometimes, the land-rich-but-cash-poor easement donor cannot afford to hire a consultant to document the property's condition. Sometimes the easement is so attractive to the agency or organization that it will offer to shoulder the cost of preparing baseline data in order to close the deal. Even when the grantor does pay the expenses, the physical task of compiling the data often falls to the grantee by default, as the grantor is not likely to know anyone else who knows how to compile baseline data.

In any case, it is in the best interest of the organization or agency that buys or accepts the donation of an easement to set its own standards for what must go into its baseline data files. By shouldering this responsibility, the grantee can control the quality of the information. Ultimately, it is the grantee's responsibility to make sure that the documentation contains all the information necessary to manage and enforce the easement.

When to Compile— Before or After?

IRS regulations require an easement donor to provide the donee with documentation of the property's condition *prior to* the time of the gift. *See* Treas. Reg. § 1.170A-14(g)(5)(i). Whether required beforehand or not, it is excellent policy to compile baseline data before accepting an easement—if for no other reason than it gives both grantor and grantee a clear idea of what they are getting into. This is good planning even when you are buying the easement and tax considerations are irrelevant.

Some grantees record the baseline data as an exhibit when they record the easement itself. Some states, however, do not allow the recordation of photographs, overlays, and the other nonstandard materials that typically comprise baseline data. This handbook's model easement documents incorporate the baseline data by reference into the text of the easement and stipulate that the documentation is on file with the grantee or attached to the document as an exhibit. Leaving the data on file with the grantee gives it the flexibility to meet any future needs to amend the data—within the limits of acceptable change established by the easement.

How Complete Must an Inventory Be?

A baseline data inventory is complete when it contains enough information to define each right and restriction written into the easement. Four basic considerations described below will help you determine what is "enough." The data should be sufficient to meet IRS requirements, if they apply. The data should be specific, but should include no more detail than necessary. And it should be objective and easy to duplicate. Ultimately, however, what exactly is "enough" must be determined on a case-by-case basis.

The detailed nature of some easements requires that baseline data be prepared by professionals. Professional architects, for example, might be necessary to document the exact condition of a historic commercial building. A particularly fragile habitat may require documentation by a naturalist or biolo-

A historic preservation easement held by the National Trust for Historic Preservation protects this 18th century manor house known as Mt. Harmon, a National Historic Landmark located on Maryland's eastern shore. The Natural Lands Trust, based in Philadelphia, holds the easement on the 80-acre land parcel surrounding the house. The protection of an additional 300 acres that was originally part of the farm was financed by ecologically sensitive development of a portion of the property, also restricted by easements held by NLT.

COURTESY OF THE NATIONAL TRUST FOR HISTORIC PRESERVATION

gist. Many easements, however, can be documented effectively by informed nonprofessionals.

IRS Requirements

IRS regulations state that an easement donor must make available to the donee "documentation sufficient to establish the condition of the property at the time of the gift." The regulations specify that such documentation *may* include:

(A) The appropriate survey maps from the United States Geological Survey, showing the property lines and other contiguous or nearby protected areas;

(B) A map of the area drawn to scale, showing all existing man-made improvements or incursions (such as roads, buildings, fences, or gravel pits), vegetation and identification of flora and fauna (including, for example, rare species locations, animal breeding and roosting areas, and migration routes), land use history (including present uses and recent past disturbances), and distinct natural features (such as large trees and aquatic areas);

(C) An aerial photograph of the property at an appropriate scale taken as close as possible to the date the donation is made; and

(D) On-site photographs taken at appropriate locations on the property. *See* Treas. Reg. § 1.170A-14(g)(5)(i)(A)-(D).

The key word in this section of the regulations is *may*. As Stephen Small explains in *The Federal Tax Law of Conservation Easements* (p. 16-3):

Say what you will about the IRS, but never accuse the Service of inadvertent use of the word "may." Must, shall, can't, won't, will, and don't flow off the IRS draftsman's pen with ease; the use of "may" represents a carefully considered decision and the word means what it says. In this case, if the donor can document the condition of the property in some other way sufficient to satisfy the donee organization (for whom this section of the Regulation provides the primary benefit), the donor is free to do so.

There are, however, two *musts* in this section of the regulations:

If the terms of the donation contain restrictions with regard to a particular natural resource to be protected, such as water quality or air quality, the condition of the resource at or near the time of the gift must be established. *See* Treas. Reg. § 1.170A-14(g)(5)(i)(D).

And:

The documentation, including the maps and photographs, must be accompanied by a statement signed by the donor and a representative of the donee clearly referencing the documentation and in substance saying, "This natural resources inventory is an accurate representation of [the protected property] at the time of the [conveyance of the easement]." *See* Treas. Reg. § 1.170A-14(g)(5)(i)(D).

Beyond these requirements, the volume and specificity of the information that the grantee should record in the baseline data depend on the terms of each easement.

Data Should Be Specific

It is not enough to record in the baseline data that a piece of property is in "good" condition, or that the view the property affords is "scenic." What, for example, is "good" elk habitat? To a rancher it may mean one thing, to a wildlife biologist, another. And "scenic" certainly is in the eye of the beholder.

For the purposes of baseline data, such phrases need to be clearly defined, in enough detail to allow for meaningful future comparison. This usually requires quantitative documentation. Habitat, for example, may be described as "so many" acres, planted with "such and such" forage, comprised of "x, y, and z" species, in "so many" pounds per square foot. "Scenic" may be described by documenting exactly what can be seen, how many people regularly enjoy the view, and any official recognition the property's scenic values may have received.

Include No More than Necessary

The degree of detail necessary for a baseline data file depends on the latitude that the rights reserved in the document give the landowner to alter the property's resources and on the sensitivity of the resources that the easement protects.

An example of a potentially threatening reserved right is when a landowner donates an easement but keeps the right to extract subsurface minerals on his or her property. Reserved mineral rights appear to the IRS as a future threat to the conservation values of the protected property. That threat can be reduced by having thorough documentation on file of the resource's condition at the time of the gift. This is what the regulations require.

If, on the other hand, the rights that the landowner retains are not potentially threatening, painstaking documentation is not necessary. Again, from Small (p. 16-3):

> When the donor reserves the subsurface mineral rights, or the right to do selective timber cutting, documentation is clearly necessary. When the easement is a "no further building" easement and the donor simply reserves the right to enter and leave the property and to use it in the usual manner, some donee organizations may be quite comfortable without the documentation suggested by this section of the Regulation. When the landowner reserves the right to build two more houses on a 100-acre parcel [however], documentation seems to be appropriate and necessary.

No one expects grantors or grantees to document every plant, animal, ditch, and fence post. Only the resources that the easement seeks to protect must be documented. The more delicate the resource, the more specific the documentation must be. Remember the simplicity of your goal: to document the state of the land to the degree necessary to provide a common reference point for future inspections.

Keep in mind that this is primarily a legal, not a biological, document. Write descriptions according to professional standards, but in terms that the nonbiologist can understand.

Data Should Be Objective and Easy to Duplicate

Over the years, different people will monitor the land. In order for baseline data to allow for meaningful comparisons 50 years from now, the data must be objective and easily understood, and the methods of monitoring must be easily replicable. If the vantage points of each photograph are not recorded, they will be of no use to future monitors. If the height of the forage is measured one year and a sample of the forage is cut and weighed the next, no meaningful comparison will be possible.

Sample Baseline Data Documents

Two model baseline data documents—one used by The Nature Conservancy, the other by the National Trust for Historic Preservation—are included at the end of this chapter. Another excellent baseline data document for land conservation easements is available from the Maine Coast Heritage Trust. This excellent document makes use of a mock conservation easement over a rural island to illustrate the type and breadth of information that the trust puts into its baseline data documents.

Baseline Data Checklist

The following checklist draws heavily on information from two private organizations that are experts in the easement field: The Nature Conservancy and the Maine Coast Heritage Trust. Keep in mind that no generic baseline data document can fit every easement. Tailor the following checklist to develop the baseline data necessary for each easement that your organization or agency acquires.

This is not to say that you should ignore the merits of uniformity. As Elizabeth Watson, former government relations specialist for the Land Trust Exchange, explains:

Uniformity in developing baseline data can help to lower administrative confusion and cost, as the easement program grows. Yes, the easement should be tailored to the property, and yes, the monitor should be aware of the particulars of any one property when he or she goes into the field, but it certainly simplifies things from an administrative standpoint if the same things can mostly be expected from easement record to easement record. A lot of programs haven't thought this through because they don't have a lot of easements, yet. But talk to those who do compile baseline data for a lot of easements!

Checklist

1. COVER PAGE

Should state: "Baseline Data for Conservation Easement granted by _____ on _____ property, _____ County, _____(state)_____ to _____(grantee)_____ ." The signature of the author/collector and the date should also appear.

2. TABLE OF CONTENTS

3. OWNER ACKNOWLEDGMENT OF CONDITION

This is an IRS requirement if the easement is a gift for which a deduction will be claimed. The regulations require that this statement must clearly reference the baseline data. It must say, "in substance . . . [t]his natural resources inventory is an accurate representation of [the protected property] at the time of the transfer." *See* Treas. Reg. § 1.170A-14(g)(5)(i)(D).

The statement must be notarized and signed by both grantor and representative of grantee. (The Nature Conservancy uses a standard letter that lists all of the documents included in the baseline data package.)

4. BACKGROUND INFORMATION

☐ Ownership information (name, address, and phone number of property owner)

☐ Historical information on the donation/acquisition (brief chronological description of events that led to the protection of the property)

☐ Summary of easement provisions (specific prohibitions, restrictions, retained rights, as derived from the language of the easement document)

☐ Purpose of easement

☐ Evidence of the significance of the protected property, as established either by government policy (include copies of documents) or by the long-term protection strategy developed by the grantee

☐ Corporate or agency resolution accepting gift (minutes of the meeting at which a gift is accepted or acquisition approved are adequate)

5. LEGAL CONDITION

Some grantees include in the baseline data file:

☐ A copy of the signed, recorded easement document

☐ An assessor's parcel map

☐ A clear title statement or preliminary title report, noting any liens against the property that could compromise its natural qualities or invalidate the easement

☐ Copies of any other relevant easements or water rights associated with the property.

6. ECOLOGICAL FEATURES

☐ An inventory of rare, endangered, and/or threatened species

☐ Reports from wildlife biologists or other specialists that document the status of significant natural elements

☐ A very general description of plant cover, soils, etc.

Include only those ecological features that the easement seeks to protect. The Nature Conservancy advises in its training material: "The only time a quantitative vegetation analysis . . . needs to be done is if the grantor/owner is now, will, or may be using the property in a way that is potentially damaging to the element(s), e.g. grazing or farming."

7. AGRICULTURAL FEATURES

☐ Intensity of grazing (can be determined by experts and expressed in "animal units" per acre)

☐ Level of pesticide use (The American Farmland Trust usually provides that the landowner must comply with all applicable federal, state, and local laws and regulations governing application of pesticides, herbicides, and other chemicals.)

☐ Soil quality (The American Farmland Trust encourages landowners to ask the Soil Conservation Service to prepare a soil conservation plan; this serves as the easement's benchmark for acceptable practices on erodible land.)

Grantees of easements over productive agricultural lands typically set a level of "acceptable" pesticide or herbicide use—a subject of constant debate. For comments on IRS treatment of this question, see chapter 12 of *The Federal Tax Law of Conservation Easements*.

Another difficult task for agricultural easement grantees is defining when grazing becomes overgrazing. The local office of the Soil Conservation Service and similar state agencies may be able to help.

8. SCENIC FEATURES

☐ Official policies citing property's scenic value

☐ Number of people who frequent nearby public places (roads, trails, parks) from which they can view property

9. MAN-MADE FEATURES

☐ Improvements (structures, trails, fences, wells, power lines, pipelines, irrigation systems, etc.)

☐ Recreation/tourism attractions

☐ Trespass damage and disturbed land (stray animals, introduced species, evidence of vehicular trespass, etc.)

10. PHOTOGRAPHS

☐ Aerial photos, if appropriate (Have aerial photos enlarged, if necessary, to correspond to the scale of the maps included in the baseline data.)

☐ On-site photos (Be sure to record key photo points on a map, record distance and azimuth from structures or other fixed points, and sign and date all photos; see appendix E for tips on taking documentary ground photographs.)

One easement grantee, the Society for the Preservation of New England Antiquities, records with the easement deed a separate affidavit signed by the photographer attesting to the accuracy of the photographs they record.

11. **MAPS**

Without good maps, baseline data are useless. Include at least:

☐ A state map showing easement location

☐ An 8 ½″ x 11″ section of a local road map showing easement location

☐ The largest-scale U.S. Geological Survey topographical map available (usually at a scale of 1:24,000, called a 7-1/2 minute scale), showing easement boundaries

Mark all key ecological, scenic, archeological, historic, and man-made features on the "base" topographical map, on separate maps as necessary, or on a clear plastic (mylar) overlay. Make sure map scales correspond. Key all maps and drawings to base map, and identify location, scale, and north arrow.

12. **SURVEYS**

☐ Surveys generally are not required, but they may be helpful.

Special Conditions for Historic Preservation Easements

The National Trust for Historic Preservation requires that suitable photographic and written documentation accompany easements accepted by it. In addition to items numbered 1 through 5 and 10 through 11 identified in the above checklist, documentation for historic sites may also include architectural depictions using the documentation standards and format of the Historic American Buildings Survey (HABS) of the U.S. Department of the Interior, as shown at the end of this chapter.

Before the National Trust accepts an easement, the HABS description form, as well as photographic documentation that includes all features covered by the easement, are completed. Another form used by the National Trust supplements the HABS form in that it identifies the *condition* of the property at the time the Trust accepts the easement.

Photographic documentation for properties that are National Historic Landmarks consists of a representative series of views using 4″ x 5″ negatives developed as 8″ x 10″ black-and-white glossy prints. Where the significance of the property is primarily architectural, documentation may also include measured drawings to HABS standards. For properties within historic districts or whose significance is primarily associative, 35 mm black-and-white photographs developed as 8″ x 10″ glossy prints and 35 mm color slides are acceptable. Measured drawings are normally not required, unless those properties are also of national significance architecturally.

BASELINE DATA CHECKLIST

All items below must be provided on the documentation report. However, the volume and specificity of information required by this checklist will vary depending on the terms of the easement. The intent of this format is to allow flexibility in your documentation technique and to key the quantity and nature of the documentation to the terms of the easement. Some conservation easements may require very general description of plant cover, geology, soils, etc., whereas others may need to be narrower in scope and more detailed as necessary to ensure adequate monitoring of specific elements. In such an instance, the legal and biological monitoring functions may overlap to some extent.

Checklist:
_____ cover page
_____ owner acknowledgment of condition (standard form letter must be notarized and should list all documents included in the documentation package)
_____ background information (brief narrative history of easement acquisition: summary of current status; location of/directions to easement)
_____ legal (list of restrictions and retained rights, benefited preserve, easement recordation data)
_____ ecological features (narrative description keyed to restrictions and retained rights)
    _____ target elements   _____ plant cover types
    _____ wildlife   _____ aquatic resources
    _____ geology and soils
_____ manmade features (narrative description of improvements, structures, trails, wells, power lines, pipelines, etc., include historic use if appropriate)
_____ photographs (aerial photo [recommended]; on-site photos should be keyed to restrictions and retained rights)
    _____ aerial   _____ on-site
_____ maps
    _____ location of easement (state map easement location; 8 1/2″ x 11″ section of local road map showing easement location; 8 1/2″ x 11″ or larger topo map section showing easement boundary)
    _____ ecological and manmade features as needed (can be mapped on topo map above or on separate maps as necessary to ensure clarity and adequacy of documentation)
      _____ element locations   _____ structures/buildings
      _____ plant cover types   _____ trails
      _____ geology and soils   _____ wells
      _____ aquatic resources   etc.

1800 North Kent Street
Arlington, Virginia 22209
703 841-8749

The Trustees of Reservations
Conserving the
Massachusetts Landscape

572 Essex Street
Beverly, Massachusetts
01915

Telephone
617-921-1944

CONSERVATION EASEMENT
BASELINE DOCUMENTATION REPORT

Please complete to satisfy Section 1.170A-14(g)(5) of the federal tax regulations.

Donor Name _____   Property Location:

Address _____   Road _____

_____   Town _____

Donee Name _____   County _____

Address _____

Land Types
     # Acres _____   % Forestland _____   % Farmland _____
     % Wetland _____   % Buildings & Grounds _____   % Other _____

Buildings and Structures on Property
     Describe size, type, and condition of structures including houses, sheds, towers, docks, barns, man-made ponds, roads, utilities, etc. Map location of improvements on attached map.

Condition of Land
     Describe condition and management status of forest or farmland, health of wetlands or waterways, unusual features, rare species; note erosion, gravel pits or pollution.

In compliance with Section 1.170A-14(g)(5) of the federal tax regulations this natural resources inventory is an accurate representation of the property at the time of the conservation easement donation.

_____   _____
Donor   Donee

_____   _____
Date   Date

Attachments: USGS topographic map _____
             (showing property line and other nearby protected land)
             Aerial photograph _____
             On-site photographs _____
             (showing man-made features)

APPENDIX D   Sample Baseline Data Documents

 National Trust for Historic Preservation

ARCHITECTURAL DATA FORM

STATE	COUNTY	TOWN OR VICINITY

HISTORIC NAME OF STRUCTURE *(INCLUDE SOURCE FOR NAME)*	HABS NO.

SECONDARY OR COMMON NAMES OF STRUCTURE

COMPLETE ADDRESS *(DESCRIBE LOCATION FOR RURAL SITES)*

DATE OF CONSTRUCTION *(INCLUDE SOURCE)*	ARCHITECT(S) *(INCLUDE SOURCE)*

SIGNIFICANCE *(ARCHITECTURAL AND HISTORICAL, INCLUDE ORIGINAL USE OF STRUCTURE)*

STYLE *(IF APPROPRIATE)*

MATERIAL OF CONSTRUCTION *(INCLUDE STRUCTURAL SYSTEMS)*

SHAPE AND DIMENSIONS OF STRUCTURE *(SKETCHED FLOOR PLANS ON SEPARATE PAGES ARE ACCEPTABLE)*

EXTERIOR FEATURES OF NOTE

INTERIOR FEATURES OF NOTE *(DESCRIBE FLOOR PLANS, IF NOT SKETCHED)*

MAJOR ALTERATIONS AND ADDITIONS WITH DATES

PRESENT CONDITION AND USE

OTHER INFORMATION AS APPROPRIATE

SOURCES OF INFORMATION *(INCLUDING LISTING ON NATIONAL REGISTER, STATE REGISTERS, ETC.)*

COMPILER, AFFILIATION	DATE

1785 Massachusetts Avenue, N.W.
Washington, D.C. 20036
(202) 673-4000

Taking Documentary Ground Photographs

The key to taking baseline data ground photos is to make them easy to repeat. Here are some guidelines:

Take photos from points that will be easy to locate in the future. Road intersections, edges of buildings, major fence corners, and utility poles are good spots. Be sure to note the location on each photo.

Take a compass direction for each photograph. Compass directions, of course, won't change, even if the landscape changes dramatically. A simple and accurate compass direction is an azimuth. To take an azimuth:

1. Hold the compass level at waist or chest height.

2. Align the magnetic needle pointing north with 0 degrees on the dial (veneer) of the compass.

3. Look over the veneer to the object you are photographing or to the center of your intended photo and read the degrees. Read degrees as a continuous scale, from 0° to 360°, around the circle.

4. Write down the compass direction in your notes, and label it "AZ MG" for "magnetic azimuth."

For simplicity's sake, this method uses magnetic north and makes no correction for true north. If you place this information on a topographic map, you will need to correct it according to the local variations between magnetic north and true north. The information you'll need to do this is provided in the U.S. Geological Survey map legend.

Make a comment about each photograph in your notes. Example: "This photograph shows the barn and part of the corral as seen from the intersection of the driveway and county road 409."

Note the location of all photo points on the data file's base map.

For more information, order the National Mapping Program Brochure entitled "Finding Your Way with Map and Compass," available free from the National Cartographic Information Center.

Ordering Aerial Photographs

Check these sources for ordering aerial photographs. Consider what scale you need for your particular purpose. For large properties, a scale of 1:20,000 (one mile to three inches) provides enough detail for baseline data purposes. In sensitive areas, you may need an enlargement or "blow-up." Some agencies can provide blow-ups; if they can't, they may be able to recommend a good commercial photographic printing house that can.

Soil Conservation Service. Local Soil Conservation Service district offices typically have black-and-white aerial photos of local lands. They often will provide 9″ x 9″ photos at a low cost, as well as enlargements and mosaics (single, large prints of several aerial photos of contiguous areas). District personnel can help you decide what you need. District offices are listed under "U.S. Department of Agriculture" in your local phone book.

Soil and Water Conservation Districts. In many cases, these county agencies will prepare free of charge an aerial photograph, blown up large enough for use as a base map, and also will add property lines. This map is prepared when a farmer requests a soil and water conservation plan from the district. (These nonbinding plans make recommendations for land uses and management practices to protect soil resources.) Soil Conservation Service personnel can give you more information.

U.S. Forest Service. If the property is near a national forest, your local Forest Service office may have appropriate aerial photographs. These photos typically are in color—sometimes true color, but sometimes only false-color infrared where healthy vegetation appears red. Orders are processed at Salt Lake City, but check with local personnel to determine what you need and how to order it. Look under "U.S. Department of Agriculture" in the phone book.

U.S. Geological Survey's National Cartographic Information Center. This center is a clearinghouse for all government aerial photos. Find out if the maps you need are available by using the questionnaire in the center's brochure entitled "How to Order Aerial Photographs." Staff will contact you as to the maps' availability and cost.

County Assessors. Many county assessors, especially in rural areas, have aerial photo coverage of lands under their jurisdiction. Call the local county assessor's office.

Private Professionals. Private professionals often are the best choice, for they often can produce just the photo you need. Some professional aerial photographers are experienced in the baseline data and monitoring needs of easement grantees and offer comprehensive services to meet them.

Making Mylar Overlays for Base Maps

Mylar is a transparent plastic sheeting with one roughed-up surface that holds ink. It is a handy material to use as an overlay on a base map to record buildings and other landmarks. Some tips for working with mylar:

☐ Before putting the first information on the mylar, make sure you put the base map and overlay "in register" so that you can line them up easily time after time. Put a cross on each of three corners of the base map, and on corresponding corners of the mylar. Line up the cross ticks each time you use the overlay.

☐ Use inks that are especially made for plastic. Although mylar is made to take ink, some inks for paper do not adhere to it well.

☐ Steer clear of stick-on and rub-on letters, lines, and symbols. They may make snazzy maps, but they tend to peel and chip with time.

Before beginning a mylar overlay, be sure that the scale of your base map is big enough to allow you to clearly record roads, buildings, and other improvements on the mylar. Well-equipped copy chops or other shops specializing in graphic reproduction can enlarge maps.

CHAPTER 7

Monitoring and Enforcement:

Making Easement Restrictions Stick

From a practical point of view, there is no such thing as a perpetual easement if there is not a commitment to enforce the terms of the easement. . . . I spent the first ten years of my career acquiring easements and the last ten years administering and defending the same type of easements. Believe me, acquiring the easements is the easy part.

> Paul Hartmann
> *Realty Officer*
> *U.S. Fish and Wildlife Service*

In a perfect world, there would be no easement violations. There also would be no need for easements.

That easements sometimes are violated is proof that they serve a purpose. All the trouble of negotiating the terms and drawing up the documents would hardly be worthwhile if there were not a real danger to guard against. Regrettably, though, that danger does not disappear once the easement document is signed.

You, as an easement holder, are responsible for guarding against violation, usually in perpetuity. This is a significant burden. The way to guard against such violations is to periodically check to see that the terms of the easement are being followed, a procedure called monitoring.

Monitoring puts the muscle in an easement program. Its importance, however, sometimes is overlooked by easement program planners. Again, from Paul Hartmann:

> It is very easy to underestimate the importance of this [enforcement] aspect when considering the less-than-fee method. But it all needs to come together when you first plan your easement program. *Do not allow easement enforcement to be an after-thought.* If you catch yourselves or others saying, "We'll worry about that later," STOP! You're making a big mistake.

Three Keys to Preventing Violations

As in football strategy, the best defense against lengthy and costly enforcement actions is a good offense. The three key players on a tough easement-holding organization's offensive line are:

1. A good relationship with the property owner
2. An easement document with clear and enforceable restrictions
3. A program of regular, systematic, and well-documented monitoring

With this offense in place, an easement holder may be able to keep its *defensive* players—mediation, litigation and injunction—on the bench.

Contact with the Property Owner is Critical

Because an easement is a partnership, with different entities holding separate rights to the same real estate, the potential for conflict is large. The most effective safeguard against conflict is regular and open communication between the participants.

Communication engenders cooperation. A property owner is less likely to illegally bulldoze part of his or her land or damage a protected facade when visited once a year by representatives from the easement holder. The visit serves as a regular reminder that the landowner is legally bound to keep the property in its original state. Perhaps more important, it shows that the easement holder is serious about its commitment to keep the property in the required condition. Finally, the personal visits give the property owner some names and faces to put behind the cold, legal terms of the deed.

By creating this rapport, the easement holder greatly increases the odds for a successful partnership. Acadia National Park's resource management specialist, Carroll Schell, credits the violation-free record of the park's easement program partly to luck but mostly to a cooperative landowner/agency relationship:

> I am certain that the only positive posture to take to mitigate the need for litigation is to have an effective monitoring program that includes the grantor. If the landowner knows that the grantee is interested and concerned about the well-being of his property, then that landowner will call if there are questions about interpretation of the easement and usually can anticipate what the grantee's position will be.

The one-on-one contact so essential to a healthy grantor/grantee relationship should occur regularly—at least once a year. Some grantees supplement that scheduled personal contact of the annual monitoring visit with other actions:

Recognition. Rewarding easement grantors with some tangible recognition of their generosity and good property stewardship. Historic preservation ease-

COURTESY OF LUTHER COLLEGE

The only known Woodland Indian effigy of a lizard is protected by a conservation easement held by the Clayton County Conservation Board in Iowa. Limed in white for the photo, the lizard's outline is evident by the different materials placed by the Indians.

ment donees sometimes place bronze plaques on donors' doorways. A less expensive option is a hand-lettered proclamation lauding the donor's good deed.

Advisory Services. Offering advisory services of professionals such as landscape architects, road engineers, and timber specialists who are at the grantee's disposal.

Newsletters. Sending a regular newsletter to all easement program participants. This not only provides relevant news and advice but also can acknowledge and welcome new grantors to the program.

The Strong Defense of a Well-Drawn Deed

No matter how good your property owner communication is, as an easement enforcer, you are bound to have problems. It's not a matter of if, but when. In fighting those problems, you ultimately must rely on the terms of the deed itself.

How can you draft an easement containing restrictions that are truly enforceable and will survive the courts? The model easements and commentaries provided in Part 3 of this handbook should provide a useful guide. Several sections in both commentaries address enforcement issues.

How to Monitor a Conservation Easement

The foundation of the monitoring process is the baseline data developed when the easement first was acquired (see chapter 6).

Each easement-holding organization or agency typically develops its own monitoring inspection report form or checklist that pinpoints the natural and human-caused changes that have taken place on the property since the last time it was monitored. This handbook reprints two organizations' exemplary lists at the end of this chapter. The detail or procedures that some of these reports require may present too big a burden for your staff or volunteers. Aerial monitoring, for example, may be out of the question. Tailor these examples to your needs.

Here are the steps in making a monitoring visit:

1. Notify the property owner in writing well in advance of the visit. The owner or his or her representative should accompany you on the visit if at all possible.

2. Review the easement's baseline data. Take a summary of the document's main restrictions for reference during the visit.

3. Gather the equipment you will need in making the inspection—maps, photos, camera, etc.

4. During the visit, note any changes to the property. Take photographs when they would be helpful.

5. Discuss observable changes with the property owner.

6. Complete the inspection report form and send two copies to the property owner. Ask him or her to sign and return one copy for your files.

Monitoring Historic Preservation Easements—Special Considerations. Monitoring historic preservation easements carries with it implied responsibilities that usually do not apply to monitoring land conservation easements. Through its inspection of a property under a historic preservation easement, the easement-holding organization's approval of the condition of the property or its protected elements may be construed as an implied certification of structural integrity, particularly if the inspection is undertaken by an expert, such as an architect. If, after an inspection, a piece of the inspected facade falls off, an argument could be made that the inspecting organization was negligent in not notifying the owner of the weakness or defect. Worse still, the inspecting organization may recommend some action related to the property's restoration or maintenance that leads to building damage.

To prevent such misunderstanding, the easement deed should include effective and complete hold harmless and indemnification provisions covering the above contingencies. Grantees also should have the owner sign similar hold harmless and indemnification statements at the bottom of each inspection form filled out by the easement-holding organization. Alternatively, all inspections could be conducted by licensed and insured architects who, in turn, would indemnify the easement-holding organization for any claim or costs attributable to the inspections.

Old Easements, New Owners

The further an easement passes down the line from the original grantor to subsequent property owners, the greater seems the chance that the new owners will ignore the terms of the easement. There is still too little experience with easements to generalize as to whether or not this is true. Nevertheless, experienced grantees take precautions to avoid conflict with new landowners on easement-burdened property.

The key is to involve the community in the protective spirit of the easement. Here are some tips:

Realtors. Educate local realtors about how an easement binds property in perpetuity. Offer to explain to their clients what they can and cannot do on a property under easement.

Title Companies. Ask local title companies to inform your agency or organization of title searches they do on easement-burdened property, so that you will be alerted to the potential sale of a protected property.

Legal Community. Hold meetings for the legal community—attorneys, magistrates, and judges—to describe the legal effects and the history of easements. Tell them how to order *The Federal Tax Law of Conservation Easements* and *Appraising Easements*.

Neighbors. Encourage the neighbors to be watchdogs. Neighbors are your best bet to combat easement violations. "Because we operate within a tight-knit, small-community atmosphere, landowners are often self-policing," says John Bledsoe, a district ranger in the Clearwater National Forest in Idaho. "Almost every tract along the river is under easement. So when 'Joe' does something next door that appears to be out of bounds with easement conditions, the district office phone starts ringing."

The watchdog effect can work in big cities, too. In Washington, D.C., several violations have come to the attention of the L'Enfant Trust when neighborhood residents noticed something unusual taking place on a historic house marked with a L'Enfant Trust bronze plaque.

First, though, the neighbors have to know what trouble to look out for. The organization or agency that holds the easements must make its presence and its mission known in the community. Chapter 3 on marketing easements gives suggestions on how to publicize your easement program.

It is well worth your time to try to work with landowners. "The administration of easements involves a lot of gray area, and requires a good deal of judgment, listening, and negotiation," says John Twiss, a ranger in the Nezperce National Forest in Idaho. "We do not try to force our interpretation of the easement on anyone unless the project or change is imminent."

Negotiation, however, has its limitations. Twiss continues: "But we make all grantors aware that we will not take the ostrich approach, either. We are being paid to administer these easements and cannot ignore violations. We deal with violations immediately and insist upon correction of the violation ASAP. There is a real danger in waiting."

Rectifying Violations

"While friendly compliance is the ideal situation, management should realistically expect that at some point, conflicts will arise," says B.J. Schaefer, assistant chief of the Division of Realty of the U.S. Fish and Wildlife Service.

"Times change, owners change, economic pressures change, value systems change, and the long-term relationship with [the grantee] imposed by the easement will cease to be attractive to at least some property owners. The temptation to violate will increase. The easement holder must be prepared to withstand the pressures and be blessed with a carefully drawn easement that can stand up to a court test."

Experienced easement-holding agencies and organizations offer three pieces of advice on rectifying violations:

1. Stay out of court whenever possible.

2. Make sure the easement document specifies that you can go to court under specific circumstances.

3. If you must go to court, make sure you can win.

Easement grantees have two big incentives to stay out of court. First, like any private citizen, they would prefer to spend their limited resources on more constructive pursuits. Second, the hard feelings that inevitably result from a lawsuit can cripple the landowner/grantee relationship to the point where the incentive to cooperate is destroyed. The result can be more violations—and more time in court.

Litigation

Preventing litigation is not always possible. Some cases demand legal action. The quickest and most effective way to stop an action that imperils the integrity of the protected property's resources is to seek an injunction. An injunction is a writ granted by a court of equity, which requires someone to do or refrain from doing a certain act. If, for example, you realize that a landowner is cutting virgin redwood trees that the easement over his property protects, an injunction will stop him in his tracks.

Alternatives to the Courtroom

Restoration. The example of the timber cutting landowner points out an overriding problem with trying to rectify a violation. The damage is usually done by the time the easement holder learns about it. Often, no remedy will restore the originally protected resource. Halting the timber cutting midway cannot bring back to life the 500-year-old trees that already were cut. The IRS regulations require that an easement deed specify restoration as one of the available remedies for violation. *See* Treas. Reg. § 1.170A-14(g)(5)(ii). What restoration is adequate, however, is often difficult to determine.

Arbitration. As court costs continue to spiral and cases back up for months, professional third-party arbitration becomes a more attractive option for prompt settlement of disputes. When a case is settled by arbitration, the two parties choose a disinterested third party, who hears both sides of an issue and dictates a solution, typically a compromise. Arbitration can cost less money and take less time than litigation. That does not mean, however, that it is cheap and quick. The time that arbitration proceedings take—and the money it costs to pay an arbitrator for that time—depends on the complexity of the issue.

A critical factor in deciding between arbitration and litigation is the issue of appeal. Most organizations feel that, for arbitration to be useful at all, it must be binding. If the parties can appeal, the arbitration process loses its attractive swiftness. In some violation cases, the right to appeal is not significant; in others it is.

Often the grantee may feel that winning in court, and setting a legal precedent, is essential. Relying on a disinterested third party can be too risky. When issues involve a large amount of money, a critical legal issue, or both, litigation is a surer course than arbitration.

Arbitration cannot be an easement holder's only defense. Indeed, some easement holders cannot use arbitration at all; federal and state agencies usually cannot agree to arbitration because it is perceived as an illegal delegation of authority.

Mediation. While arbitration depends on a disinterested third party to dictate a solution, mediation involves the parties themselves. A third-party mediator is hired to guide the disputing parties in working out their own solution to their problem. Where some federal and state agencies cannot use arbitration, mediation *is* an option. In mediation, like arbitration, however, the solution can set no legal precedent.

A grantee's bottom line must be to defend the terms of the easement. Never compromise the integrity of an easement simply to stay out of court. How well you defend your easements affects more than just your program. Your responsibility, or lack thereof, contributes to the national reputation of easement programs.

A Commitment to Defense

Neither arbitration nor litigation is inexpensive. Easement holders must be prepared to handle the costs of settling disputes. For details on how grantees plan for enforcement costs, see chapter 8.

Monitoring and defending easements sounds like a lot of work, and it is. But organizations and agencies should never accept conservation easements without a strong commitment and ability to monitor them.

The monitoring, management, and enforcement of the easements acquired will be the most difficult and long-term stage of the process. It has been assumed in the past that once the department has acquired an easement, our involvement in that particular easement is finished. The fact is that once we have acquired an easement, our involvement in the easement has just begun. With every right acquired . . . a corresponding responsibility is assumed.

Art Reese
Chief of Habitat and Technical Services
Wyoming Department of Game and Fish

The Trustees of Reservations
Conserving the
Massachusetts Landscape

572 Essex Street
Beverly, Massachusetts
01915

Telephone
617-921-1944

CONSERVATION RESTRICTION INSPECTION REPORT

1. Date (year only) _____

2. Name of property _____

3. Location _____
   street address

_____
city or town   county

4. Day and date restricted area inspected _____

5. Size in acres _____

6. Date conservation restriction acquired (month and year recorded) _____

_____

7. Name and address of owner at that time _____

_____

8. Name and address of present owner (if different from that of original donor,

_____

9. Length of time in present ownership _____

10. Names of members of inspection team _____

11. Did the owner of the land accompany you on the inspection? If not, give the
    name and address of his/her authorized representative or identify permission
    given (whether by letter, telephone or personally). _____

_____

12. Are the terms of the conservation restriction being observed? Describe details
    of your inspection. _____

_____

13. Did you note any possible violations of the terms of the conservation restric-
    tion? Be as specific as you can. _____

_____

14. Describe acts or uses permitted by the terms of the restriction that have taken place since the last inspection. _____

_____

_____

15. Number and description of photographs accompanying this report. Be sure to identify each photograph. _____

_____

16. Time spent on the property _____

17. Present use of restricted property _____

_____

18. Uses of surrounding properties _____

_____

19. Remarks (particularly as to present condition of property) _____

_____

_____

_____

20. Superintendent's name _____

   Signature _____

21. One member of inspection team should also sign here. _____

_____

APPENDIX F   Sample Monitoring Inspection Forms

 National Trust for Historic Preservation

EASEMENT INSPECTION FORM

BUILDING/SITE:
ADDRESS:
CURRENT OWNER:
ADDRESS:
PHONE:
INSPECTION DATE:

A: Protected Features or Restrictions   Compliance

B: General Conditions and Potential Problem Areas

C: Did Inspector meet with the property owner or his representative during the
      inspection visit?

      If yes, name of owner or representative:

D.   Inspected by:
      Title/Affiliation:
      Phone:
      Date:

E.   I, _____ , owner of the above property, agree that the
      description prepared by _____ is an accurate represen-
      tation of the physical condition of the property as of _____ .

1785 Massachusetts Avenue, N.W.
Washington, D.C. 20036
(202) 673-4000

96

National Trust for Historic Preservation

OPTIONAL OWNER STATEMENT FORM

Building/Site:

Address:

Current Owner:

Address:

Inspection Date:

Inspected By:

Title:

A.   General Conditions and Potential Problems:

B.   Owner Statement:

1. Construction, restoration, major maintenance, or changes in use or owner-ship contemplated within the next 12 months:

2. Comments on Easement Inspection Procedure:

C.   Signature of Owner:

_____   _____

Signature   Date

1785 Massachusetts Avenue, N.W.
Washington, D.C. 20036
(202) 673-4000

```
        N A P A
       C O U N T Y
        L A N D
        T R U S T
```

EASEMENT MONITORING PROGRAM
INSPECTION REPORT: 19 ___

Easement Name:
Address:

Owner:
Address:

Manager:
Address:

1. If property is currently being used for any of the following purposes, please describe.

    ECOSYSTEM/SPECIES PRESERVATION: (nesting site protection, etc.)

    SCIENTIFIC/EDUCATIONAL: (research, nature study, etc.)

    WILDLIFE/HABITAT MANAGEMENT: (planting, selective cutting, etc.)

    RECREATIONAL: (hiking, hunting, camping, etc.)

    FORESTRY: (harvesting, reforestation, nursery, etc.)

    AGRICULTURAL: (orchard, vineyard, horse pasture, etc.)

    RESIDENTIAL: (permanent residences, guest houses, mobile homes, etc.)

    COMMERCIAL: (sales to the public, concessions, etc.)

    INDUSTRIAL: (mining, etc.)

2. If manmade alterations of the property have taken place, please note location, extent, purpose, and individual or groups responsible.

    CONSTRUCTION:

    FILLING:

    EXCAVATION:

    OTHER:

3. If the property has been altered by natural causes, please note location and nature of changes.

    FIRE:

    FLOODING:

    LANDSLIDE:

    EROSION:

    OTHER:

P.O. BOX 2903   •   YOUNTVILLE   •   CALIFORNIA   •   94599

4.   If any new documentation was made, indicate below.

           Map I.D.#   Description Photos   Drawings

BUILDINGS:

STRUCTURES:

ROADS & TRAILS:

FILLING:

EXCAVATION:

OTHER:

5.   Are special restrictions in the conservation easement, if any, being complied with?

6.   Describe current land use and condition of appurtenant property, if any, and note any significant changes since last monitoring report.

7.   Is there a plaque on the property acknowledging Land Trust involvement?

8.   What are the current status and known plans concerning management of the property?

9.   Further observations.

Date of Inspection:

Signed by Monitor(s): _____   _____

     Address: _____   _____

                  _____   _____

     Phone: _____   _____

Signed by Landowner: _____

PLEASE INDICATE THE NUMBER OF THE FOLLOWING ATTACHED TO THIS RE-PORT:

                                          aerial photo   _____
                                          ground photos   _____
                                          maps   _____
                                          illustrations   _____
                                          additional pages   _____
                                          other   _____
                        TOTAL NUMBER OF ATTACHMENTS   _____

CHAPTER 8

Funds for Monitoring:

Ensuring Long-Term Protection

Somehow, people got the idea that the easement was a "lesser" protection tool, and because of that, it was less expensive and required less participation [from the conservation organization]. The fact is, easements are the *most* complicated land protection tool. Owning land in fee is the simplest way to protect it. Holding an easement—which is actually like owning land in a partnership—is at least twice as complicated, and it can turn out to be more expensive.

Walt Matia
former Director of Stewardship
The Nature Conservancy

Landowners who grant easements perform the opposite of alchemy. They start with development rights of golden value. But once they give those development rights away, the rights lose their golden value and turn into the grantee's muddy monitoring responsibility.

That's a fanciful way of looking at the fact that every easement program administrator must anticipate: an easement is no quick fix. Routine monitoring costs money. Defending easements against legal challenges costs even more. In accepting an easement, your organization or agency assumes a perpetual financial liability. The Jackson Hole Land Trust explains this paradox well in a handout entitled "Stewardship Funds":

In accepting an easement, the Land Trust assumes the legal obligation to carry out the donor's desires by upholding the terms of the easement—forever. So although the easement donor has given something of great significance, the Land Trust has, in a sense, assumed a perpetual liability. The donor is not likely to violate his own easement, of course, but eventually others will own the property. Someone who wants to put condominiums on the hay meadow or dredge the spawning stream may try to violate the easement. The Trust must be prepared to monitor and defend all of its easements, including taking on legal battles when necessary. It *will* happen and it *will* be costly. It's only good business to plan for it now.

Not only is it good business to plan for the costs of monitoring and enforcement, but if the donor claims a tax deduction for the easement, it is an IRS requirement. The IRS regulations state that an "eligible donee" of tax-deductible conservation easements "must . . . have the resources to enforce the restrictions" of the easements. *See* Treas. Reg. § 1.170A-14(c)(1). Although the regulations say that donees "need not set aside funds to enforce the restrictions that are the subject of the contribution," many donees believe that the most important resource for enforcing easement restrictions is cash in the bank.

Of course, the best way to avoid costly monitoring and enforcement problems is to plan ahead. Make sure that an easement is the right tool for the property and that the terms are neither too restrictive nor too loose. Assuming, though, that an easement is the right tool and that the document is carefully drawn, how do grantees plan for the inevitable costs of monitoring?

Many organizations and agencies set aside funds solely for monitoring and defending easements. They term this separate pot of money a monitoring fund, a stewardship fund, an enforcement fund, or an endowment. Again, from the Jackson Hole Land Trust:

> The Stewardship Fund is set aside solely to cover the costs of monitoring and defending our conservation easements. It enables us to make annual visits to each property and to gather current information about the land. Most important, as the Fund builds, it will insure our ability to take whatever actions are necessary to uphold the terms of every easement.

Many grantees build this fund easement by easement at the time of each gift by either soliciting a cash contribution from the donor or raising money from other sources. Others simply set aside a certain percentage of each year's revenue as a monitoring fund. Some keep their monitoring funds separate from their operating funds. Others do not. The pros and cons of each method are outlined in this chapter.

Regardless of how they raise or administer monitoring funds, all easement administrators agree that financial planning for easement upkeep is crucial. "No matter how you raise the money," says The Nature Conservancy's Walt Matia, "the real issue is to acknowledge that there will be some cost."

Asking a Donor for a Cash Gift

Program administrators who accept the generous donation of an easement and then turn around and ask the donor to give cash as well may feel like King Lear's ungrateful children. They also run the risk of being perceived that way— "sharper than a serpent's tooth"—by the property owner.

"It has happened that we've priced ourselves right out of an easement" by asking for a cash donation to accompany the gift of easement, says Brian Steen, executive director of the Big Sur Land Trust. "And it wasn't because the landowner couldn't afford it. It was a conceptual disagreement. There were public agencies who offered to take the easement for nothing. The landowner accused us of being mercenary."

With most easement donors, however, the Big Sur Land Trust has been more successful. "We've encountered the whole range of acceptance, from zero percent to one hundred percent," says Steen. On the average, he estimates, about three in four easement donors agree to give cash.

Three in four also seems to be the success rate for the Society for the Protection of New Hampshire Forests, according to Bruce Hovland, the society's director of forestry and land protection. When the forest society started its easement program, it did not push the request for a general contribution. "We didn't want money to be a limiting factor," says Hovland. "Now, though, we've realized that it's important for donors to recognize the commitment we make to monitoring their easements. We've found it valuable to discuss with landowners their contributions to a restricted fund, to be used only for monitoring and defending easements."

On Boston's north shore, thousands of acres of productive wildlife habitat bordering tidal rivers and the Massachusetts coast are protected by conservation easements held by two land trusts, Essex County Greenbelt Association and The Trustees of Reservations.

EDWARD MONNELLY

Indeed, many organizations make the point to easement donors that their contribution of cash to a monitoring fund acts as security that their protective intent will be carried out. "I usually describe the endowment as an insurance policy," says Steen. "The landowner's contribution is the premium." The Napa County Land Trust reprinted in its newsletter these words from a donor's letter: "In keeping with my desire to preserve the natural, scenic, agricultural, and open space values of the lands over which I am donating an easement, I would like to create an underlying endowment with your organization to ensure that you will be able to carry out your monitoring and oversight functions and to enforce the terms of the easement in perpetuity." What more persuasive words than those from a satisfied customer?

No matter how you say it, say it early in your negotiations. "I make sure to tell a donor right away that we always ask for some kind of a cash contribution," says Brian Steen. "The worst thing you can do is spring it on them right before they sign the deed."

But none of the dozen easement program administrators surveyed informally turns down an easement simply because the owner can't or won't give cash to accompany it. "Some people just aren't in a position to make a donation," says Bruce Hovland. "Lots of people are cash-poor and land-rich. But that doesn't mean the easement isn't worth taking. You have to be flexible."

Asking Others for Contributions

Many easement administrators prefer to raise monitoring funds from sources other than the property owner, such as the general public or philanthropic foundations. They reason that the easement provides a significant public benefit, and the public should support its enforcement.

That reasoning, however, does not always bear fruit. To be realistic, some grantees aim to raise monitoring funds from the general public, but keep open the option of asking the donor. The Peconic Land Trust in New York explains such a policy in a handout entitled "Guidelines for Gifts of Easements":

> For each gift of an easement, the Board of Directors will set a target amount of cash contributions to be raised. Fifty percent of such funds will be put into the Peconic Stewardship Fund, the income from which will support the ongoing monitoring expenses of the Trust. With the cooperation of the donor, the Trust will attempt to raise the target amount of contributions from the local community. However, such contributions may also be requested of donors to assure that the Trust will have the resources necessary to fulfill its present and future responsibilities.

Formulas for Contributions

Different organizations use different guidelines as a starting point for negotiations over contributions to a monitoring fund. Most formulas, however, fit into one of these four categories:

☐ a percentage of the donor's tax savings

☐ a portion of the value of the gift

☐ a portion of the value of the rights the landowner retains

☐ a flat or fixed recommended amount

To determine the right amount for fixed, one-time contributions, organizations usually try to determine how much easement monitoring will cost. Expenses for each easement vary. Here are some considerations that affect monitoring costs:

☐ Size and accessibility of the property. Can monitoring be accomplished by walking the property or is aerial monitoring necessary? Can you drive to the property in a few minutes or does it take hours?

☐ Proximity to the grantee's other properties. Can several monitoring visits be accomplished on one trip?

☐ Quality of baseline data. Are the data complete and clear, or will it take substantial time in the field to determine if changes have occurred?

☐ Potential enforcement problems. Will several monitoring visits be required each year or will once a year suffice? Are costly violations likely?

☐ Need for professional monitors. Are the easement restrictions so technical in nature that they require specialists (botanists, architects, etc.) to see that they are being upheld?

Look also at the practices of peer organizations. If your organization requests a donation of $5,000 per easement, does a similar organization nearby ask for only $4,000? If so, why?

Sample Formulas

Here are the formulas that several conservation and preservation organizations use to determine how much money to solicit for monitoring funds:

The L'Enfant Trust in Washington, D.C., requests a "Fair Share Contribution" of $1,500 or 10 percent of the easement value, whichever is greater. The trust requests a $500 "contribution deposit" to cover the administrative costs of evaluating whether the potential easement is eligible for a donation to the Trust. That $500 is applicable to the Fair Share Contribution.

The Napa County Land Trust asks for 5 percent of the easement's appraised value or 5 percent of the easement-restricted property's appraised value, whichever is greater. Originally the trust requested 10 percent of the donor's tax savings but has found that its current policy comes closer to reflecting the costs of monitoring.

The Philadelphia Historic Preservation Corporation covers monitoring costs from two sources. First, the corporation places a portion of its general fund each year into a separate endowment to cover easement monitoring costs—the amount depending on the number and characteristics of the easements the corporation acquires that year. Second, it charges the donor for the legal and architectural expenses incurred in preparing the easement document, plus .05 percent of the building's fair market value (with a cap of $100,000).

Two other sample guidelines are reprinted at the end of this chapter.

How Separate? How Equal?
And How Managed?

Try telling this to a dozen volunteers who have incorporated as a land trust in order to acquire rapidly developing local wetlands: instead of buying another piece of wetlands, you should lock your money up in an endowment fund, so you'll be able to monitor your easements. And instead of paying the office utility bills, put your money into an easement endowment fund.

Balancing the pressing costs of buying land and running an office with the potential costs of defending an easement—all on a tight budget—is not easy. To compound the problem, people rarely like to give money to support operating expenses. It's far more exciting to donate $50 to help the local preservation society buy the town's 200-year-old schoolhouse than it is to help it buy light bulbs. The temptation is to spend some of the money that might accompany an easement donation on buying light bulbs or more land, rather than locking it up in an easement monitoring fund.

Some organizations, especially those on a shoestring budget, do not formally separate enforcement money. They count instead on the strength of their general fund to cover enforcement costs that might arise. Or they may have attorneys on their boards of directors who have volunteered to donate their time to defending an easement should the need arise.

Most experienced grantees, however, place at least a portion of the cash received from an easement donor into a distinct easement monitoring fund. A portion often also goes toward reimbursing the organization for the expenses of accepting the easement—such as legal fees, filing fees, and baseline data development costs—and covering routine operating expenses not associated directly with the easement program. Given a $5,000 grant, for example, a portion—perhaps $3,000—might go toward general reimbursement and operating costs, while the remaining $2,000 might be placed in an easement management fund. The interest from the $2,000 also could support operating costs.

Grantees must be careful, however, of the representations they make concerning the use of an easement endowment obtained from donors. If contributions are diverted to uses other than those represented, the donors may have grounds to accuse the donee of fraud.

Finally, how should a monitoring fund be managed? Although these funds often are called *endowments,* few organizations manage their funds as true endowments. In a true endowment, the donation would be invested and only the interest on the investment would be available to the organization. A donation of $4000 invested at 7.5 percent, for example, would yield just $300 annually that would be available to the organization. Typically, only high-budget organizations can afford the luxury of locking away so much money.

However you raise and manage the money, easement monitoring needs to have its own operational priority. Without sufficient, distinct monitoring funds, "you rob Peter to pay Paul," says Acadia National Park's chief of resource management, Carroll Schell. "Your monitoring program, and therefore your rapport with the grantor, may fall into jeopardy."

Jackson Hole Land Trust

THE STEWARDSHIP FUND

The donation of a conservation easement is a major commitment for any landowner. Although tax benefits may be a strong incentive for some, no property owner gives an easement without a real desire to see his land protected.

In accepting an easement, the Land Trust assumes the legal obligation to carry out the donor's desires by upholding the terms of the easement—forever. So although the easement donor has given something of great significance, the Land Trust has in a sense assumed a perpetual liability. The donor is not likely to violate his own easement, of course, but eventually others will own the property. Someone who wants to put condominiums on the hay meadow or dredge the spawning stream may try to violate the easement. The Trust must be prepared to monitor and defend all its easements, including taking on legal battles when necessary. It will happen and it will be costly. It's only good business to plan for it now.

The Stewardship Fund has been established for that very purpose. The Fund is set aside solely to cover the costs of monitoring and defending our conservation easements. It enables us to make annual visits to each property and to gather current information about the land. Most important, as the Fund builds, it will insure our ability to take whatever actions are necessary to uphold the terms of every easement.

The initial cost to the Trust for taking an easement can also be considerable. in order to be sure the easement is legally sound and suitable for the property, we must spend money for such things as baseline studies, title searches, aerial photos, maps, legal fees, and staff time. Although these expenses vary, the average cost of accepting an easement is about $1,500.

Because the Land Trust must operate on a businesslike basis, the Board has established a policy of endowing each easement at the time it is accepted, both to cover initial costs and to increase the Stewardship Fund for future costs. Thus, when circumstances permit, we ask each easement donor to also make a cash contribution for these purposes. This contribution is in no way a condition of our accepting

POST OFFICE BOX 2897   JACKSON   WYOMING   83001   PHONE 307-733-4707

an easement, and we know that it may not always be possible. However, we do ask every easement donor to review the following guidelines.

1. Please consider a minimum donation of $3,000. Of this, $1,500 will be credited to the general operating fund to cover initial costs; the remaining $1,500 will go to the Stewardship Fund.

2. If $3,000 is not possible, please give what you can. Half will go to the operating fund and half to the Stewardship Fund.

3. If you can, please give more. A contribution can be spread out over two or more years, if that is desirable. In determining what is possible and fair, consider not only your own resources, but the size and complexity of the easement, its fair market value and the amount of tax saving resulting from the easement donation. Of larger gifts, $1,500 will go to the operating fund and the remainder to the Stewardship Fund.

We invite questions and comments about these policies and guidelines, and hope you will feel free to discuss them with us.

SOCIETY
FOR THE
PROTECTION
OF
NEW HAMPSHIRE
FORESTS

54 PORTSMOUTH STREET
CONCORD, N. H. 03301-5486
(603) 224-9945

CONSERVATION EASEMENT
MONITORING AND ENFORCEMENT FUND

Since 1974 the Forest Society has been granted over 130 conservation easements covering more that 15,000 acres. We are responsible for monitoring these properties to ensure the easements are upheld now and forever.

THE PROGRAM

If our Society is the Grantee of your Conservation Easement we will monitor the status of your land by plane every spring. Aerial monitoring, after snow melt and before leaf out, is the fastest and most comprehensive way to see the whole parcel. On the first monitoring flight an aerial photo is taken, which is used for comparison in future years. If any questions or discrepancies arise, we check the land on the ground and talk with the landowner. Should there be a violation that the current landowner does not willingly correct, legal action may be necessary. Every spring the current landowner is notified after we have monitored their land. This is especially important when the land changes hands.

If our Society has an Executory Interest in your Conservation Easement we check with the grantee every spring to be sure the necessary monitoring has been done. Should the grantee be unresponsive or find any violation, we visit the site to ensure the terms of the easement are being upheld. If the grantee is unable to uphold the terms of the easement, our Society could take on grantee responsibilities as called for in the easement.

Our monitoring and enforcement program has proved effective in regularly viewing the easement properties, enforcing the restrictions, and keeping the landowners informed. To date we have only had two violations and both have been quickly responded to and corrected.

THE COST

Our experience indicates the cost of monitoring and enforcing grantee interests in conservation easements is about $1/acre/year for the first 50 acres and nearly $.25/acre/year for additional acres in the same easement. If our Society acquires an executory interest in an easement, our cost is cut in half.

A permanent endowment for each easement is necessary to ensure adequate funds are always available for monitoring and enforcement. Our Board of Trustees has pooled the endowments for all easements into the Conservation Easement Monitoring and Enforcement Fund.

Our Fund is invested according to investment strategies approved by our Board. Up to 6.5% of the annual earnings from the Fund is spent on easement monitoring. The remaining income is returned to the Fund as a hedge against inflation. If enforcement is necessary, unexpended monitoring income of the Fund principal may be drawn upon for legal or other enforcement expenses. Your contribution to the Fund supports the monitoring and enforcement of your Conservation Easement forever. The table below shows the recommended Fund contribution by parcel size.

| | —Suggested Contributions— | |
Parcel Size (acres)	Society as Grantee	Society Receives Executory Interest
≤ 50	$ 900	$ 450
51 - 100	1080	540
101 - 150	1260	630
151 - 200	1440	720
201 - 250	1620	810
251 - 300	1800	900
301 - 350	1980	990
351 - 400	2160	1080
401 - 600	2880	1440
601 - 800	3600	1800
801 - 1000	5000	2500
1001 +	—Negotiable—	

CHAPTER 9

Back-Up Grantees:

Transferring Easements to Other Holders

The day will come when the original grantors of an easement will either want to or have to transfer ownership of their property. The easement document provides for this eventuality by clearly defining the terms of protection that will bind both present and subsequent owners.

But what if the *grantee* someday wants to or has to transfer ownership of the easement? What if the easement-holding nonprofit goes out of business? Or what if the easement-holding agency is reorganized and can no longer fulfill its commitment to monitoring easements? Or what if a new nonprofit or agency is established that is better suited to act as easement caretaker?

Like grantors, grantees too can transfer their interests in their easement-restricted properties—if the integrity of the easement is not affected by the transfer and if the new grantee meets state statutory requirements. Just as a deed of easement limits any future property owner's actions, so it restricts future organizations or agencies that might someday hold the easement.

How do grantees prepare for this eventuality? Some grantees wait to decide how to transfer their easements until a need arises. Others plan in advance and line up a specific secondary defense called a back-up grantee.

Transferring an Easement

IRS Requirements

Responsible easement holders transfer their easements only to those organizations or agencies that will take equally good care of them. If the easement was a gift and the donor claimed an income tax deduction, this precaution is more than a moral obligation; it's an IRS requirement.

For tax-deductible gifts, the easement document must state that the donee will never transfer the easement unless the organization to which it is transferred, the "transferee," meets two tests:

1. The transferee must be qualified to hold easements under the relevant state and federal laws; *and*

2. The transferee must agree to continue to enforce the easement restrictions. *See* Treas. Reg. § 1.170A-14(c)(2).

This handbook's model easements include language that meets this IRS requirement.

The Legal Process of Assigning

The legal term for transferring a property interest such as an easement is "assigning." It's a relatively simple process. The assignment document is signed, notarized, and recorded in the public records.

The sunlight, scale, and ambience of New York City's Greenacre Park are protected by the first scenic easement applied to an urban landscape. The easement, donated to the New York Landmarks Conservancy by the owner of a four-story building opposite the park, prohibits any construction that would exceed the height of the current building and prohibits the use of the site's development rights to support construction on any other site that would shadow the park or block its view.

WILLIAM H. WHYTE

With an assignment document goes an agreement. The agreement covers practical concerns—such as transferring monitoring funds to the assignee and requiring reports from the assignee to the assigner—that are incidental to the actual assignment. These types of concerns need not be recorded in the county records and can be outlined in a side agreement, or they can be incorporated in the recorded assignment. It's a matter of preference. One legal reason for keeping them separate is that an agreement is a bilateral contract, enforceable by both parties. A standard assignment is a unilateral instrument and may not represent a "contract" if the assigner needs to enforce the terms under which the assignment was made.

A more generic legal mechanism used to transfer easement ownership is the quitclaim deed. This handbook recommends the more specific path of using assignment and agreement documents, which spell out the responsibilities of the two parties in greater detail.

Sample assignment and agreement documents are reprinted at the end of this chapter. Use them for guidance only. As with any legal procedure, consult an attorney for the particulars of your case.

Passing the Buck(s)—and the Good Will

Whenever possible, the grantee should have the owner of the easement-restricted property participate in the transfer process. It is critical to the new grantee's effectiveness as easement steward that the property owner have confidence in the new grantee. If the issue is approached with sensitivity and if the transfer does indeed further the intent of the easement, the property owner is unlikely to object to the transfer.

If the grantor donated cash to cover the costs of monitoring the easement, that money should stay with the easement. Whatever amount has not already been spent on monitoring should be transferred to the next grantee. Take special care to explain to the original donor where the money is going, and why.

Planning Ahead: Back-Up Grantees

Many easement programs are small and low on cash. They may have voluntary boards of directors that turn over every few years or they may be run by overburdened town or county staff. The easements they hold, however, typically are required to last forever.

To make sure that their easements will be enforced over the long term, many small easement programs rely on larger organizations or agencies to act as partners in holding their easements. The larger organizations sometimes act as "co-donees"—splitting in half both the title to the easement and the steward-ship responsibilities that go with it. More often, however, the larger programs agree to be a back-up and to hold an executory or reversionary interest in the smaller programs' easements. (See this handbook's model easements for specific language on back-up grantees.)

A back-up grantee is a complement, not a substitute, for a strong monitoring fund. A monitoring fund is an easement program's defensive line; a back-up grantee is its secondary defense.

A back-up grantee is empowered to enforce an easement if the original grantee fails to do so or to take over an easement if the original grantee can no longer manage it. The original grantee has the primary responsibility for holding the easement and for monitoring it. The back-up organization or agency keeps on file a second set of all of the documentation relevant to the easement, so that it is prepared to act if and when the primary grantee can no longer manage and defend the easement.

Even without a specifically designated back-up grantee, the courts have the power to ensure that the purposes of the easement are carried out in the event of the original organization's demise. It is safer, however, for grantees to take the matter into their own hands.

Why Enlist a Back-Up Grantee?

Here are some of the reasons why grantees enlist a back-up grantee:

Greater defense resources. A primary reason to use a back-up grantee is to be able to draw on the defense resources of another entity. Because the back-up organization has a legal interest in the easement, it has the legal standing to defend the easement in court.

Strong selling point to landowners. Some property owners balk at the idea of granting an easement to a local organization or agency without the security of a larger entity to back it up. The more assurance you can offer landowners that their land will indeed be protected forever, the more inclined they may be to grant an easement. A back-up grantee adds to this assurance.

Access to expertise. When the grantee is not fully versed in topics such as land use management, natural area supervision, or architectural review, consultation with a more experienced back-up grantee can be useful.

Protection against public taking. For private easement-holding organizations, using a government agency as a back-up may provide protection against public takings through eminent domain or condemnation proceedings. Private organizations cannot prevent public takings of their properties. Federal property interests, however, usually cannot be condemned by a state, and state property interests usually cannot be condemned by a local government. If an agency has a legal interest in your easement-protected property, it may be able to fight condemnation proceedings stemming from a "lesser" agency.

Not all easement grantees, however, think that back-ups are a great idea. Some grantees say that potential grantors can be put off by the mention of a back-up grantee. It's hard enough to get some landowners to trust them, these grantees say. Bring another organization into the picture and the deal can fall through. Grantees who feel this way say it is unnecessary to consider the issue of choosing a successor until there is a specific need.

What's In It for the Back-Up Grantee?

It's easy to see the advantages that a back-up grantee offers the primary grantee. But what's in it for the back-up? Why would one organization want to offer its resources to another?

When one grantee offers its resources as a back-up to another, it strengthens the cause of land protection in the back-up organization's back yard, as well as the general cause of easement programs. An easement violation that is allowed to stand sets a precedent that damages the integrity of easement programs everywhere. It is in every easement holder's interest to ensure that the terms of every easement across the country are upheld.

Where to Find a Back-Up Grantee

Several states, especially those in the East, have statewide private organizations and/or public agencies that assume the responsibility of backing-up local easement grantees. The Maryland Environmental Trust is a prime example. Often the willingness of regional organizations to assist local easement holders goes way beyond serving as a back-up. Some, such as the Society for the Protection of New Hampshire Forests, act as matchmakers for easement donors and more suitable recipients. In a similar vein, the New Jersey Conservation Foundation accepts its easements with reserved assignment rights so that it can assign them to appropriate local organizations at a later date.

National organizations have similar practices. The Nature Conservancy is the prime example of an organization that serves both as a matchmaker— sometimes "pre-acquiring" easements for later assignment to local grantees— and as a back-up grantee. The National Trust for Historic Preservation does the same.

Most easement grantees know who else is in the easement business in their areas. For those who do not, two resources may help: the Land Trust Exchange's *National Directory of Local and Regional Land Conservation Organizations* and staff at the National Trust for Historic Preservation. In some cases, however, an easement holder will not be able to find a willing back-up.

The Ultimate Back-Ups:
The Courts and the People

Since the purpose of conservation easements is to benefit the general public, it makes sense that local citizens and the attorney general have the right to enforce an easement.

In most states, the attorney general's supervisory powers over charitable institutions give him or her the right to enforce an easement when the grantee is not meeting that task. In many states, local citizens can sue to enforce an easement. The California Open Space Easements Act of 1969, for example, allows property owners and local residents to enforce easements in equity if the city or county holding the easements fails to enforce or honor the restrictions (California Government Code Section 51058). Such procedures are cumbersome, however, and you cannot be sure of the results.

The issue of public enforcement also raises a sticky question: Who decides when an easement grantee is failing to meet its stewardship responsibility? Leaving that determination to the court is a cumbersome process. It is not guaranteed to work. Clearly, the intent of the easement is best served when the grantee itself recognizes the need to assign the easement to another's stewardship.

[Sample Document]

ASSIGNMENT OF DEED OF CONSERVATION EASEMENT

WHEREAS, Land Trust A ("LTA"), a nonprofit California public benefit corporation, holds a Deed of Conservation Easement (the Ocean Ranch Easement) over certain property in Marin County, California;

WHEREAS, Land Trust B ("LTB"), a nonprofit California public benefit corporation organized for the purpose of encouraging the conservation of resources, is a "qualified organization" within the meaning of Section 170(h)(3) of the Internal Revenue Code of 1986, as amended, and an organization eligible under California law to hold a conservation easement;

WHEREAS, LTB wishes to hold and enforce the terms of the Ocean Ranch Easement; and

WHEREAS, it is consistent with the charitable purpose of LTA to transfer the Ocean Ranch Easement to LTB and it is consistent with the charitable purposes of LTB to hold and enforce the Ocean Ranch Easement;

NOW THEREFORE, effective upon the recordation of this document in the Official Records of Marin County, California, LTA hereby assigns and conveys to LTB all of its right, title, and interest in that certain Deed of Conservation Easement which was executed on December 30, 1987, and recorded on December 31, 1987, in Book 419, Pages 522 through 531, of the Official Records of Marin County, California.

Executed in San Francisco, California, this 10th day of June 1988.

LAND TRUST A

By: _____

Title: _____

[insert appropriate corporate acknowledgement]

[Sample Form of Acceptance,
which should be part of same document]

ACCEPTANCE

Land Trust B hereby accepts the above Assignment of Deed of Conservation Easement and agrees to diligently exercise all of the responsibilities of the Grantee thereunder.

Executed at San Francisco, California the 11th day of June 1988.

Land Trust B

By: _____

Title: _____

[insert appropriate corporate acknowledgement]

[Prepared by Trust for Public Land]

[Sample Document]
AGREEMENT FOR THE ASSIGNMENT
OF A CONSERVATION EASEMENT
FROM LAND TRUST A TO
LAND TRUST B

This is an agreement dated June 9, 1988, between Land Trust A, a nonprofit California public benefit corporation (having its principal address at 101 Main Street, San Francisco, California 94105), and Land Trust B, a nonprofit California public benefit corporation (having its principal address at 102 Main Street, San Francisco, California 94105).

RECITALS

A. LTA holds a conservation easement over certain real property in Marin County, California. Said conservation easement is referred to as the "Ocean Ranch Easement."

B. LTB was organized for the purpose of encouraging the conservation of environmental and productive resources.

C. It is consistent with the charitable purposes of LTA to transfer the Ocean Ranch Easement to LTB and it is consistent with the charitable purposes of LTB to hold and enforce the Ocean Ranch Easement.

D. LTB is both a "qualified organization" within the meaning of Section 170(h)(3) of the Internal Revenue Code of 1986, as amended, and an organization eligible under California law to hold conservation easements.

E. LTB has inspected the property subject to the Ocean Ranch Easement and has reviewed the terms of the Ocean Ranch Easement.

F. LTB wishes to hold and enforce the Ocean Ranch Easement.

THEREFORE THE PARTIES AGREE AS FOLLOWS:

1. LTA will assign the Ocean Ranch Easement to LTB.

2. LTB will promptly accept the Ocean Ranch Easement from LTA.

3. LTA will grant to LTB the sum of $5,000, to be delivered with the executed assignment, to be used for preparing baseline data on the property subject to the Ocean Ranch Easement and for monitoring and reporting on the Ocean Ranch Easement.

4. LTB will diligently monitor the Ocean Ranch Easement and take such steps as it deems appropriate to vigorously enforce the terms of the Ocean Ranch Easement so as to protect the conservation values which the Ocean Ranch Easement is intended to protect. Said monitoring shall include at a minimum an annual inspection of the property subject to the Ocean Ranch Easement and the preparation of a written report based upon said inspection which notes the conditions of the property in relation to the Ocean Ranch Easement and the baseline data relating to the

Ocean Ranch Easement maintained by LTB. LTB agrees to send LTA copies of any such reports if and when LTA should find them necessary for evaluating the assignment of easements to other conservation organizations.

In witness of the foregoing provisions the parties have signed this agreement below.

LAND TRUST A

By: _____

Title: _____

LAND TRUST B

By: _____

Title: _____

[Prepared by Trust for Public Land]

CHAPTER 10

Amending Easements:

The Question of Accommodating Change

When the terms of an easement are negotiated, both the grantor and the grantee should consider those provisions as unchangeable. Although altered circumstances and conditions *may* someday justify an amendment to the document, amendments should be viewed with extreme caution. No organization or property owner should ever agree to a conservation easement with the idea that its terms will be changed later.

The question of when it is acceptable to amend an easement is just beginning to be raised. The records show little experience with the issue. In 1985, only 15 percent of easement holders responding to the Land Trust Exchange easement survey reported permitting amendments. The answers are being developed now, case by case.

And plenty of people are paying attention. Easement grantors want to know what will happen if a drastic need for change in their easements' terms arises. Grantees want examples of how others have handled this sticky situation. Most important, the courts, the state and local legislatures, and the Internal Revenue Service may judge the integrity of the entire easement concept by the way the issue of amendments is handled.

The implications of amendment go far beyond any one easement. Abuse of the right to amend can raise charges as serious as tax fraud. The issue is fraught with such ominous complexities that it is tempting just to avoid it. Responsible easement holders, however, must confront the issue and develop a policy to guide their amendment decisions, easement by easement.

Determining When to Amend

Changes Should Strengthen the Easement or Be Neutral

The ideal amendment policy would be: "Change it for the better or don't change it at all." The only amendments permitted would be those that strengthen the protective terms of the easement document. In practice, however, the merits of a proposed change may rarely be that clear-cut. In such cases, a workable policy should be: "Either change it for the better or change it for the neutral." But the amendment must never result in net degradation of the conservation values the easement is designed to protect.

The Maryland Environmental Trust (MET) follows a policy along these lines. As senior easement planner Jody Roesler explains:

It is the policy of MET to amend an easement only if:

1. The amendment would strengthen the easement provisions—that is, the amendment changes the original easement terms so that permitted uses on the land would have fewer environmental impacts than the uses permitted under the terms of the original deed; or

2. The amendment would have a neutral effect on the easement provisions—that is, it would neither strengthen nor weaken the original easement terms. For example, the amendment might include new preservation benefits which MET determines to be of equivalent value to increased environmental impacts.

Determining what is neutral is a tough call. At the Maryland Environmental Trust, amendments that meet these tests must be approved by MET's board of trustees and, because the trust is associated with state government, by the Maryland Board of Public Works.

Two Examples: Approved and Denied

Two examples from the Maryland Environmental Trust show the type of considerations that go into an amendment decision. In one example, the trust approved an amendment for a 300-acre property where the easement reserved for the grantor the right to build private educational and recreational camp facilities on 23 designated acres. The amendment replaced this right with the right to build one single-family residence with accessory structures confined to a two-acre site, reducing the potential impact on the property.

An amendment that did not win MET approval proposed to eliminate two paragraphs from the deed of easement that the trust held jointly with the Maryland Historical Trust over a 290-acre historic farm. The first paragraph the grantor wished to delete prohibited all industrial or commercial activities, except for farming, forestry, and activities that could be conducted from existing residential or farm buildings without alteration of their external appearances. The second required the written approval of the joint grantees as to the location, design, and appearance prior to the start of construction on all permitted buildings, structures, and improvements. Because deleting these paragraphs would have been neither neutral nor more restrictive with respect to protection of the environment and the historical integrity of the site, the boards of trustees of both organizations turned the proposed amendment down.

Easement Amendment Practices to Date

The record is sketchy on who has approved what amendments. The most complete data were compiled by the Land Trust Exchange in 1985 from 15 private and 12 public programs that reported accepting amendments. (Easement programs devoted exclusively to the preservation of historic buildings were not included in this survey.) These grantees reported the five following reasons for amending easements:

Clarification of terms. Most of these amendments were made to clarify the terms found in the easement document. Two cases involved the resolution of violations. In one case, for example, the construction of a barn prompted the need to clarify the term "accessory building." Three other cases involved adding provisions that accidentally had been omitted. One grantee amended each of its easements to require property owners to notify it of changes in ownership at least 30 days in advance.

Boundary adjustments. Several amendments involved boundary adjustments; one case corrected a surveying error. (The survey had the easement boundary running through the middle of a barn!) Another case involved an owner who was not the original grantor and wanted to build a swimming pool extending into a restricted area. The grantee released the restriction on the affected area in return for an equal amount of land added to the easement elsewhere on the property.

Site change of permitted activities. Four grantees permitted a change in site of a permitted activity—for two, the siting of house lots, for the other two, the siting of roads. Another case involved the permission to cut timber to foster the best management of the forested portion of a property.

Easing conflicts with local zoning. Two amendments were prompted by conflicts with local zoning. In one case, a house lot was changed so that the landowner could comply with septic and setback requirements in the zoning ordinance. In the other, the easement had allowed construction of a small house for the mother of the donor, so long as the house was not sold separately. Zoning, however, required that separate dwelling units be subdivided. The amendment permitted the subdivision but provided that the house could not be sold separately.

Increasing restrictions. Amendments also have increased the restrictiveness of easements. An easement on a waterfront property, for example, was amended to increase the required setback of any structures from the high-water mark. At Acadia National Park, an easement grantor went from a limited development posture to a forever-wild posture, much to the surprise and satisfaction of the park.

Why would easement grantors ask for tighter restrictions on the use of their property? Grantors may become more conservation-minded over time, as the natural value of the land becomes more and more important to them. Also, their family and financial situations may change, encouraging them to put more restrictions on the property.

Appraisals and Tax Deductions

An amendment that changes the uses specified in the original document may affect the property's value. When someone agrees to tighten a conservation easement, there may be an additional deduction allowable, although the IRS might conceivably take the position that the amendment document does not meet all the tests of a deductible conservation easement.

Donated easements must not be amended in a manner that *increases* the property value by restoring rights that the original easement prohibited. Not only are such amendments unethical, they may also subject both the grantor and grantee to penalties from the IRS.

Grantees must take it upon themselves to police their amendment practices. Be certain that the changes proposed by an amendment will not jeopardize the intent of the easement. Include the advice of an attorney and an appraiser in any discussion, however minor. Carefully record all deliberations over amendments in case there are questions later. Bear in mind that the only changes allowed should be those that are for the better or for the neutral.

The Legal Process of Making an Amendment

Like the easement document itself, an amendment must be recorded. Some states require a court's supervision to modify an easement, unless amendment is expressly provided for in the document.

This handbook's model easement documents expressly provide for amendment. The model historic preservation easement document refers to the "Standards for Rehabilitation and Guidelines for Rehabilitating Historic Buildings" issued by the Secretary of the Interior. It also reserves for the grantee the right to substitute reasonable alternative standards. This language complies with the January 1986 federal tax regulations, which state:

> When restrictions to preserve a building or land area within a registered historic district permit future development on the site, a deduction will be allowed under this section only if the terms of the restrictions require that such development conform with appropriate local, state or federal standards for construction or rehabilitation within the district. *See* Treas. Reg. § 1.170A-14(d)(5)(i).

Any amendments also must adhere to these standards.

Proceed with Caution and Equity

The right to amend an easement carries with it the potential for abuse. It also allows for changes that are necessary to make an easement workable "in perpetuity." Grantees must be judicious.

Treat grantors' requests for amendments with equity and scrutiny. Remember that each amendment sets a precedent. Where one person's request is approved, others with similar plans may expect to get similar approvals. Document your reasons for approving or denying each proposed amendment.

Use your right to amend easements sparingly, and only for the good of the easement. Make your easement program's policy clear: accept only those amendments that add to the integrity of your easements.

PART 2

Two Legal Issues

The Armour-Stiner Carmer Octagon House in Irvington, New York, a property listed on the National Register of Historic Sites, is protected by a historic preservation easement held by the National Trust for Historic Preservation.

CHAPTER 11

Term and Termination:

When Easements Aren't Forever

William R. Ginsberg

Most conservation easements will be of potentially infinite duration. State enabling statutes in the field are usually flexible—generally permitting any term desired by the parties, although a few require a minimum life such as 10 or 15 years.[1] But to obtain a federal tax deduction for the contribution of a conservation easement, it must be granted in perpetuity. In addition, maximum real property tax benefits will be available only if the easement is permanent. A shorter specified term may result in a smaller reduction in assessed valuation or the gradual phase-out of any reduction. Since the purpose of conservation restrictions is usually the permanent protection of a historic structure or open space, it would seem that restrictions should be of infinite duration.

Easements with Limited Terms

In certain circumstances, however, a limited term on conservation restrictions may be necessary or even desirable. Suppose, for example, a property is the habitat of a rare and endangered species of plant. The owner wishes to continue to occupy the property for a few years, but is willing ultimately to sell it to a conservation organization or a governmental agency. An interested conservation organization may be able to raise the necessary funds to purchase the property if it has sufficient time but wants to protect the habitat in the interim by limiting the uses of the land. If the funds cannot be raised within a certain period of time, the owner wants to be free to sell the property on the open market. The owner and the conservation organization might agree on an option to purchase, coupled with conservation restrictions to protect the parcel during the option period.

---

1. For example, Virginia requires a minimum of five years, Michigan and California at least 10, and Montana 15. The New York statute provides that a minimum term will be set by regulations, which have not yet been issued.

More simply, some owners will be unwilling to restrict their property in perpetuity but may be willing to do so for a period of years. The hope would be that, with the passage of time, the owner might have a change of heart and be willing to donate or sell the land or conservation restrictions on the land. A conservation easement for a period of years will establish a relationship with an interested conservation organization and protect the property while the owner makes a longer-term decision.

In almost all circumstances, however, conservation easements should be perpetual. Short-term arrangements may give the illusion of protection and establish a false sense of security. Furthermore, it takes as much time and money to negotiate and process an easement that lasts 10 years as one in perpetuity. Most conservation organizations and governments have limited staff time and should expend it on projects that will have long-term impact. Similarly, owners will often be unwilling to pay the costs associated with the placing of short-term restrictions or to contribute adequate funds for overhead and monitoring expenses of short-term conservation easements.

Methods of Termination

Because most conservation easements are designed to run in perpetuity, the question of how or when an easement can be extinguished is usually far from the minds of the grantor and grantee. The subject, however, is an important one. Conservation easements are frequently resisted by property owners or government officials simply because they are, theoretically, to be held in perpetuity, and perpetuity is a very long time. There is a concern that mistakes may be made or that circumstances may change, and the permanent restrictions may be a cause for regret. Fears have even been expressed that the use of conservation easements might be so widespread in a community that they would prevent the construction of necessary public facilities such as schools, hospitals, and housing.

Such concerns might have some validity if, in fact or in law, anything were truly permanent. But this is rarely the case, and conservation easements are no exception. They should, as already indicated, potentially be of infinite duration, but that is very different than *actually* being of infinite duration.

Conservation easements granted to run in perpetuity can be terminated by several methods and in a variety of circumstances, some of which are under the control of the grantor and grantee, and others not. Some states have anticipated that issues may arise with respect to the termination of conservation restrictions, and several statutes, as well as the Uniform Conservation Easement Act, provide that they may be terminated "in the same manner as other easements."[2] Other state statutes are silent on the question, probably assuming that

---

2. See, for example, Arizona, Colorado, Maryland, New Hampshire, and Utah.

there is no need to restate the obvious, and therefore pre-existing legal doctrines apply.[3] In a small number of states, statutory provisions are ambiguous or suggest that termination provisions, if desired, should be included in the easement document. New York, in particular, requires care in this respect. The following methods of termination, however, will be relevant in all states.

Eminent Domain (Condemnation)

If land is needed for a public purpose such as a school, road, or even a sports stadium, it may be taken by government, even against the wishes of the private owner. In such an event, the owner must be compensated for the value of the property. If the land is restricted by a conservation easement that prevents the proposed use, the restrictions may also be terminated by condemnation.[4] The nature and extent of compensation to the holder for the termination of the restrictions is a matter of some legal complexity and may vary from state to state. The definition of *public purpose* is very broad; thus the government's power of eminent domain makes it unlikely that a conservation easement will, at some future time, prevent necessary public activity.

Foreclosure

Another means whereby conservation restrictions may be terminated without the consent of the holder or landowner is through the foreclosure of a pre-existing lien on the property, such as a mortgage, mechanic's lien, or lien for unpaid taxes. At the foreclosure sale, the purchaser will take title free of restrictions placed on the property after the creation of the lien being foreclosed. This unfortunate result can be avoided with respect to a mortgage if, at the time the conservation easement is placed on the property, a subordination agreement is obtained from the holder of the mortgage. Such a subordination agreement is required by Internal Revenue Service regulations if the grantor is donating the easement and wishes to take a federal tax deduction for its value.

In a minority of states, the foreclosure of a tax lien placed on property *after* the conservation easement is recorded may also terminate the prior existing conservation restrictions. Fortunately this approach is changing, but the law of the state in which the property is located must be consulted on this point. In any event, if there is a pre-existing, unsubordinated mortgage on the property, or if state law with respect to tax liens is in doubt, a conservation easement should provide that the holder has the right to make mortgage and tax payments if the owner fails to do so, and that such payments will then become a lien on the

---

3. For example, Connecticut, Delaware, Louisiana, Michigan, Missouri, Montana, North Carolina, Ohio, and Washington.

4. In most states with conservation easement statutes, a conservation easement can also be created through the condemnation of the restrictions by a governmental entity.

restricted property. Such a provision will give the holder of the easement an opportunity to protect the restrictions should the need arise.

Funds allocated to the state of California from the federal Land and Water Conservation Fund helped purchase this conservation easement on California's northern coast, near Trinidad. The easement is held by the Humboldt North Coast Land Trust.

Marketable Title Acts

More than a third of the states have passed legislation providing that, after a certain number of years, claims to or restrictions on real property are automatically extinguished.[5] While Massachusetts and Wisconsin have such statutes, they specifically exempt conservation easements. In other states, however, the holder of the conservation easement may find that it is automatically voided after 20 to 30 years, notwithstanding that it was intended to restrict the land in perpetuity. The provisions of these statutes vary, but if one is on the books in your state, you might consider joining with other organizations to try to have the law amended in order to exempt conservation easements and other restrictions placed on property for public benefit purposes.

---

5. Connecticut, Florida, Illinois, Indiana, Iowa, Massachusetts, Michigan, Minnesota, Nebraska, North Carolina, North Dakota, Ohio, Oklahoma, South Dakota, Utah, Vermont, Wisconsin, and Wyoming.

Changed Conditions

The uses of land change with time. Farms may be turned into residential subdivisions. Residential areas may become commercial and commercial areas may become residential. It is this very process of change that conservation easements are intended to prevent, at least on the property subject to the easement. There is, however, a legal doctrine that permits the owner of property to prevent the enforcement of restrictions on the land if the surrounding area has changed so that the restrictions can no longer fulfill their original purposes. This is known, appropriately, as the doctrine of changed conditions.

There is some question whether this doctrine applies to conservation easements. It was not originally intended to do so, since it evolved before conservation easements were first used. Clearly it should not apply in most instances, since it is highly unlikely that the purposes of a conservation easement will be frustrated by changes in the surrounding neighborhood. Conservation easements are intended to preserve landmark structures or open space for historic, scenic, educational, recreational, or environmental reasons. It is quite likely that achieving these objectives will become more important if the character of the surrounding area changes. Because of the doctrine of changed conditions, it is important, however, to state the purposes of the restrictions clearly and to indicate, when it is appropriate to do so, that several objectives are to be achieved.

Release, Inaction, and Merger

The holder of a conservation easement may terminate it through its own action or, in some instances, inaction. The right of a holder to extinguish an easement by voluntarily releasing the restrictions on the land is sometimes limited by statute. In Arizona, the written consent of the property owner as well as the holder of any enforcement right is required. Most owners will not object to ending restrictions on their property. If they have taken a federal tax deduction for the value of a donated easement, however, they may lose the deduction if the restrictions are terminated. In Massachusetts, termination requires a public hearing, and in Nebraska, the approval of the governmental body that originally approved the easement is needed.

No nonprofit conservation organization or government should release an easement on privately held land without receiving adequate compensation. To do so would probably violate state law, be contrary to the purpose for which the organization was formed, and jeopardize the organization's tax-exempt status. The compensation should at least be equal to the increase in the value of the land resulting from the termination of the restrictions. Thus, in theory, a conservation organization or the governmental holder of a conservation easement could negotiate with the owner of restricted property on a price for which it would release the easement. It could then use the proceeds to purchase land or another conservation easement.

In practice, however, such a procedure would be dangerous and undesirable. It might result in a lawsuit by the state attorney general and could cast doubt on the integrity of the organization and of the easement process. As a matter of policy, a holding organization should not consider releasing a conservation easement, even for compensation, except under the most extraordinary circumstances. In such a situation it should consider obtaining an advisory opinion from a court or appropriate governmental agency.

If the owner of restricted property violates the restrictions, and the holder of the conservation easement fails to bring suit within the period of time set forth in the state's statutes, the right to bring an enforcement action expires. As a result, the easement will be extinguished through the holder's inaction. This is the primary legal and practical reason why adherence to the provisions of a conservation easement must be carefully and consistently monitored by the holder, at least on an annual basis.

If the holder of a conservation easement on a piece of property becomes the owner of that restricted property by gift or purchase, the right to enforce the restrictions "merges" with the rights of ownership, and the easement will be extinguished. This result is logical and necessary, since it would be unrealistic to expect the holder-owner to enforce restrictions against itself and, in any event, it could agree with itself to release the restrictions, as discussed above. This situation will not occur often and is of little importance since the holder-owner's interest is to protect the property. Trouble could arise, however, if the owning organization subsequently were to sell the property. In such a case, the owning organization should impose any restrictions that are agreed upon with the purchaser by including them in the deed of sale.

The Holder's Responsibility

Even when a conservation easement provides that it will run in perpetuity, the easement may be terminated by the holder or without the holder's consent and notwithstanding its objections. When an easement is accepted by a conservation organization or government, it accepts the responsibility of enforcement and the duty to prevent termination, accidentally or otherwise. If questions of termination arise, the holder should promptly discuss them with a knowledgeable attorney.

CHAPTER 12

Easements as Public Support:

The "Zero-Value" Approach

William T. Hutton

A nonprofit land trust or historic preservation organization that seeks to play in the conservation easement arena must vigilantly monitor its fiscal diet to assure that it continues to qualify as a "public charity."[1] Under Section 170(h)(3) of the Internal Revenue Code, only conservation organizations that receive adequate public support, as elaborately defined by statute and regulations, will qualify to receive tax-deductible easement donations.[2] Yet, paradoxically, the receipt of easements themselves—the *raison d'être* for many a land trust's establishment—may jeopardize its continuing ability to solicit and accept such gifts.

Of all the properties susceptible of charitable conveyance, the typical conservation easement is unique in furnishing little or no measurable benefit to the donee.[3] Under the "before and after" appraisal method, the donor ordinarily determines the proper charitable deduction according to the reduction in value that results from the creation of a "perpetual conservation restriction." *See* Treas. Reg. § 1.170A-14(h)(3). But the donee rarely finds its balance sheet enhanced by the receipt of such an easement; indeed, most nonprofit easement managers are all too aware that monitoring and enforcement of easement

---

1. As used herein, "public charity" connotes an organization entitled to be considered an organization other than a private foundation by reason of its satisfaction of the public support requirements of I.R.C. § 170(b)(1)(A)(iv) or § 509(a)(2) and corresponding Treasury regulations. A § 509(a)(3) organization (colloquially known as a "satellite") attains immunity from private foundation status via exclusive support rendered to another public charity, and thus need not be concerned with the relative amounts of its sources of sustenance.

2. See I.R.C. § 170(b)(A)(vi) and Treas. Reg. § 1.170A-9(e); I.R.C. § 509(a)(2) and Treas. Reg. § 1.509(a)-3. Although the issue discussed herein is of equal theoretical concern to both I.R.C. § 170(b)(1)(A)(vi) and § 509(a)(2) organizations, few conservation organizations in fact seek to maintain public charity status under the latter provision.

3. "Donee" is perhaps a misnomer here, but is used in deference to custom.

obligations create net balance sheet liabilities (see chapter 7). From the donee's perspective, then, the donated silk purse is transformed, at the moment of conveyance, into a sow's ear destined for perpetual care.

Governmental and Public Support Requirements

In order to illustrate the problem that metamorphosis may pose for the donee organization, let us suppose that the Sturdley Valley Land Trust was incorporated on January 2, 1983, and has just completed its five-year advance ruling period, during which it has intended to establish its entitlement to "public charity" status under I.R.C. § 170(b)(1)(a)(vi) by receiving a "substantial" part of its total support from a combination of government grants and public donations.[4]

Under the regulations, Sturdley Valley will be guaranteed continuance of its public charity status if it can demonstrate that at least one-third of its total support is from governmental and public sources. *See* Treas. Reg. §§ 1.170A-9(e)(2), (5)(iii)(*a*). Failing to reach that level is not necessarily fatal; provided that at least 10 percent of the land trust's total support is from governmental and public sources, the trust may qualify upon consideration of all relevant "facts and circumstances." *See* Treas. Reg. §§ 1.170A-9(e)(3), (5)(iii)(*a*).

For a land trust that attracts substantial easements but little cash, meeting the regulations' threshold may be difficult. Government grants to private land trusts are rare, and private support weighs favorably in the support balance only to the extent that total gifts from a single source, determined with reference to certain aggregation rules, do not exceed 2 percent of total support for the measuring period. *See* Treas. Reg. § 1.170A-9(e)(6). But substantial contributions or bequests from "disinterested parties" may be excluded from the total support calculation if they are "unusual or unexpected" and, by reason of their size, would adversely affect the organization's support status. *See* Treas. Reg. § 1.170A-9(e)(6)(ii). The regulations that provide this exception are amplified by Revenue Procedure 81-7, which sets out certain factors guaranteeing, where met, that an easement donation will escape the support calculation as "unusual."[5] Among the most troublesome of those factors, particularly for a newly established land trust, is the prohibition against the donor's being a creator, former contributor, or relative of such a person.

---

4. A new organization generally has five years to establish public charity status. Thereafter, an organization must show that contributions averaged over the preceding four years meet the tests of the regulations.

5. 1981-1 C.B. 621. Six factors must be satisfied; the precise requirements of the revenue procedure should be consulted in respect of any easement (or other donation)

Results Using Donors' Deduction Values:
Certain Easements Excluded as "Unusual Grants"

Now suppose that for the years 1983-1987 Sturdley Valley received the following in contributions: a number of small cash contributions (none larger than $100) totaling $5,000; five easements valued by their donors for charitable contribution purposes at an aggregate of $640,000; and one gift of land in fee worth $15,000 (see Table 1). Two of the five easements, at a combined value of $370,000, and the single land donation were received from members of the land trust's board.

TABLE 1
Contributions to Sturdley Valley, 1983-1987

Small cash donations (none exceeding $100)	$ 5,000
One gift of land (from board member)	15,000
Five easements:	
Easement A (from board member)	150,000
Easement B (from board member)	220,000
Easement C	70,000
Easement D	90,000
Easement E	110,000
TOTAL	$660,000

Unfortunately for Sturdley Valley, the two easement donations from board members are almost certainly barred under IRS guidelines from removal from the total support calculation as unusual grants. Eliminating the other three easements produces a "total support" figure of $390,000, based entirely on charitable contribution amounts: $5,000 cash, $370,000 included easements, and $15,000 real estate in fee (see Table 2). In calculating the amount of "favorable support," each gift from a single private source must be limited to 2

---

sought to be excluded. In general, the procedural guidelines require that (1) the donor neither have created the donee organization, have previously contributed substantially to it, nor be related to a creator or substantial contributor; (2) the donor not occupy a managerial role with the donee, be related to a manager (e.g., a director or officer), or be in a position to exercise control over the organization; (3) the donation be in the form of cash, marketable securities, or function-related property (e.g., a conservation easement to a land trust); (4) the donee's entitlement to exempt status as a public charity has been recognized by the IRS; (5) no material restrictions on the gift have been imposed by the donor (the fact that the donation itself may be an aggregate of restrictions upon the donor's use will not violate this requirement); and (6) if the gift is made to underwrite operating expenses, it is limited to not more than one year's budget.

percent of total support, in this case $7,800 (2 percent of $390,000). That limitation applies to each of the included easement gifts as well as to the fee transfer. Thus the aggregate of favorable support is a mere $28,400. Sturdley Valley fails, therefore, even to meet the 10 percent threshold requisite to making a "facts and circumstances" argument.[6]

TABLE 2

Results Using Donors' Deduction Values:
Certain Easements Excluded as "Unusual Grants"

	Total Support	Favorable Support
Small cash gifts	$ 5,000	$ 5,000
Land gift	15,000	7,800*
Easements from board members		
Easement A	150,000	7,800*
Easement B	220,000	7,800*
TOTAL	$390,000	$28,400

Percent Favorable Support: $28,400/$390,000 = 7.28 %

*Favorable support from a single source is limited to 2 percent of total support.

Easements Valued at Donors' Deduction Values:
All Donations Included

Another, slightly better, alternative is available. By including all of the easement donations at their charitable contribution values (nothing in the regulations *compels* exclusion of unusual grants), the total support becomes $660,000, and the 2 percent limit on gifts from each private source increases to $13,200. Applying that ceiling to all five easement gifts and the fee donation, favorable support increases to $84,200 or 12.76 percent of total support (see Table 3)—not a comfortable leap over the 10 percent benchmark but sufficient to permit a plea for IRS mercy.

All Easements Valued at Zero:
The Zero-Value Approach

Now let us contemplate "support" from the donee's vantage. While neither the statute nor the regulations provide definitional help (*see* I.R.C. § 509(d) and

---

6. For a description of the factors relevant to a "facts and circumstances" determination, see Treas. Reg. § 1.170A-9(e)(3).

TABLE 3

Easements Valued at Donors' Deduction Values:
All Donations Included

	Total Support	Favorable Support
Small cash gifts	$ 5,000	$ 5,000
Land gift	15,000	13,200*
All five easements:		
Easement A	150,000	13,200*
Easement B	220,000	13,200*
Easement C	70,000	13,200*
Easement D	90,000	13,200*
Easement E	110,000	13,200*
TOTAL	$660,000	$84,200

Percent Favorable Support: $84,200/$660,000 = 12.76 %

*Favorable support from a single source is limited to 2 percent of total support.

Treas. Reg. § 1.509(d)-1), the *Oxford English Dictionary* offers several possibly relevant meanings: "bearing or defraying of charge or expense;" "spiritual help;" and "contributing to the success . . . of something." It is submitted that to solve Sturdley Valley's problem, the first of those definitions should be applied. Only by adopting a definition that compels a measurement of value *to the donee* is it possible sensibly to apply the mechanical test of the regulations. Under that approach, the typical conservation easement, carrying no affirmative rights, will have no measurable value.

This "zero-value" approach is further justified by a common-sense comparison of motives. The donor of cash or securities obviously intends to furnish sustenance to the charitable donee, but the donor of an easement cannot be presumed to have the donee's fiscal welfare in mind. Although the donor satisfies a conservation objective and achieves a tax benefit by a sacrifice of property, in so doing he or she typically imposes a financial *burden* upon the donee. The spiritual satisfactions of easement acceptance may heighten the organization's claim to exempt status, but they should not weigh in a balance intended to test the public pocketbook appeal of a charitable cause.

In at least one situation, the IRS has evidently accepted this line of reasoning. A local land trust in a western state had attracted very little financial support during its advance ruling period, yet had accepted certain easements not permitted to be excluded from the support calculation as unusual grants. For annual reporting purposes, the organization had booked easements at their contribution value, and it was therefore not surprising that the IRS first proposed to reject the organization's claim to continuing public charity status. Upon review, however, the zero-value approach was endorsed. The examining agent's report simply states that "it was further determined that conservation easements donated to the organization have no market value in the hands of the organization and will not be considered as support."

Elimination of all easement values, in Sturdley Valley's situation, produces a total support figure of $20,000, of which $5,400, or 27 percent, counts favorably (see Table 4). Although Sturdley Valley still falls short of the one-third safe harbor, this substantial level of public support, in combination with the organization's public aspects, should suffice.

Organizations that have the opportunity to attract a significant number of easement gifts in their early years may be tempted to take a different tack and value easements with reference to donors' appraisals, since an adequate volume of easement transactions could conceivably protect public charity status, based upon contribution amounts, quite without regard to cash or other property donations.

TABLE 4
All Easements Valued at Zero:
The "Zero-Value" Approach

	Total Support	Favorable Support
Small cash gifts	$ 5,000	$5,000
Land gift	15,000	400*
All five easements		
Easement A	-0-	-0-
Easement B	-0-	-0-
Easement C	-0-	-0-
Easement D	-0-	-0-
Easement E	-0-	-0-
TOTAL	$20,000	$5,400
Percent Favorable Support:	$5,400/$20,000 = 27 %	

*Favorable support from a single source is limited to 2 percent of total support.

Yet over the long term, the zero-value approach may be a safer strategy. The struggle for public charity status, upon which the land trust or historic preservation organization relies for its lifeblood under I.R.C. § 170(h)(3)(A), is a perpetual one, based upon a four-year moving average of support calculations. *See* Treas. Reg. § 1.170A-9(e)(4). A slowing of the flow of easements is likely sooner or later to raise the measurement problem discussed here.

PART 3

Model Easements and Commentaries

141

PART 3 · Model Easements and Commentaries

Many people are surprised to learn that most of California's Big Sur Coast is privately owned. The Big Sur Land Trust, to encourage private land stewardship for public benefit, seeks and holds conservation easements on scenic properties such as the one shown here.

Introduction to
Model Easements

Russell L. Brenneman

If you were to purchase some property—let's say a house—together with me so that we would own and use it jointly, we would want to be very careful about spelling out in writing the rules that would tell us what things each of us could and could not do with it. If we are careful and compatible, this might work out as long as both of us are around, but if we transfer our interest in the property to another person—or if we die and the interest passes to our heirs—we introduce people who were not parties to our transaction and who may or may not agree with our views of it. If we assume further that we want our co-ownership to last "forever," we enhance the possibilities of misunderstanding.

The example is not an exact analogy to a conservation or historic preservation easement in the sense that the holder of such an easement does not ordinarily have the affirmative right to use property that we would expect a co-owner to have. But otherwise the example is very useful. Conservation and preservation easements set up a long-term relationship between parties who have a legal interest in the same piece of property. Because of an easement's expected longevity, future parties (or at least their representatives) who had no involvement in the original transaction are guaranteed to share concurrent interests in that property.

Two other aspects suggest warning signals for the creators of easement transactions.

First, the goals of the parties in all likelihood will diverge over time. Presumably when Owner donates a conservation easement in Greenacre to Landsaver Foundation, the objectives of the parties are identical. Owner wants to protect the same aspects of the property that Landsaver does. Owner's children may share their parent's point of view. However, the likelihood that all the grandchildren will share it uniformly and to the same degree is much less certain. Some certainly will have moved away from the area of Greenacre and will not share their parent's fondness for it. Others will become subject to the customary proclivities of property owners to maximize economic gain from all of the property that they own, including Greenacre. Landsaver Foundation is also not immune from change. Corporations do not die, but their officers, directors, and staff members do tend to change, and none as yet has proved immortal. The passage of time increases the likelihood that people who were not involved in the original easement transaction will be dealing with each other about Greenacre.

Second, the private benefits of the easement transaction will be dissipated over time. The benefit to Owner of an income tax deduction for her charitable contribution may be very real; so also, the estate tax deduction to her heirs, if the easement is transferred by will. In the case of a lifetime gift, Owner also will have enjoyed the very real satisfaction that comes from a generous gift for a prized cause. Successive generations, when they think of the burden that the easement imposes on Greenacre, may not have that sense of an offsetting personal benefit. Again, the interest of Owner's successors in confining the easement to its narrowest terms may well run counter to the expectations of Landsaver Foundation.

While not as applicable to specific easement transactions, a third factor provides a basis for additional caution: we really have not had much experience with conservation or historic preservation easements. It was not until the 1960s that this protection approach began to be cautiously used by nongovernmental conservation and preservation groups, and prior government applications of the technique had not been particularly happy, at least for the agencies involved. While the use of and interest in easements has burgeoned and the legal underpinnings for them are now, in my view, firmly established, in point of fact we do not have several generations' worth of experience to guide us.

Do these concerns suggest that conservation and preservation easements are not useful tools or that we should turn away from them as a protection technique until more time has passed? Certainly not. In many situations easements are the *most* useful tool to accomplish the reasonable goals of owners and their families and preservation and conservation groups, public and private. We have certainly had enough experience to establish that.

These concerns, however, do authenticate the absolute need for clarity and precision in the document that establishes the restrictions of the property—the grant (in whatever form) of the conservation or preservation easement. This instrument, we must remember, is to control Greenacre's fate over time and is to govern the behavior of people who are not present at the outset. Not only Greenacre is at stake. Whether or not the relationships among those future participants are to be peaceful or stormy, efficient or costly, privately resolved or the basis for expensive strife, will also be fundamentally affected by the quality of the original grant of the conservation easement.

This discussion underscores the importance of the following model easements and associated commentaries. The easement documents are not presented in "off the shelf" form. Precision in the document for the particular transaction requires clarity of thinking among the parties as well as drafting skill; fuzziness in legal phrasing can emanate from failing to think carefully and patiently enough about just what might happen. Both cautionary prefaces should be read with care. The comments provide an agenda for thought as well as wording. The texts in themselves are another step in a longer journey. Twenty years ago, such "models" did not exist. Twenty years from now, we shall have learned still more. That learning will rest in no small measure on the experience of the users of this handbook and their contributions to the collective knowledge of the land conservation and historic preservation community. That said, we can be grateful for the solid guidance provided along the way by the following model easements.

CHAPTER 13

Model Conservation Easement and Commentary

Thomas S. Barrett

Introduction

The model conservation easement is an abstraction. It is not the product of negotiation on specific facts but a studious synthesis of responses by the land conservation community, on diverse facts, to recurring drafting concerns.* The intention is that it serve as a reliable standard reference on drafting issues. Of course, no one document can hope to serve as a standard for all situations. There is no way, once and for all, to fix the variables that come with context—legal jurisdiction, character of land and resources, productive uses, conservation objectives, motivation, financial terms, degree of governmental involvement, to name the most obvious. The model's function is not to provide a solution to the puzzle each easement transaction presents but to offer an analytical framework for solving the puzzle on its own terms. It is a guide, not a rule; one approach among many.

The Checklists: A Key to Structure

The emphasis is on structure. As the checklists that follow illustrate, the model is constructed of a succession of overlaying provisions that can be grouped according to the nature of the concerns they address. In its most fundamental form, a conservation easement is a straightforward conveyance, and the short

---

* In the course of preparing the model easement and commentary, the author reviewed over 100 conservation easements, considered responses by some 40 practitioners to a questionnaire on the subject, and consulted directly with more than 20 recognized authorities in this field, including representatives of conservation organizations, governmental agencies, and the private bar.

form, outlined in Checklist II, indicates the essential terms. These provisions are the core of the model and, depending on the circumstances, may be all that is required.

As experience with managing conservation easements has developed over the years, however, the terms of the instrument have evolved. The unilateral conveyance, sufficient in some cases, may fall short in others where bilateral rights and obligations are appropriate. Analogous to what occurred over time in the development of real property leasing law, the conservation easement has begun to take on the characteristics of a contract as well as a conveyance. A conservation easement creates a relationship of shared control over the future of land. The perpetual nature of that relationship, designed as it is to outlast the original parties, suggests the need for a governing document in which predictable points of potential friction are anticipated and provided for and in which behavioral ground rules—for the grantee as well as the grantor—are established. These are contractual considerations, and Checklist III indicates the provisions in the model that are intended to address them.

At the same time, perpetuity counsels flexibility—the need for a mechanism for adapting to the unforeseen, a capacity for stretch. An easement is more than the sum of its restrictions; it is a right to protect certain values. The more drafters focus on the future, which cannot be known, the more emphasis they place on articulating those values in the easement. As critical for an easement's long-term enforceability as its express restrictions, the thinking goes, is the clarity with which its purpose and intent are set out. The provisions that are most indicative of purpose and intent are shown in Checklist IV.

Finally, of course, where deductibility for income or estate tax purposes is an issue, the Internal Revenue Service's detailed requirements must be met. Provisions responsive to the IRS requirements are outlined in Checklist V.

Drafting to Fit the Facts

The model is not exhaustive. There are bound to be concerns, on some facts, that it does not address. Likewise, some of the concerns it does address may not be an issue in some cases. As for the language chosen, there is no magic to it. Even the IRS, though it does require certain provisions, does not require any particular language. Drafters of legal documents develop their own individual styles, and the model in no way seeks to impose the author's. The shared goal, an elusive one, is formal clarity. Rare is the document that cannot be improved upon in this regard. The hope is that even where the model falls short of the goal, the commitment to pursuing it will be sufficiently apparent to serve as a source of encouragement to others.

Ultimately, the facts determine what should go into an easement. Some terms are more fact-dependent than others, though, and they are the hardest to deal with in a model intended for general application. Recitals of specific conservation values, and the express restrictions and reservations, are inextricable from the facts—a distinction that the model calls attention to by leaving them out. They are dealt with, instead, in the commentary. In an easement negotiation, the parties, for good reason, are likely to focus more on the express restrictions than any other aspect of the agreement—particulary if they are negotiating an open-space easement that requires a careful balancing of permitted and prohibited uses. Accordingly, the commentary devotes considerable space to the discussion of hypothetical restrictions. It should be understood, however, that there is such a wide disparity of views on how to approach the drafting of these provisions—resulting mostly from the wide divergence of objectives people bring to them—that there is little in the way of real substantive guidance to pass on. As section 16 of the commentary states, the sample restrictions strive for two virtues: balance and coherence. Beyond that—like everything else in the easement, but more so—drafters have to think it all through for themselves, carefully, critically, case by case.

Trial and Error

People who work in this field are aware that, in terms of the legal development of the concept, they are present at the creation of the conservation easement. State enabling statutes are all of recent vintage and there is no case law to speak of, which makes these—to the satisfaction, no doubt, of those who do not wish us well—"interesting times." But newness can be a blessing as well as a curse. The opportunity to shape the concept, to give it definition, is an exciting one and drafters should be stimulated by the fact that, in a real sense, the conservation easement is, for now at least, whatever they say it is. There will be mistakes, of course, unavoidably, and as the concept matures and the courts become involved, there will be a welcome narrowing of approaches, and the lines of a "right way" will become clearer.

The process, though, will take time and will involve—day by day, year by year—practitioners learning, by trial and error, what it is an easement can and cannot do. All the while, their understanding of the land and the relationship of people to the land—and through the land, to each other—will be deepening, to the end that future generations may benefit not only from the open spaces they protected but from their hard won knowledge of how—and how not—to go about it. The model conservation easement and commentary are presented to the land conservation community in the hope that, by bringing this solitary exercise in trial and error to light, the author will have contributed in some small way to the winning of that knowledge.

Checklists

Checklist I
Model Conservation Easement
Complete Outline*

CAPTION (Parties and Date)

RECITALS

- Title Representation
- Legal Description of Property
- Generic Conservation Values
- Qualitative Description of Property
- Baseline Documentation
- Continuation of Existing Uses
- Conveyance of Right to Protect Conservation Values
- Qualifications of Grantee
- Grantee's Commitment

GRANT

PROVISIONS

1. Purpose
2. Rights of Grantee
   (a) Protection of Conservation Values
   (b) Inspection
   (c) Enforcement (Including Restoration)
3. Prohibited Uses
   [Insert Express Restrictions]
4. Reserved Rights
   [Insert Express Reservations, if desired]
5. Notice of Intention to Undertake Certain Permitted Actions
5.1 Grantee's Approval
6. Grantee's Remedies
6.1 Costs of Enforcement
6.2 Grantee's Discretion
6.3 Waiver of Certain Defenses
6.4 Acts Beyond Grantors' Control
7. Access
8. Costs and Liabilities
8.1 Taxes
8.2 Hold Harmless

9.   Extinguishment

9.1   Proceeds

9.2   Condemnation

10.   Assignment

11.   Subsequent Transfers

12.   Estoppel Certificates

13.   Notices

14.   Recordation

15.   General Provisions
       (a) Controlling Law
       (b) Liberal Construction
       (c) Severability
       (d) Entire Agreement
       (e) No Forfeiture
       (f) Joint Obligation
       (g) Successors (and Run with the Land)
       (h) Termination of Rights and Obligations
       (i) Captions
       (j) Counterparts

HABENDUM

SIGNATURES AND ACKNOWLEDGEMENTS

SCHEDULE OF EXHIBITS

SUPPLEMENTARY PROVISIONS**

[5.2] Arbitration

[Between 9/10] Amendment

[10.1] Executory Limitation

[Between 10/11] Subordination

---

*This is a generic outline; formal requirements for a conservation easement vary from state to state.

**The designation of these provisions as "supplementary" is not meant to imply that everthing else is essential, but only that a decision to include them is likely to turn more on particular facts or involve stronger preferences than the other provisions.

Checklist II
Short Form Conservation Easement
The Essentials of Conveyance*

CAPTION (Parties and Date)

RECITALS

- Title Representation
- Legal Description of Property

GRANT

PROVISIONS

    1.   Purpose

    2(b) Right of Entry for Inspection

    3.   Prohibited Uses

    4.   Reserved Rights

    7.   Access (if desired)

    15(g) Successors (and Run with the Land)

HABENDUM

SIGNATURES AND ACKNOWLEDGEMENTS

SUPPLEMENTARY PROVISIONS

    [10.1] Executory Limitation (if desired)

---

*Other provisions may be required by state law.

Checklist III
Additional Covenants
Ground Rules for a Perpetual Relationship

PROVISIONS

    2(b) Inspection (Prior Notice)

    5.   Notice of Intention to Undertake Certain Permitted Actions

    5.1   Grantee's Approval

    6.   Grantee's Remedies

    6.1   Costs of Enforcement

    6.2   Grantee's Discretion

    6.3   Waiver of Certain Defenses

    6.4   Acts Beyond Grantors' Control

    8.   Costs and Liabilities

    8.1   Taxes

    8.2   Hold Harmless

    9.2   Condemnation

    10.   Assignment

    11.   Subsequent Transfers

    12.   Estoppel Certificates

    13.   Notices

    14.   Recordation

    15.   General Provisions
         (a) Controlling Law
         (b) Liberal Construction
         (c) Severability
         (d) Entire Agreement
         (e) No Forfeiture
         (f) Joint Obligation
         (h) Termination of Rights and Obligations
         (i) Captions
         (j) Counterparts

SUPPLEMENTARY PROVISIONS

    [5.2]   Arbitration

    [Between 9/10] Amendment

    [Between 10/11] Subordination

Checklist IV
Clarifying Terms
Purpose and Intent

RECITALS

- Qualitative Description of Property (Conservation Values/Public Benefit)
- Baseline Documentation
- Continuation of Existing Uses
- Conveyance of Right to Protect Conservation Values
- Grantee's Commitment

PROVISIONS

1. Purpose

2. Rights of Grantee

   (a) Protection of Conservation Values
   (c) Enforcement (Consistency)

3. Prohibited Uses

4. Reserved Rights

Checklist V
Provisions Relating to IRS Requirements
(Treas. Reg. § 1.170A-14)

RECITALS
- Generic Conservation Values
- Qualitative Description of Property (Conservation Values/Governmental Policy/Public Benefit)
- Baseline Documentation
- Qualifications of Grantee

GRANT (Perpetuity)*

PROVISIONS

1.	Purpose
2(b)	Right of Entry for Inspection *
3.	Prohibited Uses (No Inconsistent Use; No Surface Mining) *
5.	Notice of Intention to Undertake Certain Permitted Actions *
6.	Grantee's Remedies (Enforcement, Including Restoration) *
7.	Access **
9.	Extinguishment *
9.1	Proceeds ***
10.	Assignment *
14.	Recordation

SUPPLEMENTARY PROVISIONS

[Between 10/11]. Subordination

---

* Mandatory. (Paragraph 5 required if reserved rights might have an adverse impact on conservation values.)

** Mandatory for certain types of easements (e.g., those with a recreational or educational purpose).

*** Donor must agree "at the time of the gift;" unclear if agreement must be in easement instrument.

Note: Other provisions listed here are optional from a drafting standpoint, though substantive compliance is required. They are included, among other reasons, to make the model a convenient single source of reference to all IRS requirements.

Model Conservation Easement

Note: The boxed numbers inserted in the text of the easement correspond with the subheading numbers in the commentary that follows.

DEED OF CONSERVATION EASEMENT ☐1

THIS GRANT DEED OF CONSERVATION EASEMENT is made this _____ day of _____ ,19 _____ , by _____ and _____ , husband and wife, having an address at _____ ("Grantors"), in favor of _____ a nonprofit __[state of incorporation]__ corporation [qualified to do business in __(state where property is located)]__ , having an address at _____ _____ ("Grantee"). ☐2

WITNESSETH:

WHEREAS, ☐3 grantors are the sole owners in fee simple of certain real property in _____ County, _____[state]_____ , more particulary described in Exhibit A attached hereto and incorporated by this reference (the "Property"); ☐4 and

WHEREAS, the property possesses __[e.g., natural, scenic, open space,__ __historical, educational, and/or recreational]__ values (collectively, "conservation values") of great importance to Grantors, the people of __[county, locale,__ __or region]__ and the people of the State of _____ ; ☐5 and

WHEREAS, in particular, _____[describe specific conservation __values]__ _____ ; ☐6 and

WHEREAS, the specific conservation values of the Property are documented in an inventory of relevant features of the Property, dated _____ _____ , 19 _____ , _____[on file at the offices of Grantee–or– __attached hereto as Exhibit B]__ and incorporated by this reference ("Baseline Documentation"), which consists of reports, maps, photographs, and other documentation that the parties agree provide, collectively, an accurate representation of the Property at the time of this grant and which is intended to serve as an objective information baseline for monitoring compliance with the terms of this grant; and ☐7

WHEREAS, Grantors intend that the conservation values of the Property be preserved and maintained by the continuation of land use patterns, including, without limitation, those relating to ___[e.g., farming, ranching, or___ __timber production]__ existing at the time of this grant, that do not significantly impair or interfere with those values; and ☐8

WHEREAS, Grantors further intend, as owners of the Property, to convey to Grantee the right to preserve and protect the conservation values of the Property in perpetuity; and ⑨

WHEREAS, Grantee is a publicly supported, tax-exempt nonprofit organization, qualified under Section 501(c)(3) and 170(h) of the Internal Revenue Code, whose primary purpose is _____[e.g., the preservation, protection, ___ or enhancement of land in its natural, scenic, historical, agricultural, ___ forested, and/or open space condition] ; and ⑩

WHEREAS, Grantee agrees by accepting this grant to honor the intentions of Grantors stated herein and to preserve and protect in perpetuity the conservation values of the Property for the benefit of this generation and the generations to come; ⑪

NOW, THEREFORE, in consideration of the above and the mutual covenants, terms, conditions, and restrictions contained herein, and pursuant to the laws of [state where property is located] and in particular [specific state statutory authority] , Grantors hereby voluntarily grant and convey to Grantee a conservation easement in perpetuity over the Property of the nature and character and to the extent hereinafter set forth ("Easement"). ⑫

1. Purpose. It is the purpose of this Easement to assure that the Property will be retained forever [predominantly] in its [e.g., natural, scenic, historic, agricultural, forested, and/or open space] condition and to prevent any use of the Property that will significantly impair or interfere with the conservation values of the Property. Grantors intend that this Easement will confine the use of the Property to such activities, including, without limitation, those involving [e.g., farming, ranching, timber production, public recreation, or education] , as are consistent with the purpose of this Easement. ⑬

2. Rights of Grantee. To accomplish the purpose of this Easement the following rights are conveyed to Grantee by this Easement:

(a) To preserve and protect the conservation values of the Property;

(b) To enter upon the Property at reasonable times in order to monitor Grantors' compliance with and otherwise enforce the terms of this Easement; provided that such entry shall be upon prior reasonable notice to Grantors, and Grantee shall not unreasonably interfere with Grantors' use and quiet enjoyment of the Property; and

(c) To prevent any activity on or use of the Property that is inconsistent with the purpose of this Easement and to require the restoration of such areas or features of the Property that may be damaged by any inconsistent activity or use, pursuant to paragraph 6. ⑭

3. Prohibited Uses. Any activity on or use of the Property inconsistent with the purpose of this Easement is prohibited. Without limiting the generality of the foregoing, the following activities and uses are expressly prohibited: ⑮

[Insert Express Restrictions] ⑯

4. Reserved Rights. Grantors reserve to themselves, and to their personal representatives, heirs, successors, and assigns, all rights accruing from their

ownership of the Property, including the right to engage in or permit or invite others to engage in all uses of the Property that are not expressly prohibited herein and are not inconsistent with the purpose of this Easement. [Without limiting the generality of the foregoing, the following rights are expressly reserved:] 17

[Insert Express Reservations, if desired] 18

5. <u>Notice of Intention to Undertake Certain Permitted Actions.</u> The purpose of requiring Grantors to notify Grantee prior to undertaking certain permitted activities, as provided in paragraphs _____ , is to afford Grantee an opportunity to ensure that the activities in question are designed and carried out in a manner consistent with the purpose of this Easement. Whenever notice is required Grantors shall notify Grantee in writing not less than [e.g., sixty (60)] days prior to the date Grantors intend to undertake the activity in question. The notice shall describe the nature, scope, design, location, timetable, and any other material aspect of the proposed activity in sufficient detail to permit Grantee to make an informed judgment as to its consistency with the purpose of this Easement.

5.1 <u>Grantee's Approval.</u> Where Grantee's approval is required, as set forth in paragraphs _____ , Grantee shall grant or withhold its approval in writing within   [e.g., sixty (60)]   days of receipt of Grantors' written request therefor. Grantee's approval may be withheld only upon a reasonable determination by Grantee that the action as proposed would be inconsistent with the purpose of this Easement. 19

6. <u>Grantee's Remedies.</u> If Grantee determines that Grantors are in violation of the terms of this Easement or that a violation is threatened, Grantee shall give written notice to Grantors of such violation and demand corrective action sufficient to cure the violation and, where the violation involves injury to the Property resulting from any use or activity inconsistent with the purpose of this Easement, to restore the portion of the Property so injured. If Grantors fail to cure the violation within   [e.g., thirty (30)]   days after receipt of notice thereof from Grantee, or under circumstances where the violation cannot reasonably be cured within a [thirty (30)] day period, fail to begin curing such violation within the [thirty (30)] day period, or fail to continue diligently to cure such violation until finally cured, Grantee may bring an action at law or in equity in a court of competent jurisdiction to enforce the terms of this Easement, to enjoin the violation, *ex parte* as necessary, by temporary or permanent injunction, to recover any damages to which it may be entitled for violation of the terms of this Easement or injury to any conservation values protected by this Easement, including damages for the loss of scenic, aesthetic, or environmental values, and to require the restoration of the Property to the condition that existed prior to any such injury. Without limiting Grantors' liability therefor, Grantee, in its sole discretion, may apply any damages recovered to the cost of undertaking any corrective action on the Property. If Grantee, in its sole discretion, determines that circumstances require immediate action to prevent

or mitigate significant damage to the conservation values of the Property, Grantee may pursue its remedies under this paragraph without prior notice to Grantors or without waiting for the period provided for cure to expire. Grantee's rights under this paragraph apply equally in the event of either actual or threatened violations of the terms of this Easement, and Grantors agree that Grantee's remedies at law for any violation of the terms of this Easement are inadequate and that Grantee shall be entitled to the injunctive relief described in this paragraph, both prohibitive and mandatory, in addition to such other relief to which Grantee may be entitled, including specific performance of the terms of this Easement, without the necessity of proving either actual damages or the inadequacy of otherwise available legal remedies. Grantee's remedies described in this paragraph shall be cumulative and shall be in addition to all remedies now or hereafter existing at law or in equity. [20]

6.1 <u>Costs of Enforcement</u>. Any costs incurred by Grantee in enforcing the terms of this Easement against Grantors, including, without limitation, costs of suit and attorneys' fees, and any costs of restoration necessitated by Grantors' violation of the terms of this Easement shall be borne by Grantors. If Grantors prevail in any action to enforce the terms of this Easement, Grantors' costs of suit, including, without limitation, attorneys' fees, shall be borne by Grantee. [21]

6.2 <u>Grantee's Discretion</u>. Enforcement of the terms of this Easement shall be at the discretion of Grantee, and any forbearance by Grantee to exercise its rights under this Easement in the event of any breach of any term of this Easement by Grantors shall not be deemed or construed to be a waiver by Grantee of such term or of any subsequent breach of the same or any other term of this Easement or of any of Grantee's rights under this Easement. No delay or omission by Grantee in the exercise of any right or remedy upon any breach by Grantors shall impair such right or remedy or be construed as a waiver.

6.3 <u>Waiver of Certain Defenses</u>. Grantors hereby waive any defense of laches, estoppel, or prescription. [22]

6.4 <u>Acts Beyond Grantors' Control</u>. Nothing contained in this Easement shall be construed to entitle Grantee to bring any action against Grantors for any injury to or change in the Property resulting from causes beyond Grantors' control, including, without limitation, fire, flood, storm, and earth movement, or from any prudent action taken by Grantors under emergency conditions to prevent, abate, or mitigate significant injury to the Property resulting from such causes. [23]

7. <u>Access</u>. No right of access by the general public to any portion of the Property is conveyed by this Easement. [24]

8. <u>Costs and Liabilities</u>. Grantors retain all responsibilities and shall bear all costs and liabilities of any kind related to the ownership, operation, upkeep, and maintenance of the Property, including the maintenance of adequate comprehensive general liability insurance coverage. Grantors shall keep the Property free of any liens arising out of any work performed for, materials furnished to, or obligations incurred by Grantors. [25]

8.1 <u>Taxes.</u> Grantors shall pay before delinquency all taxes, assessments, fees, and charges of whatever description levied on or assessed against the Property by competent authority (collectively "taxes"), including any taxes imposed upon, or incurred as a result of, this Easement, and shall furnish Grantee with satisfactory evidence of payment upon request. [Grantee is authorized but in no event obligated to make or advance any payment of taxes, upon ___[e.g., three (3)]___ days prior written notice to Grantors, in accordance with any bill, statement, or estimate procured from the appropriate authority, without inquiry into the validity of the taxes or the accuracy of the bill, statement, or estimate, and the obligation created by such payment shall bear interest until paid by Grantors at the lesser of ___ percentage points over the prime rate of interest from time to time charged by ___[designated bank]___ or the maximum rate allowed by law.] 26

8.2 <u>Hold Harmless.</u> Grantors shall hold harmless, indemnify, and defend Grantee and its members, directors, officers, employees, agents, and contractors and the heirs, personal representatives, successors, and assigns of each of them (collectively "Indemnified Parties") from and against all liabilities, penalties, costs, losses, damages, expenses, causes of action, claims, demands, or judgments, including, without limitation, reasonable attorneys' fees, arising from or in any way connected with: (1) injury to or the death of any person, or physical damage to any property, resulting from any act, omission, condition, or other matter related to or occurring on or about the Property, regardless of cause, unless due solely to the negligence of any of the Indemnified Parties; (2) the obligations specified in paragraphs 8 and 8.1; and (3) the existence or administration of this Easement. 27

9. <u>Extinguishment.</u> If circumstances arise in the future such as render the purpose of this Easement impossible to accomplish, this Easement can only be terminated or extinguished, whether in whole or in part, by judicial proceedings in a court of competent jurisdiction, and the amount of the proceeds to which Grantee shall be entitled, after the satisfaction of prior claims, from any sale, exchange, or involuntary conversion of all or any portion of the Property subsequent to such termination or extinguishment, shall be determined, unless otherwise provided by___[state]___ law at the time, in accordance with paragraph 9.1. Grantee shall use all such proceeds in a manner consistent with the conservation purposes of this grant. 28

9.1 <u>Proceeds.</u> This Easement constitutes a real property interest immediately vested in Grantee, which, for the purposes of paragraph 9, the parties stipulate to have a fair market value determined by multiplying the fair market value of the Property unencumbered by the Easement (minus any increase in value after the date of this grant attributable to improvements) by the ratio of the value of the Easement at the time of this grant to the value of the Property, without deduction for the value of the Easement, at the time of this grant. The values at the time of this grant shall be those values used to calculate the deduction for federal income tax purposes allowable by reason of this grant, pursuant to Section 170(h) of the Internal Revenue Code of 1954, as amended.

For the purposes of this paragraph, the ratio of the value of the Easement to the value of the Property unencumbered by the Easement shall remain constant. [29]

9.2 <u>Condemnation</u>. If the Easement is taken, in whole or in part, by exercise of the power of eminent domain, Grantee shall be entitled to compensation in accordance with applicable law. [30]

10. <u>Assignment</u>. This Easement is transferable, but Grantee may assign its rights and obligations under this Easement only to an organization that is a qualified organization at the time of transfer under Section 170(h) of the Internal Revenue Code of 1954, as amended (or any successor provision then applicable), and the applicable regulations promulgated thereunder, and authorized to acquire and hold conservation easements under [state statute] (or any successor provision then applicable). As a condition of such transfer, Grantee shall require that the conservation purposes that this grant is intended to advance continue to be carried out. [31]

11. <u>Subsequent Transfers</u>. Grantors agree to incorporate the terms of this Easement in any deed or other legal instrument by which they divest themselves of any interest in all or a portion of the Property, including, without limitation, a leasehold interest. Grantors further agree to give written notice to Grantee of the transfer of any interest at least [e.g., twenty (20)] days prior to the date of such transfer. The failure of Grantors to perform any act required by this paragraph shall not impair the validity of this Easement or limit its enforceability in any way. [32]

12. <u>Estoppel Certificates</u>. Upon request by Grantors, Grantee shall within [e.g., twenty (20)] days execute and deliver to grantors any document, including an estoppel certificate, which certifies Grantors' compliance with any obligation of Grantors contained in this Easement and otherwise evidences the status of this Easement as may be requested by Grantors. [33]

13. <u>Notices</u>. Any notice, demand, request, consent, approval, or communication that either party desires or is required to give to the other shall be in writing and either served personally or sent by first class mail, postage prepaid, addressed as follows:

To Grantors: _____

_____

_____

To Grantee: _____

_____

_____

or to such other address as either party from time to time shall designate by written notice to the other. 34

14. Recordation. Grantee shall record this instrument in timely fashion in the official records of _____ County, ___[state]___ and may re-record it at any time as may be required to preserve its rights in this Easement. 35

15. General Provisions.

(a) Controlling Law. The interpretation and performance of this Easement shall be governed by the laws of the State of ___[state]___ .

(b) Liberal Construction. Any general rule of construction to the contrary notwithstanding, this Easement shall be liberally construed in favor of the grant to effect the purpose of this Easement and the policy and purpose of [state statute] . If any provision in this instrument is found to be ambiguous, an interpretation consistent with the purpose of this Easement that would render the provision valid shall be favored over any interpretation that would render it invalid.

(c) Severability. If any provision of this Easement, or the application thereof to any person or circumstance, is found to be invalid, the remainder of the provisions of this Easement, or the application of such provision to persons or circumstances other than those as to which it is found to be invalid, as the case may be, shall not be affected thereby.

(d) Entire Agreement. This instrument sets forth the entire agreement of the parties with respect to the Easement and supersedes all prior discussions, negotiations, understandings, or agreements relating to the Easement, all of which are merged herein. [No alteration or variation of this instrument shall be valid or binding unless contained in an amendment that complies with paragraph ____ (see supplementary provisions re: Amendment.]

(e) No Forfeiture. Nothing contained herein will result in a forfeiture or reversion of Grantor's title in any respect.

(f) Joint Obligation. The obligations imposed by this Easement upon Grantors shall be joint and several.

(g) Successors. The covenants, terms, conditions, and restrictions of this Easement shall be binding upon, and inure to the benefit of, the parties hereto and their respective personal representatives, heirs, successors, and assigns and shall continue as a servitude running in perpetuity with the Property.

(h) Termination of Rights and Obligations. A party's rights and obligations under this Easement terminate upon transfer of the party's interest in the Easement or Property, except that liability for acts or omissions occurring prior to transfer shall survive transfer.

(i) Captions. The captions in this instrument have been inserted solely for convenience of reference and are not a part of this instrument and shall have no effect upon construction or interpretation.

(j) Counterparts. The parties may execute this instrument in two or more counterparts, which shall, in the aggregate, be signed by both parties; each counterpart shall be deemed an original instrument as against any party who has signed it. In the event of any disparity between the counterparts produced, the recorded counterpart shall be controlling. ☒36

TO HAVE AND TO HOLD unto Grantee, its successors, and assigns forever. ☒37

IN WITNESS WHEREOF Grantors and Grantee have set their hands on the day and year first above written.

_____

_____

Grantors

_____

Grantee

by _____

its ____[Official Capacity]____ ☒38

[Acknowledgments]

SCHEDULE OF EXHIBITS

A.   Legal Description of Property Subject to Easement

[B.   Baseline Documentation]

B. or C. Site Descriptions/Map

[C. or D. Identification of Prior Mortgage]

Supplementary Provisions ☒39

(Paragraph numbers indicate relative position in model.)

[5.2] <u>Arbitration.</u> If a dispute arises between the parties concerning the consistency of any proposed use or activity with the purpose of this Easement, and Grantors agree not to proceed with the use or activity pending resolution of the dispute, either party may refer the dispute to arbitration by request made in writing upon the other. Within   [e.g., thirty (30)]   days of the receipt of such a request, the parties shall select a single arbitrator to hear the matter. If the parties are unable to agree on the selection of a single arbitrator, then each party shall name one arbitrator and the two arbitrators thus selected shall select a third arbitrator; provided, however, if either party fails to select an arbitrator, or if the two arbitrators selected by the parties fail to select the third arbitrator within ___[e.g., fourteen (14)]___ days after the appointment of the second arbitrator, then in each such instance a proper court, on petition of a party, shall appoint the second or third arbitrator or both, as the case may be, in accordance with _[state arbitration statute]_ , or any successor statute then in effect. The matter shall be settled in accordance with the ___[state arbitration statute or other appropriate body of rules]___ then in effect, and a judgment on the arbitration award may be entered in any court having jurisdiction thereof. The prevailing party shall be entitled, in addition to such other relief as may be granted, to a reasonable sum as and for all its costs and expenses related to such arbitration, including, without limitation, the fees and expenses of the arbitrator(s) and attorneys' fees, which shall be determined by the arbitrator(s) and any court of competent jurisdiction that may be called upon to enforce or review the award. [40]

[Between 9 and 10] Amendment. If circumstances arise under which an amendment to or modification of this Easement would be appropriate, Grantors and Grantee are free to jointly amend this Easement; provided that no amendment shall be allowed that will affect the qualification of this Easement or the status of Grantee under any applicable laws, including [state statute] or Section 170(h) of the Internal Revenue Code of 1954, as amended, and any amendment shall be consistent with the purpose of this Easement, and shall not affect its perpetual duration. Any such amendment shall be recorded in the official records of _____ County, ____[state]____ . [41]

[10.1] Executory Limitation. If Grantee shall cease to exist or to be a qualified organization under Section 170(h) of the Internal Revenue Code of 1954, as amended, or to be authorized to acquire and hold conservation easements under _[state statute]_ , and a prior assignment is not made pursuant to paragraph 10, then Grantee's rights and obligations under this Easement shall become immediately vested in _[designated back-up grantee]_ . If _[designated back-up grantee]_ is no longer in existence at the time the rights and obligations under this Easement would otherwise vest in it, or if [designated back-up grantee] is not qualified or authorized to hold conservation easements as provided for an assignment pursuant to paragraph 10, or if it shall refuse such rights and obligations, then the rights and obligations under this Easement shall vest in such organization as a court of competent jurisdiction shall direct pursuant to the applicable ___[state]___ law and with due regard to the requirements for an assignment pursuant to paragraph 10. [42]

[Between 10 and 11] Subordination. At the time of conveyance of this Easement, the Property is subject to the mortgage identified in Exhibit _[C or D]_ attached hereto and incorporated by this reference, the holder of which has agreed by separate instrument, which will be recorded immediately after this Easement, to subordinate its rights in the Property to this Easement to the extent necessary to permit the Grantee to enforce the purpose of the Easement in perpetuity and to prevent any modification or extinguishment of this Easement by the exercise of any rights of the mortgage holder. The priority of the existing mortgage with respect to any valid claim on the part of the existing mortgage holder to the proceeds of any sale, condemnation proceedings, or insurance or to the leases, rents, and profits of the Property shall not be affected thereby, and any lien that may be created by Grantee's exercise of any of its rights under this Easement shall be junior to the existing mortgage. Upon request, Grantee agrees to subordinate its rights under this Easement to the rights of any future mortgage holders or beneficiaries of deeds of trust to the proceeds, leases, rents, and profits described above and likewise to subordinate its rights under any lien and to execute any documents required with respect to such subordination, except that the priority of any lien created by Grantee's exercise of any of its rights under this Easement prior to the creation of a mortgage or deed of trust shall not be affected thereby, nor shall this Easement be subordinated in any other respect. [43]

Commentary

Note: The numbers at the beginning of the subheads in this section correspond with the boxed numbers inserted in the text of the model conservation easement preceding this commentary.

1. Title of Document

A deed is a written instrument for effecting the transfer of title to real property, which consists of land and interests in land. "Conservation easement" is the name used in most jurisdictions to describe the real property interest that is the subject of the instrument at hand, although in some states it may be designated, variously, a conservation, open space, or scenic easement, restriction, covenant, or servitude. The requirements for and some of the technical legal attributes of conservation interests vary from state to state.[1] Even the practice of creating a conservation interest through a transfer by deed is not universally followed. Under some circumstances, or in some jurisdictions, conservation restrictions may be imposed by simply recording them against the property to be protected without a formal conveyance. It is, of course, of fundamental importance that each conservation interest be drawn to reflect the law of the jurisdiction where the subject property is located.

2. Preliminary Identification of Parties

The date of conveyance and the names and addresses of the parties are given up front for ease of reference. The status of the parties is indicated for the same reason, to be expanded on in the recitals to follow. The phrase "husband and wife" that appears in the model is significant in the community property states of the West where both must be joined in the conveyance to effect a fully valid transfer of title to an interest in community real property. Other joint ownership relationships, such as those involving joint tenants, cotenants or tenants by the entirety (another form of title sometimes employed by marriage partners), should be indicated, as appropriate, and all necessary parties joined in the conveyance. The nonprofit corporate status of the grantee and its state of incorporation should be shown. If the grantor is a corporation, corresponding status information should be supplied. If the state of incorporation of a grantor or grantee is different from the state in which the property is situated, depending on the jurisdiction, formal qualification to do business in the state where the property is situated may be required to effect a valid transfer. In addition, for out-of-state grantees, qualification may be an independent requirement of a state's conservation easement enabling legislation. Qualification typically in-

---

1. For a concise review of the law relating to conservation easements, see Richard R. Powell, *The Law of Real Property,* vol. 3 (New York: Matthew Bender and Co., 1987), 430.1 - 430.6.

volves little more than filing the corporate charter and appointing an agent for service of process. The fact of qualification should be stated as indicated in brackets. Proof of these matters is customarily provided at closing, along with proof of corporate authority to execute the easement instrument (such as approval of the board of directors).

3. Recitals

The recitals or "whereas" clauses function as a preamble to the easement, setting forth background information essential for understanding both the legal and factual basis for its creation. Use of the conjunction "whereas" to introduce the recitals is a traditional but by no means obligatory conveyancing convention. The model follows traditional form here and elsewhere because, as a practical matter, when reviewing multi-page documents, being able to tell at a glance where you are at any given point is something you quickly come to appreciate, and the familiar structural guideposts, like the "whereas" introducing each recital, are a real help. Matters of style are largely governed by taste, of course, although there may be something to be gained from giving the relatively "novel" conservation easement a traditional look. Judges and lawyers otherwise unfamiliar with the conservation easement will at least recognize the form if not the substance. For a perpetual agreement to have the ritualistic solemnity about it that the use of traditional language tends to bring is probably not such a bad idea in any case.

4. Title Representation and Legal Description of the Property

In this first recital the grantors' "fee simple" ownership of the property indicates that they own the rights that are being transferred by means of the easement—a fact that the grantee should corroborate by a search of the property records of the county in which the property is situated. A title search will also reveal the existence of any recorded liens or other encumbrances on the property that might jeopardize the easement. Often landowners are willing to provide, at their own expense, a title report prepared by an attorney or title company.

The legal description of the property must be set forth and must conform exactly to the description appearing in the title records. If the easement covers only part of a larger parcel, a survey delimiting its precise boundaries should be obtained, unless the area can be identified with certainty by reference to existing governmental survey subdivisions or maps, photographs, or prominent natural features. Of course, as a practical matter, the easier it is to identify the land under easement on the ground, the easier it will be to administer the easement, and the boundaries of an easement should be chosen with that fact in mind. Attaching an exhibit containing the description and incorporating it by reference is a useful drafting device, particularly if the description is long or is not available during preparation of the early drafts.

In the few states without conservation easement enabling legislation, a small parcel is ordinarily carved out of the property and conveyed in fee to the grantee so that, in order to circumvent common law limitations on the enforceability of negative easements in gross (i.e., not running to the benefit of another property), the easement can be described as "appurtenant" to the parcel conveyed.

5. Generic Conservation Values

The generic conservation values introduced here, in brackets, mimic the conservation purpose categories of Section 170(h) of the Internal Revenue Code, which governs the deductibility of gifts of conservation easements. The conservation values of a given property might include one or more of these, or subcategories of these (e.g., agricultural or silvicultural), or other values, depending on the circumstances.

6. Qualitative Description of Property

The purpose of this paragraph, which is likely in practice to extend to several paragraphs, is to lay the foundation for the easement by summarizing, concisely, the characteristics of the subject property that have been identified for protection and the rationale for protecting them. They should be drafted with great care since they will function over time as the primary reference point for determining what the easement is all about. Each resource (and its location, if confined to a fixed area within the property) should be clearly described (a particular view to or from a mountain range, a stand of virgin timber, a critical wetland, an ocean access way, prime farmland, an historical or archaeological site) so that the parties, their successors, and if necessary, the courts—however they may differ under a given set of circumstances on how it should be achieved—will always be able to determine with some certainty the underlying purpose of the easement.

Clarity here can go a long way to compensate for a built-in limitation all fallible easement drafters face: the impossibility of anticipating in the restrictive section of the easement every conceivable potentially conflicting variation in use of the property that might create problems in the future. This is not to say that all protected resources must be narrowly defined. Typically an easement serves broad purposes (a community's need for open space) as well as narrow (protection of significant habitat for an endangered species, for example). The point is only that an easement that is silent or vague about the resources to be protected, whether specific or general in character, may provide an inadequate level of protection for one or the other under the stress of unforeseen circumstances.

The conservation values of the subject property should be highlighted in the context of any applicable governmental policies or programs designed to promote their protection, and the public benefit to be derived from their protection should be emphasized. For a helpful listing of some factors that warrant mention, if applicable, see the conservation purposes section of the Internal Revenue Service conservation easement regulations found at Treasury Regulations Section 1.170A-14(d). (See also chapter 2 of this handbook.) In addition, where the parties have met requirements for qualifying the easement under a federal, state, or local program that has specific legal consequences of its own (such as, for example, automatic preferential property tax treatment), express reference to compliance with these requirements should be made here.

The content of these public benefit recitals should be the product of careful research and should be as site-specific as possible. This is not only because in them the grantors suggest their case for meeting the conservation purpose test for the deductibility of their easement donation under federal and state tax laws (a case for which they should be able to provide detailed supporting evidence if questioned) but also because they provide a public policy rationale for enforcing the easement that will assist the courts in any future dispute over its terms. Our law does not favor long-term private restrictions on the exercise of property rights and provides numerous mechanisms for removing them. In the years to come, conservation easements are likely to stand or fall on the strength of their identification with the public interest—the premise on which the statutory authority for conservation easements, now established in all but a few states, is built.

Sample Qualitative Description Recitals

The following paragraphs, loosely adapted from sample conservation easement forms prepared by the Maine Coast Heritage Trust for its coastal island resource protection program, illustrate the approach in the context of a hypothetical island property that exhibits both natural and scenic qualities of substantial significance:

> . . . WHEREAS, in particular, the Maine coast, and that portion of the Maine coast in which the Property is located known as the Five Bay tidal region, is a relatively intact coastal ecosystem and, as such, provides important habitat for a wide variety of birds, fishes, and both marine and terrestrial mammals and plants; and
>
> WHEREAS, the Property, which exists in a substantially undisturbed natural state, harbors a diversity of plant and animal life in an unusually broad range of habitats for property of its size, including a cobble barrier beach and associated wetlands, nesting ledges, a spruce fir forest, and open meadows, the locations of which are indicated in Exhibit _____ attached hereto and incorporated by this reference; and
>
> WHEREAS, the Five Bay tidal region is an active nesting territory for the endangered bald eagle as documented by the United States Fish and Wildlife Service, *An Ecological Characterization of Coastal Maine,* FWS/OBS-80/29 (October 1980); and
>
> WHEREAS, a bald eagle nesting site is located on the Property as indicated in Exhibit _____, which site has been identified, surveyed, and documented as nest site 20C by the Maine Eagle Project, a project of the Maine Department of Inland Fisheries and Wildlife and the

Wildlife Division, College of Natural Resources, University of Maine at Orono, under agreement with the U.S. Fish and Wildlife Service; and

WHEREAS, the Property lies in close proximity to Eagle Island, Little Mar Island, and Whale Rock, all of which are in public ownership by either the Maine Department of Inland Fisheries and Wildlife or the Maine Bureau of Public Lands and which contain nesting sites for a diversity of coastal waterbirds, including black guillemots, common eiders, common terns, least terns, and double-crested cormorants, as documented by the United States Fish and Wildlife Service, Biological Services Program, *Coastal Waterbird Colonies* (1977); and

WHEREAS, because of the integrated nature of the coastal ecosystem, the use made of the Property will affect not only the conservation values of the Property but those of these and other neighboring islands as well; and

WHEREAS, in recognition of the importance of the Property as an ecological and scenic resource, a major portion of the Property, as indicated in Exhibit ____, has been designated a Critical Area by the State of Maine in the Register of Maine Critical Areas and the entire property is classified by the same registry as a scenic coastal island; and

WHEREAS, the town of Big Bay in its comprehensive plan has designated the area where the Property is located as a Scenic Coastal District; and

WHEREAS, the Property is situated on and prominently visible from the public waterways of Long Sound, which sustain substantial recreational boating traffic; and . . .

Needless to say these provisions are entirely fact dependent. The important thing, for drafting purposes, is that they contain sufficient detail to provide both a factual context and a public policy rationale for the use restrictions to follow.

7. Baseline Documentation

The IRS requires a donor who retains rights in the property whose exercise could impair the property's conservation values to provide documentation prior to the grant "sufficient to establish the condition of the property at the time of the gift," including the condition of any resources, such as soil and water, specifically identified for protection. Both parties must acknowledge in a signed statement accompanying the baseline documentation that the documentation accurately represents the condition of the property at the time of the transfer. *See* Treas. Reg. § 1.170A-14(g)(5)(i).

There is no requirement that the documentation be made part of the easement itself. It is important, however, as a practical matter, that the relationship of this material to the easement be made clear in the easement, since its function is to provide the grantee with a starting point for monitoring the grantor's compliance with the terms of the easement. Some practitioners attach the baseline documentation to and record it with the easement. Rules governing the recordation of photographs, overlays, and other graphic material that is not of standard size or quality vary from jurisdiction to jurisdiction. In some states, this material may not all be recordable. If the baseline documentation is not to be recorded, it should be incorporated by reference and grantee's custodianship noted. In most jurisdictions, assuming the documentation is where it is represented to be, this is sufficient to put subsequent purchasers and encumbrancers on notice of its contents to the same extent as if it were recorded.

The use of formal baseline documentation in support of a conservation easement is a relatively new development. Were it not for the 1986 IRS requirements it is unlikely the practice would have become pervasive among land trusts and other conservation grantees for some time to come. There is no doubt that carefully prepared baseline material can be a considerable aid to monitoring and enforcing a grantor's performance of an easement's terms. Easement drafters should be careful, however, not to become too dependent on it. Good baseline documentation presents a "snapshot" of the property at the time of the grant, but even if it were possible, the purpose of an easement is not to freeze the land at one moment in time. With limited exceptions (as when affirmative maintenance obligations or rights are involved—to preserve a meadow against forest encroachment, for example), an easement is not intended to interrupt the cycles of change on the land but rather to restrict, to varying degrees, a landowner's freedom to interfere with those cycles.

Consequently, given the dynamic nature of land and the subtlety and complexity of the forces that effect changes in the land, "the condition of the property at the time of the gift" is likely to become a decreasingly useful reference point over the long haul. For this reason among others (the baseline documentation, if not recorded, could be lost, damaged, or destroyed, and whether recorded or not it could prove to be a less than perfect, or even wholly inadequate, reference source in some cases), a drafter should approach the task of drafting an easement as if there were to be no supporting documentation. All that is necessary to understand and enforce the easement should be contained within the four corners of the easement instrument. Although the baseline documentation, ideally, will provide useful evidence of the conservation values of a property, typically it will not be considered the exclusive source of evidence, and in any case, it should not be necessary to look beyond the easement itself to identify what those values are.

The utility of the baseline data is extended by the updating provided by monitoring reports, which are the product of a grantee's regular inspections of the property. The IRS regulations give a useful catalogue of what the baseline documentation might include. *See* Treas. Reg. § 1.170A-14(g)(5)(i). Whether baseline documentation is required at all and if so how detailed it should be are questions that can be answered only on a case-by-case basis. The variables include the potential for conflict that exists between a grantor's reserved rights and the conservation resources to be protected as well as the sensitivity and complexity of those resources. (For more on the subject of baseline documentation, see chapter 6 of this handbook.)

8. Continuation of Existing Uses

The intention to permit the existing uses of the property to continue is made clear.

9. Conveyance of Right to Protect Conservation Values: Affirmative Purpose

Although most people think of conservation easements as essentially negative in character because of the many restrictions on land use they typically contain, it may be useful, conceptually, to remember that, in the usual case (buffer-type easements are an exception), the restrictions in an easement are in support of an overarching affirmative purpose to see to the preservation of the conservation values of the restricted property itself. This affirmative purpose distinguishes the typical conservation easement from traditional negative easements, covenants, and servitudes, whose primary purpose is in some way to enhance or protect the value of property outside the boundaries of the property subject to them.

Enabling legislation in most states has made speculation regarding the nature of a conservation easement a matter of little more than theoretical interest. It is at least conceivable, however, that in states that have not enacted such legislation, this technical distinction could have a bearing on the enforceability of the "novel" conservation easement, particularly in light of the fact that the courts have been reluctant, traditionally, to expand the exceedingly narrow category of negative easements that are considered valid under the common law. Arguably, a right to protect certain features of a property is no less "affirmative," conceptually, than a right-of-way across it and should be no less enforceable. In any case, emphasizing this affirmative aspect of the easement is a subtle way of encouraging the parties to think of the conservation values it protects as something as real and positive, in their way, as the development rights it restricts.

10. Qualifications of Grantee

The grantee must be shown to meet all state and federal qualifying requirements relevant to the easement transaction in question. This paragraph (including the bracketed portion) tracks the language of one state's enabling statute almost word for word, with the addition of the clause stating the grantee's qualification under Section 170(h) of the Internal Revenue Code. The federal tax regulations require that a grantee have both the commitment and resources to enforce the easement. *See* Treas. Reg. § 1.170A-14(c)(1). An organization "organized or operated primarily or substantially" for a qualified conservation purpose meets the commitment test automatically. Whether the organization's resources are sufficient is a separate question of fact, but a dedicated monitoring fund is expressly not required.

11. Grantee's Commitment

The grantee's acceptance of the easement puts it on the hook to enforce it. The attorney general of the state in which the property is situated has the power, through his general supervisory authority over charitable institutions, to hold the grantee to this commitment. The somewhat elevated, ceremonial tone of the recitals peaks in this paragraph, which marks the end of the preamble.

12. Grant

This formal clause is, from a property lawyer's perspective, where the real business of the easement begins, because it is here that the transfer of the property interest is effected. Care must be taken to use language that complies with the conveyancing requirements of the jurisdiction in which the subject property is located, which in some cases may mean strict adherence to seemingly archaic formulae. One variable is the way in which consideration is recited. In some states a nominal dollar amount (for example, $10.00) is customarily stated to have changed hands; in others, gift language may be appropriate. Although discussion of the issue is beyond the scope of this commentary, it is to be noted that, under certain circumstances, the common law favors transfers for consideration over gift transfers. The model follows the modern practice, which is broadly if not universally accepted, of reciting that it is the exchange of promises contained in the agreement that provides the consideration for the grant.

Where there is statutory authority for the easement, and in some states more than one statute may apply, this authority should be invoked to ensure that the easement will benefit from it in the event of a challenge. Of course, state easement statutes may impose certain conveyancing requirements of their own, and in the model the grantors are characterized as "voluntarily" making the grant to comply with a requirement to that effect in one such statute. That the grant be made "in perpetuity" is a statutory requirement in some states as it is under Section 170(h) of the Internal Revenue Code. It is not a universal requirement, however, and there are instances where a term easement is appropriate (see chapter 11 of this handbook). In addition to whatever statutory authority may exist, some practitioners invoke the common law, presumably as insurance against the failure of the easement to meet statutory requirements or the failure of the supporting statutes themselves. In light of the fact that the common law authority for conservation easements has never been established, this does not seem to be a particularly helpful practice. Out of caution for the concerns just raised, the model makes general reference to the laws of the state where the property is located in addition to the specific statutory authority. Whether the courts will enforce a conservation easement without specific statutory authority, however, is an open question.[2]

Use of the term "grant" in a deed implies in most jurisdictions that the grantor has not previously conveyed or encumbered the interest being transferred. Infrequently, the grantor gives title warranties to insure the grantee against defects in the title to the interest conveyed. More commonly, the grantee satisfies itself as to the condition of title by searching the title record down to the date of closing or, depending on the financial stakes, obtaining title insurance.

13. Purpose

Although it appears on first reading to be nothing more than an innocuous recapitulation of the recitals, the purpose clause is, in fact, the touchstone of the easement. Everything turns on the "consistency" test that is introduced here. Only uses consistent with protection of the conservation values of the property are now permitted. In the provisions to follow, the parties' judgment concerning the consistency of specific uses will be made express. So, for example, farming, ranching, or timber production, with or without qualification as appropriate, may be permitted, while residential and commercial development, additional construction, and mining may be prohibited or restricted. It is likely to be impossible, however, to foresee every conceivable future use or variation of use. Unless the parties intend that either the specific restrictions imposed or the grantor's expressly reserved rights are to be exclusive, there must be some mechanism for dealing with the unforeseen. The consistency test is that mechanism. If the easement is reasonably clear about the conservation values to be protected, it should provide a workable standard.

It should be noted that in this paragraph, as elsewhere, the choice of language is influenced by relevant statutory and regulatory provisions. Stating the purpose of the easement to be, in part, the retention of land "predominantly" in its, for example, natural, scenic, and open space condition is to key into a state enabling statute (caveat: the appropriate language will vary from state to state). Reference to preventing uses of the property that "significantly impair or interfere with conservation values" echoes similar language in the IRS regulations. *See* Treas. Reg. §§ 1.170A-14(d)(4)(v), (e)(2), (g)(4), and (g)(5).

14. Rights of Grantee

The scope of the rights conveyed to the grantee depends on the type of easement in question. Recreational or educational easements, for example,

---

2. For a discussion of the common law problems that have led to a statutory solution in most states see the Uniform Conservation Easement Act, 12. U.L.A. 51 (supp. 1986). *See also* Thomas S. Barrett and Putnam Livermore for the Trust for Public Land, *The Conservation Easement in California* (Covelo, California: Island Press, 1983), 27-28 and 113-118.

might contain highly detailed descriptions of permitted activities, circumscribed by specific conditions and qualifications and confined to precisely delineated time periods. Natural ecosystem easements, on the other hand, might delegate broad authority to the grantee to manage the property and to make its own determination regarding limitations on access. The model provides the essentials, giving the grantee the broad power to protect the conservation values of the property but confining the grantee's supporting rights to those that are necessary for proper monitoring and enforcement of the easement (inspection, injunctive relief, and restoration). Recognizing that the typical open space easement is over property that is being put to some productive use by its owners, the model requires that the grantee's rights be exercised without undue interference with the landowner's use and enjoyment of the property. Conveyance of the rights of inspection, enforcement, and restoration is dictated not only by common sense but by the IRS. *See* Treas. Reg. § 1.170A-14(g)(5)(ii). If the parties so desire, the permitted frequency of inspection and the length of the required notice period can be specified.

The continuing right to "identify" the conservation values of the property is sometimes conveyed, particularly in natural ecosystem easements. In the typical open space easement, however, the conservation values are identified up front, and it would be an impermissible enlargement of the burden of the easement to identify new values after the conveyance. A grantee may desire the right to make scientific studies of the conservation values of the property. If so, care should be taken to carefully delimit the scope of the right in order to allay any concerns a grantor might have that it could become too intrusive. Finally, under certain circumstances the parties may contemplate engaging in specific projects to restore or enhance the conservation values of the property. If so, a right of enhancement should be included to prevent a change of ownership from undercutting the planned projects.

Some easements, usually natural ecosystems easements, empower the grantee, in its sole discretion, to determine the consistency of any activity or use for which no express provision is made with the purpose of the easement or the protection of particular resources. More typically, however, the grantor will wish to preserve a say in the matter. In the model, the issue is left open to negotiation and, if necessary, arbitration (see paragraph 5.2 of the supplementary provisions) or litigation through the grantee's exercise of the paragraph 6 remedies referred to in subparagraph (c).

15. Prohibited Uses

There are three basic approaches to structuring the restrictive provisions of a conservation easement. The first is to make the restrictions exclusive; anything not expressly prohibited is permitted. This approach is seen most frequently in simple, single purpose easements, such as the "pothole" easements taken by the U.S. Fish and Wildlife Service to protect the wetlands along the migratory waterfowl flyway of the upper Great Plains. In the pothole easements the draining, filling, leveling, or burning of wetlands is prohibited, but no other obligations or restrictions are imposed, and all other rights are reserved to the grantors. The second approach is to make the reservations exclusive and convey all other rights to the grantee. This approach—which it is more accurate to characterize as the grant of a fee subject to reserved rights than a grant of a conservation easement—is suggested by the National Park Service in its easement program guidelines.[3] "Reserved interest deeds," as the Park Service calls them, have been acquired by the Park Service at some locations along the Appalachian Trail—presumably at a premium above the standard price for conservation easements. An advantage of both these approaches is their certainty; they leave little doubt as to the scope of the easement. But, as always, there is a cost. By fixing the terms of either the restrictions or reservations, these easements allocate the risk of an omission entirely to one party or the other. In a complicated easement, where conservation concerns and productive uses require careful balancing in perpetuity, a one-way allocation of risk may be unacceptable. Not surprisingly, the third approach, which the model adopts, and which is found in one variation or another in most of the easements reviewed for this commentary, follows a middle course. It prohibits all uses inconsistent with the purpose of the easement and reserves to the grantor the right to engage in all consistent uses.

The restrictions and reservations of an actual two-acre "forever wild" easement, quoted in their entirety, illustrate the third approach in its simplest form:

> The Premises shall be kept as open space in their natural and wild state and restricted from any development with buildings or otherwise, or any use other than as open space and as sanctuary for wildlife and wild plants.
>
> It is understood, however, that the Conservation Easement herein granted permits the Grantors and their successors in interest to use the Premises for all purposes, present and future, not inconsistent with this grant.

Whether these paragraphs provide a wholly adequate basis for deciding future disputes may be open to question, but the emphasis they place on the purpose of the easement rather than the precision of its covenants is instructive.

As experience with easements grows and unexpected problems are encountered and overcome, easement practice becomes, inevitably, more sophisticated. Today's easement drafters go to great lengths to anticipate future problems and to provide for them expressly in the easement deed. Particularly where conservation values and productive uses are intermingled, it is not uncommon to find highly detailed restrictions and reservations—in some cases, in fact, so detailed that they begin to resemble zoning code provisions. The

---

3. U.S. Department of the Interior, National Park Service, Office of Park Planning and Special Studies, *Planning Process Guideline*, Release No. 3, Amendment No. 3 (March 1986), 4-5 and 38-42.

intention is to create a document that leaves as little room for interpretation as possible, one whose terms can be applied almost mechanically. Enforceability and, in the case of a deductible easement gift, an accurate, defensible appraisal are motivating goals.

But there are limits to the benefits of specificity. Too much detail can alienate the landowner, whose willing cooperation is, as a practical matter, integral to the success of an easement. And, in any case, time has a way of rendering details obsolete. A document intended to reach as far into the future as an easement must have stretch; it must have application to changing conditions—the unforeseen as well as the foreseen.

Most practitioners, recognizing the futility of trying to delimit every conceivable variation of use, activity, or practice that in the future might have an adverse impact on the resources to be protected, build in some flexibility. As in the simple easement quoted above, most easements provide that consistency with the purpose of the easement is the standard that all future actions must meet, whether dealt with expressly in the easement instrument or not. If the purpose of the easement is carefully articulated and the conservation values of the property clearly identified—and if the relationship of the specific restrictions to these values is clear—the consistency catch-all should serve to prevent the easement from being defeated for lack of clairvoyance on the part of its drafter.

16. Prohibited Uses: Express Restrictions

The content of an easement's restrictive provisions is, of course, entirely dependent on the facts at hand and must be thought through on a case-by-case basis. The requirements of natural ecosystem, recreational, educational, scenic, open space, and multipurpose easements differ, often markedly, from one another. In addition, the requirements of particular easements within a given class are as varied as the properties to which they apply, the regions of the country in which they are located, and the practical needs and temperaments of the parties who negotiate them. Seemingly infinite permutations are possible. Nevertheless, one can speak in a general way of certain basic areas of concern that are likely to come up more often than not. Restrictions regarding the following uses and resources seem to recur with the greatest frequency:

- subdivision and development
- commercial or industrial use
- new and existing buildings, structures, and improvements
- alteration of the land surface
- mineral development
- waste dumps
- utility lines
- signs
- soil and water
- wetlands
- ponds and streams
- wildlife and wildlife habitat
- trees, shrubs, and other vegetation

The degree of control imposed by an easement to regulate these uses and resources is highly variable and depends, among other things, on the conservation values identified for protection. And, of course, depending on the type of easement involved, other concerns may require attention. An agricultural easement, for example, may require conformity with a farm conservation plan prepared by the district conservationist of the Soil Conservation Service, or may go beyond that and impose specific restrictions on farming practices to protect streams, control runoff and erosion, limit the use of pesticides, and enhance soil quality. Similarly, a timberland easement is likely to impose restrictions aimed at protecting the forest resource by requiring an approved plan, by making reference to some generally accepted performance standards, or by setting forth specific requirements. Scenic easements may have provisions for maintaining open fields and meadows, preventing the obstruction of a view, and limiting parking areas. Natural habitat easements may seek to protect native vegetation from non-native encroachment and to limit hunting, fishing, or trapping. The list can be extended indefinitely, but it has little meaning in the abstract. The circumstances of a particular transaction, and the facts on the ground, are always controlling.[4]

Because the content of the restrictive provisions is entirely fact-based, the best a model can do is give some general guidance on how these provisions should be approached. There are two major concerns: balance and coherence. As to the first, which runs to policy, the grantee should be at pains not to intrude further on the landowner's beneficial use and enjoyment of the property than the protection of the conservation values of the property requires. Pride of ownership runs deep; landowners, rightly, value their prerogatives. As a general rule, grantees should not use easements to impose their own preferences in inessential matters like taste or, unless the easement is part of a comprehensive regional protection plan, to try to solve problems that transcend the boundaries of the property. The grantee should stick to restrictions that will make a substantial difference to the conservation values of the property, that it can monitor efficiently, and that it intends to enforce.

In addition, an effort should be made to scale the grantee's degree of control over the landowner's activities in a manner that corresponds to the severity of the threat the activities pose to the conservation values of the property. Fully compatible uses can be permitted without restriction; fully incompatible uses should be prohibited outright. In between, recognized performance standards, notice requirements, or approval requirements can be used, in escalating order,

---

4. A helpful discussion of typical restrictive provisions, by category, can be found in National Trust for Historic Preservation and the Land Trust Exchange, *Appraising Easements: Guidelines for Valuation of Historic Preservation and Land Conservation Easements* (October 1984). *See also* Barrett and Livermore, *The Conservation Easement in California*, 86-91; Maine Coast Heritage Trust, "Examples of Restrictive Covenant Language Used in Conservation Easements" (May 1982).

to prevent or mitigate conflicts. The more sensitive the resource to be protected, of course, the tighter the controls, but the grantee should make every effort to understand the resource, determine its tolerance to use, and give as much latitude for permitted uses, including economic uses, as possible. The less burdensome an easement's requirements, the less occasion there will be for conflict and the easier in the long run the easement will be to enforce. Particularly in the context of open space preservation, where the parties envision the coexistence of conservation values and one or more intensive productive uses, the less the landowner and the easement holder have to think about the easement in everyday situations the better.

The second concern, coherence, is a mechanical matter. The pieces of an easement should all fit together. Restrictions and permitted uses and activities should not be in conflict. Interrelationships between them should be identified, and cross-references made where appropriate. The restrictions should be presented in some logical sequence and related subjects grouped. Overly vague or ambiguous terms should be avoided. In addition, exhibits should be used as necessary to describe the location of a protected resource or permitted use.

One final note: in the restrictions, as throughout the easement, care must be taken to include any provisions required by applicable state law. Certain specific restrictions might be required, for example, to qualify under a state or local program for preferential property tax treatment.

Sample Restrictions

The following necessarily generic provisions show one way the mix might look. They are meant to approximate the contents of a typical open space easement. Natural, scenic, forest, and farmland elements are combined in them for purposes of illustration, but it should be understood that they have been assembled in a vacuum. Real negotiations over a real piece of property would very likely lead to a far different balance of concerns. What is right on one set of facts may be wrong on another. There can be no such thing as a consensus set of easement restrictions, and many experienced hands will find good reason to take issue with this one. Consequently, the reader is cautioned to bear in mind that these sample restrictions are offered not for their substance but for whatever limited guidance they might give as to form. In addition, it should be noted that these restrictions will be fully comprehensible only if read in light of the reserved rights discussed in section 17 of the commentary. Reference to paragraph 4 in these provisions should be read as reference to the reserved rights. As a matter of convenience, comments on particular provisions are interspersed.

RESIDENTIAL DEVELOPMENT

(a) The legal or *de facto* subdivision of the Property for any purpose, except as may be required by law for the uses permitted in paragraph 3(c); . . .

Residential development is the primary threat to open space. It is safe to say that the principal objective of most easements is to prohibit or control it, and in the usual case, this one provision accounts for virtually the entire diminution of market value caused by an easement. Where limited development is contemplated, the easement should delineate the areas in which it is permitted. The exception to the prohibition of this paragraph recognizes that some jurisdictions require legal subdivision for the construction of even one additional dwelling.

COMMERCIAL DEVELOPMENT

> (b) Any commercial or industrial use of or activity on the Property other than those relating to agriculture, recreation, or home occupations as permitted under paragraph 4 or mineral development meeting the requirements of paragraph 3(m); . . .

Commercial or industrial development is the second biggest threat to open space. The assumption regarding the permitted exceptions to the prohibition here, which would not hold in all cases, is that they will not change the open space character of the land or cause any significant harm to the resources the easement is intended to protect.

CONSTRUCTION AND IMPROVEMENTS

> (c) The placement or construction of any buildings, structures, or other improvements of any kind (including, without limitation, fences, roads, and parking lots) other than the following:
>
> (1) The maintenance, renovation, expansion, or replacement of existing agricultural, residential, and related buildings, structures, and improvements in substantially their present location as shown on Exhibit ____; provided that any expansion or replacement of an existing building, structure, or improvement may not substantially alter its character or function or increase its present height, or the land surface area it occupies, by more than ___[e.g., fifty (50)]___ per cent without the prior approval of Grantee;
>
> (2) The placement or construction, after prior notice to Grantee, of additional buildings, structures, and improvements for agricultural purposes in the designated agricultural area described in Exhibit ____;
>
> (3) The placement or construction, after prior notice to Grantee, of additional accessory structures and improvements for residential purposes (including, without limitation, private recreational facilities such as swimming pools and tennis courts but not including dwelling places of any kind) in the designated residential areas described in Exhibit ____;
>
> (4) The placement or construction, after prior notice to Grantee, of not more than three (3) additional single-family residences in the designated residential areas described in Exhibit ___; provided that none of such additional residences may occupy more than ___ square feet of land surface area or exceed ___ feet in height without the prior approval of Grantee; and

(5) The placement or construction, after prior notice to Grantee, of facilities for the development and utilization of energy resources, including, without limitation, wind, solar, hydroelectric, methane, wood, alcohol, and fossil fuels, for use principally on the Property; provided that the design and location of any such facilities shall be subject to the prior approval of Grantee, and provided further that the development of fossil fuel resources shall be subject to the provisions of paragraph 3(m); . . .

Generally, an easement is not intended to impinge on a grantor's existing activities or to limit their reasonable expansion—the assumption being that they are consistent with the purpose of the easement. The construction and improvements permitted by this paragraph are treated as the physical extension of permitted uses. Since the landowner is in the best position to determine what buildings, structures, and other improvements are appropriate for permitted productive activities, like farming, or for enhancing the quality of domestic life, it is prudent to give him or her as much latitude as possible to make such decisions. Sample provisions (c)(1)-(5) attempt to do just that, on the assumption that the probability of adverse impacts from these limited activities is slight. Still, by highlighting certain concerns, such as size and location, and providing for prior notice and even approval under some circumstances, these provisions illustrate a full range of control. On real facts, tighter or looser controls than those in the sample might be desirable. In addition, of course, provision for still other facilities, such as guest cabins or worker housing, may be necessary.

Some parties will prefer to agree to many of the details of permitted future development, including the precise number, location, and design of all new buildings, before executing the easement. They should realize, however, that future landowners may find the original landowner's plans unsuitable to their needs. Some easements, particularly those with a dominant scenic element, include aesthetic considerations among the grantee's concerns and seek to limit a grantor's discretion in its choice of materials and designs for new construction. Typically, however, such matters are beyond the scope of an open space easement, and a grantee will seek to influence them, if at all, by subtler methods.[5]

Control of siting, based on agricultural and residential zones, is the principal device used by the sample to assure that the activities in question do not harm the conservation values of the hypothetical property. It should be noted that the failure to control the siting of any permitted development could result in real harm to conservation values and could leave the easement vulnerable to

---

5. See Christine Carlson and Steven Durrant, *The Farm Landscape of Whatcom County: Managing Change Through Design* (San Francisco: Trust for Public Land, 1985). This remarkable study of farm landscape aesthetics is indicative of the kind of education that is likely to be the most effective means of elevating a community's awareness of the impact of individual design choices on an area's scenic quality.

attack on grounds of vagueness.[6] Site description by survey is preferred, although in some circumstances the use of maps, photographs, or natural boundaries may suffice. Alternative approaches include leaving site delineation to the future approval of the grantee or entirely excluding pre-approved sites from the area under easement. The advantage to keeping such sites within the boundaries of the easement is that it preserves the grantee's right to ensure that any permitted development will be compatible with the easement.

Paragraph (c)(5) addresses a matter on which most easements are silent but that may have increasing importance in the future if, as many foresee, the sources of energy supply become more localized and diverse. In the usual case, there are not likely to be existing plans for improvements of this type, but since, among other things, they could help to maintain the viability of a farm or other land-based enterprise over the long haul, the landowner's freedom to employ them should be preserved. Windmills, small hydroelectric dams and turbines, biomass conversion systems, and solar devices are some of the energy production options that may prove useful in the future. Since improvements of this kind can have a direct impact on certain of the conservation resources an easement seeks to protect, prior approval of both location and design is recommended to assure compatibility. The number of such facilities might also be prescribed. But providing, as the sample does, that the energy produced be used "principally" on the property, preserves some flexibility while imposing a limit that, in addition to whatever natural and practical limits there may be, ought to suffice in most cases.

The prohibition of the "placement" as well as construction of structures and "other improvements of any kind" is meant to be comprehensive, extending to trailers, towers, antennae, and the like. If any of these are of particular concern, express provision may, of course, be made for them.

The concerns addressed in paragraphs (a) - (c) are those most basic to open space preservation; they are found in one variant or another in all but the narrowest, most specialized easements. What follows, typically, are provisions addressed to management issues, concerned in part with the protection of specific resources and in part with preserving the overall scenic quality of the land. Paragraphs (d) - (m) are meant to give a sampling of the kinds of issues most frequently encountered; they are, however, neither comprehensive nor universal. In practice, the content of these provisions will vary markedly depending on the purpose of the easement, the region of the country involved, the use that the land will be put to, and most important, the particular features of the property in question.

SURFACE ALTERATION

(d) Any alteration of the surface of the land, including, without limitation, the excavation or removal of soil, sand, gravel, rock, peat,

---

6. See *Parkinson v. Board of Assessors of Medford*, 398 Mass. 112 (1986).

or sod, except as may be required in the course of any activity permitted herein; provided that construction materials, such as rock, dirt, sand, and gravel, may be taken for use on the Property from locations approved by Grantee; . . .

As this provision acknowledges, many of the activities permitted under the easement involve some disturbance of the land. In addition, it is a commonplace source of economy for farmers and other large landowners to use materials like sand and gravel that may be found on the property for their own construction projects. For most open space easements, such a limited use would not cause any problems. Where there is a scenic element involved, however, site approval—as in the sample—may be appropriate. But a note of caution: it is possible to read the prohibition against surface mining in section 170(h)(5)(B) of the Internal Revenue Code as extending to the surface removal of common construction materials, like sand and gravel, for private use. There is no support in the legislative history of this section for so broad an interpretation.[7] The clear focus of Congress was on large-scale commercial strip mining, which could destroy the conservation purpose of a gift, not the trivial impacts of a landowner's personal use of common surface materials. Even the regulations acknowledge that gravel pits may be among the existing man-made "incursions" on the property. *See* Treas. Reg. § 1.170A-14(g)(5)(i)(B). Nevertheless, some practitioners prefer to sidestep the issue by leaving the easement silent on it. Presumably, though, because this type of use is so commonplace, the parties would have to reach some understanding on the matter sooner or later. Because of the potential importance over the long term of the grantee's control over siting, the choice was made in the sample to address it openly, up front.

SOIL AND WATER

(e) Any use or activity that causes or is likely to cause significant soil degradation or erosion or significant pollution of any surface or subsurface waters; provided that this prohibition shall not be construed as extending to agricultural operations and practices (including, without limitation, the use of agrichemicals such as fertilizers, pesticides, herbicides, and fungicides) that are substantially in accordance with a farm conservation plan prepared by the _____ County District Conservationist of the United States Department of Agriculture Soil Conservation Service, or any successor or equivalent agency, which is reviewed and updated whenever a substantial

7. See U.S. Congress, House Committee on Ways and Means, *Miscellaneous Tax Bills: Charitable Deduction for Certain Contributions of Real Property for Conservation Purposes: Hearings on H.R. 4611 before the Subcommittee on Select Revenue Measures*, 96th Cong., 1st sess., 1979, and *Minor Tax Bills: Deductions for Contributions of Certain Interests in Property for Conservation Purposes: Hearings on H.R. 7318 before the Subcommittee on Select Revenue Measures*, 96th Cong., 2nd sess., 1980.

change in operations is contemplated but in any case no less often than every ten (10) years; . . .

Paragraph (e) is intentionally broad. Because soil and water are the foundation upon which the long-range health of the land rests, it cuts across every permitted use of the property. A serious protection program for these resources, however, could involve considerable time and expense. It would be likely to entail the careful compilation and analysis of complex data on a regular basis to monitor the resources as well as some kind of cooperative management mechanism for implementing any ameliorative measures that might be indicated. Few easement holders are in a position to take on that kind of responsibility, even where landowners are willing to cede it. Nevertheless, the grantee should have a hook for dealing with soil and water issues, if for no other reason than to enable it to prevent the gross harm to these resources that can result from relatively obvious causes (for example, gully erosion caused by the habitual use of off-road vehicles on severe slopes or stream pollution caused by uncontrolled stock access).

The proviso of this paragraph is intended to provide a means around the more difficult question of what to do about the cumulative effects that a land-owner's primary productive use of the land—in this case farming—can have on these resources. Such effects, because they develop slowly over many years, may take some real expertise to detect. This is a long-term management matter and there are a number of ways to approach it. On some facts, a grantee may find the risk of sustained mismanagement so negligible that it will be comfortable accepting that risk and will impose no express requirements. On other facts, a grantee may choose to require an approved plan, or compel conformity with some recognized standards, or impose specific requirements based on its own criteria. A landowner's willing cooperation, though, will always be essential for any meaningful results. For this reason, and in keeping with the preference for minimal intrusiveness discussed at the outset, the sample illustrates a middle approach. No mandatory requirements are imposed, but a safe harbor is created for operations conducted under a conservation plan, giving the landowner a strong incentive to develop and maintain such a plan. If there are deficiencies in a plan, resulting in detriment to the resource, the grantee's recourse is to work with the landowner and the agency to make appropriate adjustments. All will not agree that the Soil Conservation Service is the highest authority in these matters; other sources of expertise, where available, may be preferred. The point of the sample is only that in areas as complex as these, where knowledge and standards are evolving, the use of an objective performance standard, however imperfect, is likely to be the best approach both for the long-range management of the property and the long-range enforcement of the easement.

WETLANDS AND STREAM BUFFER

(f) The draining, filling, dredging, or diking of the wetland areas described in Exhibit____, including any enlargements thereof, or the cultivation or other disturbance of the soil within fifty (50) feet of the thread of _____ Creek, whose location is indicated on Exhibit ____; . . .

The location of any resource singled out for protection, like the creek and wetlands here, should be shown as accurately as possible on an accompanying map exhibit. Any wetlands that may develop in the future, other than as enlargements of existing wetlands, are not protected by this covenant. The cutting of trees or control of vegetation is not prohibited in the buffer area along the creek, although in some cases these additional restrictions might be appropriate.

PONDS AND WATER COURSES

(g) The alteration or manipulation of the ponds and water courses located on the Property as shown on Exhibit____, or the creation of new water impoundments or water courses, for any purpose other than permitted agricultural or residential uses of the Property or the limited energy development permitted under paragraph 3(c)(5); provided that any new water impoundments or water courses for permitted agricultural or residential uses shall be located in the designated residential and agricultural areas described in Exhibit ____; . . .

Provisions that impinge on water rights can be extremely sensitive, particularly in the more arid regions of the West. In the western states, water rights constitute a valuable form of property that can be bought and sold separately from land, and familiarity with the water law of the jurisdiction is essential before venturing into this area. Water rights are controlled, quantified, and allocated in most jurisdictions by a centralized regulatory authority, and landowners are likely to be circumspect about agreeing to any restrictions that would affect their allotment or any marketable entitlement they might have. On the other hand, a grantee will want to assure that water rights transfers have no adverse impact on the conservation values of the property. The sample makes no attempt to balance these concerns, which are raised here merely to alert drafters to their potential importance.

In the rest of the country, where the water supply is more abundant, the common law system of riparian rights governs the use of surface waters. Roughly stated, the right to use the water of a stream is incidental to and inseparable from the ownership of land adjoining the stream. It is a right held in common by all riparian landowners; downstream owners are entitled to the natural flow of a stream subject only to the reasonable diminution caused by upstream owners.

In the sample, how a landowner chooses to employ the water resources of the property for permitted uses is left to the landowner's discretion. This could be too broad a right on some facts. Some easements, for example, might require the grantee's approval of any new dam or impoundment or of its design and location, or might impose restrictions to protect fish or other water-related resources. (Note: paragraph 3(c)(5) of the sample provides for grantee control over the design and location of energy development facilities.) Other easements might prohibit any new water development altogether. The sample, however, assumes natural and practical limitations such that the landowner's exercise of rights under this provision would pose no significant threat to the conservation values of the property. The same assumption is made with respect to the landowner's right to use springs and other groundwater, which is not limited in any way by the sample provision.

TIMBER HARVESTING

> (h) The pruning, cutting down, or other destruction or removal of live trees located outside the designated residential and agricultural areas described in Exhibit____, except as necessary, in accordance with generally accepted forestry conservation practices, to control or prevent hazard, disease, or fire, to maintain the designated open space areas described in Exhibit____, or to provide firewood or construction materials for use on the Property; provided that trees may be harvested for any purpose, including, without limitation, commercial timber production or the limited energy development permitted under paragraph 3(c)(5), on a sustained yield basis in accordance with a plan prepared in consultation with a registered professional forester and approved by Grantee that is designed to protect the conservation values of the Property, including, without limitation, scenic and wildlife habitat values; . . .

The sample is premised on a hypothetical working farm with substantial but subordinate forested acreage. The commercial timber harvesting permitted by this provision is not and is never likely to be the dominant use. The easement makes no attempt to limit the landowner's discretion to remove trees in the agricultural and residential areas based on the judgment that no significant impact on the conservation values of the property would result from doing so. This, of course, would not be true for all properties. Depending on their purpose, some easements regulate these areas closely, even to the point of protecting individual trees, groves, or orchards. A provision for maintaining designated open areas is frequently encountered. This can be particularly important in the Northeast where preventing forest encroachment on meadows or certain cultural resources, such as the foundation of an ancestral homesite, is a common concern. Other provisions are sometimes included for increasing arable acreage or preserving the view from a residence. No attempt is made here to regulate the landowner's right to control shrubs and other vegetation, though again, depending on the circumstances, such regulation might be appropriate. Plan approval like that envisioned here for full-scale timber harvesting is not always feasible. Particularly in areas of the country where forest management is the dominant use, both landowners and grantees might find the requirement too burdensome.

Invoking relevant standards, such as those promulgated by the Forest Service or the Society of American Foresters, might be a workable alternative. In areas where timber harvesting is expected to be a rare occurrence, prior notice is frequently required. It should be noted that "sustained yield" forestry does not necessarily preclude clear-cutting. Where that might be a concern, a selective cutting method should be required.

COMMERCIAL FEEDLOTS

(i) The establishment or maintenance of any commercial feedlot, which is defined for the purposes of this Easement as a confined area or facility within which the land is not grazed or cropped at least annually and which is used to receive livestock that has been raised off the Property for feeding and fattening for market; . . .

This is a scenic protection provision, intended to prevent the property from becoming an unsightly stockyard. Depending on where the property is located, this kind of use might be so infeasible as to require no specific mention. Some easements go further and prohibit all husbandry practices, including certain types of poultry and dairy operations, that involve animals being kept in tightly confined environments. The judgment here, though, is that unless such uses pose a potential threat to the conservation values of the property, an easement is not the appropriate place to regulate them. It should be noted that the sample provision does not restrict the landowner's right to use permanent pens, corrals, and dry-lot feeding areas for animals raised on the property. The assumption, which may not be true in all cases, is that practical limitations would prevent such uses from having the degree of impact on the scenic quality of the property that a commercial feedlot could have.

WASTE DUMPS

(j) The dumping or other disposal of wastes, refuse, and debris on the Property, except that which is generated by activities permitted herein; provided that any such dumping or disposal shall be in accordance with applicable law and that only the site indicated in Exhibit _____ may be used for this purpose, or such other site or sites as Grantee may approve; . . .

Almost every easement has a provision dealing with dumps. When a property is especially sensitive, an absolute prohibition might be in order. Most large properties, however, have some capacity for on-site waste disposal, and the important thing is to assure that the scenic and other conservation values of the property are protected by finding an inconspicuous and otherwise appropriate place for it. Requiring waste disposal to be undertaken in accordance with applicable law gives the grantee standing to prevent or abate illegal disposal.

UTILITY SYSTEMS

(k) The above-ground installation of new utility systems or extensions of existing utility systems, including, without limitation, water, sewer, power, fuel, and communication lines and related facilities, but excluding systems for irrigating the Property; . . .

Not all landowners will agree to this prohibition, which may be more or less important depending on the degree of aesthetic refinement considered appropriate in the region of the country where the property is located. The parties should be aware, in any case, that placing utility lines under ground can be substantially more expensive than above-ground installation.

SIGNS AND BILLBOARDS

(l) The placement of any signs or billboards on the Property, except that signs, whose placement, number, and design do not significantly diminish the scenic character of the Property, may be displayed to state the name and address of the Property and the names of persons living on the Property, to advertize an on-site activity permitted pursuant to paragraph 4, to advertize the Property for sale or rent, and to post the Property to control unauthorized entry or use; and . . .

A provision of this type may serve to supplement or reinforce existing governmental regulations in some locations. Some easements arbitrarily specify the location, size, and number of permitted signs. Having prohibited billboards outright, the sample assumes that any problems that might arise over permitted signs are manageable within the stated "scenic character" constraint.

MINERAL DEVELOPMENT

(m) The exploration for, or development and extraction of, minerals and hydrocarbons by any surface mining method or any other method that would significantly impair or interfere with the conservation values of the Property. Prior to engaging in any mineral exploration, development, or extraction by any method not otherwise prohibited by this paragraph, Grantors must notify Grantee and submit a plan for Grantee's approval that provides for minimizing the adverse effects of the operation on the conservation values of the Property. In addition to such other measures as may be required to protect the conservation values of the Property, the plan must provide for: (1) concealing all facilities or otherwise locating them so as to be compatible with existing topography and landscape to the greatest practicable extent and (2) restoring any altered physical features of the land to their original state.

This provision addresses the requirements of Section 170(h)(5) of the Internal Revenue Code and Sections 1.170A-14(g)(4) and (5)(ii) of the IRS regulations, which prohibit surface mining and any other method of mining that is inconsistent with the particular purposes of an easement. The regulations contemplate that permitted mining may have "limited, localized impact" on the property so long as it is not "irremediably destructive of significant conservation interests." Designing production facilities to be compatible with existing topography and landscape and requiring reclamation to the "original state" of the land are given as examples of ways to meet this test. In addition, prior notice to the grantee is required. The sample exceeds this requirement by requiring prior approval of a mitigation plan.

There are certain long-range effects of mining, including subsidence, that may need to be considered depending on the circumstances. In addition, it should be noted that even under the best of circumstances the immediate surface impact of subsurface mining, whether for oil and gas or other minerals, can be substantial—involving, for example, roads, drill holes, well heads, pipelines, pump stations, and other temporary structures. For these reasons many grantees seek, where possible, to prohibit mining entirely or to limit it to off-site access.

In areas of the country where geothermal resources occur, express provision should be made for them in this paragraph.

17. Reserved Rights

This provision is a restatement of what is likely to be the law in most jurisdictions anyway. An easement is a conveyance of a partial interest in property; rights not conveyed are reserved. Here, as throughout the model, consistency with the purpose of the easement is expressly made the ultimate test of the landowner's rights. This is a useful expression of the parties' intent. Even without an express statement of the consistency standard, however, a court would be likely to apply it in a dispute over the scope of the grantor's reserved rights. It is a general rule of conveyancing law that a reservation inconsistent with the estate conveyed is void as repugnant to the grant. Like most common law principles, though, the repugnancy doctrine is susceptible to manipulation, and courts, in trying to carry out the intent of the instrument, seek whenever they can to reconcile reservations with the grant to give effect to both. The content of the express restrictions and reservations, along with the description of the conservation values of the property in the recitals and, if applicable, the baseline data, are collectively the best available source of guidance for applying the consistency standard to activities that have not been expressly provided for as well as those that have. They should be drafted with this secondary function in mind.

Paragraph 15(g) of the model provides that the terms of the easement apply to the grantors' successors as well as the grantors. Nevertheless, to foreclose any possibility of the reservations being construed as merely personal to the grantors, explicit reference is made to the grantors' successors here. In addition, to avoid any confusion regarding an important matter, the landowner's right to control access by third parties is made clear.

It should be noted that in certain western states, where water rights are a sensitive issue, landowners may insist on an express reservation of water rights. In the form most frequently encountered, water rights are described as "all tributary and nontributary water, water rights, and related interests in, on, under, or appurtenant to the land."

18. Reserved Rights: Express Reservations

Since consistency with the purpose of the easement is the ultimate test of the permissibility of any activity, most grantors understandably want to leave no doubt that the uses they intend to pursue are consistent with the easement they are granting. The express reservations function as a stipulation to that effect. As a formal matter, most express reservations could be drafted as qualifications of or exceptions to the express restrictions of the preceding section. In some easements that is how they appear, with the reserved rights provision then requiring no more than a brief general statement similar to the introductory portion of paragraph 4 of the model. Some permitted uses like mining or building are so heavily regulated that their logical place is among the restrictions. Many find it useful, however, for convenience of reference to isolate the most fundamental of the landowner's reserved rights from the restrictions, and the sample that follows is an example of that approach. The reservations cannot be fully understood in isolation, however, any more than the restrictions can. The two sections are interconnected and must be read together.

Sample Reservations

In keeping with the policy preference for minimizing the intrusiveness of the easement (discussed previously in section 16 of the commentary) the scope of the grantor's reserved rights should be as broad as the conservation purpose of the easement will permit. In the context of a typical open space easement, the ability of the grantor to make economically viable, productive uses of the property may be as important to the long-term preservation of the open space character of the land as the easement itself. The following paragraphs have been drafted with that consideration in mind. Again, as always, it should be understood that this represents only one mix out of an unlimited range of possibilities.

(a) To reside on the Property;

(b) To engage in any and all agricultural uses of the Property in accordance with sound, generally accepted agricultural practices. For the purposes of this Easement "agricultural uses" shall be defined as: breeding, raising, pasturing, and grazing livestock of every nature and description; breeding and raising bees, fish, poultry, and other fowl; planting, raising, harvesting, and producing agricultural, aquacultural, horticultural, and forestry crops and products of every nature and description; and the primary processing, storage, and sale, including direct retail sale to the public, of crops and products harvested and produced principally on the Property;

(c) To engage in any business that is conducted by, and in the home of, a person residing on the Property or that involves the provision of goods or services incidental to, and occupies structures used principally for, the agricultural uses of the Property; and

(d) To engage in and permit others to engage in recreational uses of the Property, including, without limitation, hunting and fishing, that require no surface alteration or other development of the land.

The sample assumes that the primary productive use of the hypothetical property for the foreseeable future will be agriculture and that agriculture is itself an open space value worthy of protection. (In some easements preserving farming is the central purpose). The intent is to authorize the continuation and reasonable expansion of existing agricultural operations with negligible interference from the grantee. In addition—in order to give the landowners as much flexibility as possible to adapt to changing market conditions over the years—the paragraph (b) definition of "agricultural uses" goes beyond conventional farming activities to embrace a broad range of productive open space uses, including, expressly or by implication, fish hatching, greenhouse cultivation, tree farming, sod farming, hydroponics, and timber production. Under a given set of circumstances one or more of these uses might be inappropriate and, if so, should be specifically restricted or prohibited. Both parties should realize, however, that existing activities are not likely to exhaust the possibilities of compatible uses and should make an effort to provide some sense of the scope of the permissible. Defining terms—even those that, like "agricultural uses," may at first blush seem self-explanatory—is likely to be the best way to do this. It will also go a long way toward preventing unnecessary misunderstandings between the original parties or their successors later on.[8]

Recognizing the economic importance of related secondary activities to many farm operations, the sample permits the processing and retail sale of products produced principally on the property. In addition, the sample permits home occupations and secondary agricultural trades, which might include, for example, farm mechanics, blacksmithing, or riding instruction. There could be reason in some cases to impose tighter restrictions on secondary activities than the sample does or to deal with them in greater detail. There may be particular concern, for example, over the number and design of structures used in the direct sale of agricultural products. Under most conditions, however, the outright prohibition of these activities is not likely to be necessary to protect the open space values of a property.

---

8. Interesting and instructive examples of detailed definitions of "agricultural" and "directly associated" uses can be found in the agricultural easement form used by the Agricultural Preserve Board of Lancaster County, Pennsylvania (which is home to the Amish community and, not by coincidence, some of the most beautiful and productive farms in the country). Available from the Land Trust Exchange.

Some easements contain provisions for fish and wildlife protection. The sample restrictions show concern for habitat protection but do not get involved in wildlife management. In some areas of the country and under some circumstances restrictions on fishing and hunting may be called for, but they can be difficult to monitor and enforce. The sample assumes a factual situation under which reliance on state regulation in this area is sufficient. The sample also assumes that using the hypothetical property for low-impact open space recreation, even on a commercial basis, would be no less compatible with the conservation values of the property than current agricultural uses.

19. Notice of Intention to Undertake Certain Permitted Actions and Grantee Approval

The IRS requires that the grantor agree to notify the grantee in writing prior to exercising reserved rights that might have an adverse impact on the conservation values the easement is intended to protect. *See* Treas. Reg. § 1.170A-14(g)(5)(ii). It is incumbent on the parties to determine which permitted activities reach that threshold and tie them into the notice provision. (See sample provisions (c)(2)-(5) and (m) of section 16 of this commentary.) The IRS requires only that the grantor notify the grantee prior to engaging in these potentially harmful activities; the grantor's prior approval is not required. Nevertheless the grantee may be able to negotiate for approval authority where it considers the activity in question to be sufficiently sensitive to warrant it. (See sample provisions (c)(1), (c)(4)-(5), (d), (h), (j), and (m).) In rare cases, particularly where sensitive natural habitats or ecosystems are involved, a right of prior approval might vest absolute discretion in the grantee to permit or prohibit a proposed activity. More commonly, as in the model, there must be a "reasonable," which means "objective," basis for withholding an approval. Here again consistency with the purpose of the easement is the determining factor. If the grantee does not have approval authority and a dispute arises concerning the consistency of a proposed activity, the grantee's only recourse is to pursue its judicial or arbitration remedies under the easement. If the grantee does have approval authority, and the grantor is to remain in compliance with the terms of the easement, it becomes the grantor's burden to seek resolution of a dispute.

20. Grantee's Remedies

This paragraph ensures that the grantee will have the full panoply of enforcement powers for protecting not only the conservation values of the property but all its rights under the easement. The IRS requires that an easement provide a right of enforcement "by appropriate legal proceedings," including the right to require restoration. *See* Treas. Reg. § 1.170A-14(g)(5)(ii).

Provision for notice and an opportunity to cure violations is customary, but the grantee should be given the right to look to its remedies without notice when necessary, in its judgment, to prevent or limit damage to the conservation values of the property. Some easements provide for recordation of the notice of violation. The model avoids this approach because of the danger that, were the landowner to prevail against the allegations referred to in the grantee's notice, the landowner might be able to sue the grantee for slander of title. In addition, such notices unnecessarily clog the record. Recordation of the easement puts the world on notice of the possibility that a violation may exist, obligating interested parties to satisfy themselves of the landowner's compliance by obtaining estoppel certificates (paragraph 12 of the model easement) or otherwise. Consequently, a recorded notice of violation is superfluous. On the other hand, once suit is filed, recording a notice of "*lis pendens*" (literally, "suit pending") is appropriate, and unless the case is frivolous, the filing is protected as a necessary adjunct of the court's exercise of jurisdiction.

One remedy not provided here that is sometimes seen in conservation easements is self-help: the right of a grantee to peaceably enter the property to abate a violation and charge any costs incurred to the landowner. There are circumstances where the availability of this remedy is appropriate, especially if the grantee has substantial management responsibilities. In a typical open space easement, however, where the landowner maintains an active, continuous presence on the property, an attempt to exercise the self-help remedy could easily create more problems than it prevents. Landowners are likely to view self-help as too invasive, and even if a grantee is selective in its use, self-help could engender hostility. In addition, it could result in increasing the grantee's exposure to liability for physical conditions on the property and for payment of contractors.

With respect to damages for loss of aesthetic or environmental values, conservation easements may break new ground in this area, particularly if support can be found in the state enabling statutes for such "creative" relief.

The paragraph is inescapably technical. The following is a brief explanation of the terms that might be puzzling to a lay reader. The distinction between "an action at law or in equity" is deeply rooted in the history of the common law. In general, an action at law is for damages; a suit in equity is for injunctive relief. In modern practice, these actions are combined and heard by the same judge who is empowered to grant both kinds of relief. Regarding injunctions, an order "*ex parte*" is one issued on the behalf of one party without notice to the other, usually under emergency circumstances, which is often the case with temporary restraining orders. A temporary restraining order is issued for only a very limited period of time, and determination of the merits is expedited. After a hearing, a preliminary injunction may be issued to preserve the status quo pending trial. Final judgment may result in a permanent injunction. Injunctions can require a person to refrain from or, more rarely, to perform some act, termed "prohibitive" and "mandatory" injunctions respectively. The model attempts to remove some of the legal obstacles to obtaining an injunction or "specific performance" of the easement agreement by having the grantors agree up front that damages are an inadequate remedy for violations of the easement. The grantee's remedies are described as cumulative and nonexclusive in order to give the grantee the widest latitude to enforce the easement. Among available remedies not expressly enumerated is the right to appeal to a court to interpret the easement and issue a "declaratory judgment" regarding its terms even if no other relief is required.

21. Costs of Enforcement

Many easements require the grantor to bear the grantee's enforcement costs. In some jurisdictions, contractual provisions for payment by one party of the other's court costs, including attorneys' fees, are made reciprocal by statute. In these jurisdictions, the prevailing party is entitled to payment of its costs and fees by the other party regardless of what the contract provides. Statutes dealing specifically with conservation easements may make independent provision for costs and fees. A concern for basic fairness would argue for reciprocity, which has the beneficial effect of forcing both parties to be equally circumspect with regard to pursuing litigation. Grantors, of course, may insist on it. The model provides for reciprocity, although the range of costs involved is not the same for both parties. By their nature, certain costs, like the costs of restoration, will always be the obligation of the grantor.

22. Grantee's Discretion and Waiver of Certain Defenses

Paragraphs 6.2 and 6.3 of the model easement attempt to remove technical defenses to enforcement of the easement. The extent to which these clauses are enforceable may vary from state to state. It should be noted that the grantee's discretion to enforce the easement is not limitless. If a grantee is seriously derelict, the attorney general of the state in which the easement is located has standing, under the state's general supervisory authority over charitable institutions, to ensure that the easement is enforced. In addition, third parties may be given enforcement rights—in some cases by statute, in others by the terms of the easement itself. The defense of "laches" is based on undue delay, "estoppel" on a prior statement or act that is deceptively inconsistent with the claim being asserted. "Prescription" is the equivalent in the easement context of "adverse possession."

23. Acts Beyond Grantor's Control

This paragraph is an important common sense limitation on a landowner's liability. Not only "acts of God," but a landowner's emergency measures in response to such acts, are beyond the scope of the easement.

24. Access

This paragraph negates any implication of third party access rights. Limitations on public access do not affect the deductibility of conservation easements, unless the conservation purpose of the easement would be undermined without public access. *See* Treas. Reg. §§ 1.170A-14(d)(2)(ii), (d)(3)(iii), (d)(4)(ii)(C), and (d)(5)(iv). Thus, for example, recreational or educational easements require "substantial and regular" public access, and scenic easements require substantial "visual" access, as do easements with an historical component. But otherwise—in the absence of any state law to the contrary—the kind and degree of public access to be conveyed, if any, is purely a matter for the parties to decide. The fact that no public access is conveyed by the easement does not preclude the landowner from permitting such access (see paragraph 4 of the model easement, regarding reserved rights) unless the easement expressly restricts the right to do so—as it might, for instance, in a natural ecosystem easement. In addition, the easement does not affect any pre-existing access rights that may have been created over the years, whether expressly or by prescription, by implied dedication, or by operation of the public trust doctrine.

25. Costs and Liabilities

Paragraphs 1 through 7 of the model easement constitute the real substance of the easement; paragraphs 8 through 15 consist of necessary but ancillary technical provisions—the fine print.

The landowner should continue to bear all the normal costs of land ownership unless the grantee is given an active role in managing the property. The grantee typically bears the cost of monitoring compliance with the easement and keeping the baseline data current, although increasingly grantees are requesting that grantors make a one-time grant of funds for these purposes.

The law regarding contractors' liens, known as mechanic's or materialman's liens, varies from jurisdiction to jurisdiction. In some states it is clear that the grantee's interest would not be affected by them. In others the language of the relevant statutes is broad enough to reach an easement, but theoretical problems having to do with the nature of conservation easements and the limitations on the kinds of entities entitled to hold them cast doubt on whether liens of this kind could ever attach to them. The model provides for them here as a matter of prudence. Drafters should consult local law to determine what steps, if any, need to be taken to protect against such liens.

26. Taxes

The special attention given to property taxes here is prompted by the fact that a grant of an easement could give rise in some jurisdictions to a shift or increase in tax liability. The law in this area is evolving. The creation of an easement might lead to a reduction in property taxes but, absent special legislation, this effect is not automatic. There may be circumstances where the transfer of an easement might trigger a reassessment of the property, which if long overdue could lead to an increase. In addition, in some jurisdictions a conservation easement might be considered a separately taxable interest. Most grantees seek to insulate themselves from any tax liability in terms similar to the model.

Special precaution is required in those jurisdictions where tax liens are senior to all other interests in the property. There, a grantee will want the authority (provided in the bracketed portion of the model provision) to pay delinquent taxes in order to protect its interest in the property against foreclosure in a tax sale. For additional protection, some easements authorize the grantee to impose a lien of its own to recover any costs the grantee may incur in this context or, in some cases, to secure all of the grantee's costs or advances relating to the easement, regardless of the context. (Although these contractual lien provisions are encountered most often in the historical easement context, where self-help provisions are common, they are beginning to find their way into open space easements.) It is an approach one associates with commercial transactions, and potential grantors may find it objectionable. Still, a contractual lien is undeniably the most efficient way to secure the grantee's position when the grantee is forced to expend funds to protect its rights under the easement, so its attraction is hard to resist, particularly if the easement includes significant self-help provisions. Where this approach is used, care must be taken to comply with local law governing the creation of a lien, as well as to structure the remedy in a way that will not interfere with the landowner's ability to use the property to secure future financing. It should be noted that even without a contractual lien, in the rare instance where a grantee elects to make a defensive expenditure it can, if necessary, sue for repayment and, if successful, record a judgment lien.

Wherever provision is made for interest payments, as in the model, the drafter should take care to stay within the limits imposed by any state usury laws.

27. Hold Harmless

This clause is intended to ensure that none of the liabilities attendant on land ownership are inadvertently transferred with the easement. Unless the grantee takes on substantial management responsibilities with respect to the property, the grantee will have no direct control over any potential hazards, making it appropriate that the risk of these liabilities remain with the landowner. It is possible that the existence of the easement relationship or one or another of the easement's provisions might marginally increase the grantor's exposure, but particularly where self-help remedies are not provided, the additional risk is likely to be minuscule and the cost of insuring against it negligible. In contrast, the effect of these liabilities being borne by the grantee, multiplied over a substantial number of properties over which the grantee exercises no management control, could be devastating for the grantee's easement program, if not for its continuing existence as a viable organization.

The degree of public access provided by the easement is, of course, likely to influence how the risk is allocated. In some jurisdictions immunity statutes protect landowners who permit public recreational access on their lands, but the scope of protection varies and is sometimes less than it seems. Where substantial public access is contemplated, it may be appropriate for the grantee to assume the liabilities relating to it and indemnify the grantor.

The model provision requires the landowner not only to indemnify the grantee but to "defend" it. The purpose of this requirement is to put these matters in the landowner's hands from the inception of a claim, rather than waiting for any actual liability or loss to be determined. The provision is further enhanced by extending its protection to certain persons who may be exposed to liability by virtue of their special relationship to the grantee.

In addition to protecting the grantee against exposure to tort liability, the model provision indemnifies the grantee against the nontort liabilities of paragraphs 8 and 8.1 (liens and taxes) and its administration of the easement, which would include its exercise of discretion with respect to enforcing the easement, or granting or withholding any consent, or any reports or advice it might give concerning the property.

Indemnity clauses are not a substitute for insurance, and all easement holders should maintain adequate coverage.[9] As added protection, depending on the circumstances, it may be feasible for the grantee to be named as an "additional insured" on the landowner's policy.

28. Extinguishment

Absent state law to the contrary, the parties to an easement would normally be free to extinguish it by private mutual agreement. However, an easement qualifying under the IRS regulations may be extinguished, as the model provides, only by a judicial proceeding. *See* Treas. Reg. § 1.170A-14(g)(6)(i).

Section 1.170A-14(g)(6)(i) of the IRS regulations describes the circumstances that might justify extinguishment as involving a "change in conditions surrounding the property" that makes the conservation purpose of the easement "impossible or impractical" to achieve. The drafter should be aware, though, that these are loaded terms in property law. Under the traditional rule, easements can be terminated only if their purpose becomes "impossible" to accomplish. The so-called "changed conditions" doctrine referred to in the IRS regulations applies not to easements but to restrictive covenants and equitable servitudes and sets a lower threshold for extinguishment, as the IRS's somewhat loose use of the term "impractical" might suggest. It may, for example, be used to terminate a restriction on grounds of economic hardship. Under that rubric, changes in the neighborhood of a restricted property that greatly increased the property's value for prohibited uses or decreased its value for permitted uses could be enough to compel termination. The model assumes that the impossibility standard is the correct one to apply to conservation easements.

---

9. *Editor's note:* The Land Trust Exchange offers land trusts access to a low-cost insurance program through membership in the Exchange. Contact the Land Trust Exchange for information.

Whether the courts will agree remains to be seen. In practice, the applicable standard is likely to vary from state to state.[10]

Technical distinctions aside, however, the outcome in an extinguishment proceeding should turn on consideration of the public benefit involved. A strong argument can be made that where the public purpose of a conservation easement has continuing vitality, economic hardship should not be a factor. The important point, from a drafting perspective, is that the range of purposes served by an easement must be clearly stated. Often conservation easements serve purposes that are both broad (e.g., a community's need for open space) and narrow (e.g., preservation of endangered species habitat). Care should be taken to express the full range of purposes in the easement so that the impossibility of fulfilling a narrow purpose (resulting, for example, from the extinction of a species) will not be allowed to defeat a broader purpose.

The IRS regulations require that the grantee's use of the proceeds it receives as the result of an extinguishment be "consistent with the conservation purposes" of the grant. *See* Treas. Reg. § 1.170A-14(g)(b)(1). Presumably, it is sufficient that the proceeds be applied to any conservation purpose of the grantee organization in the broadest sense, which for conservation organizations would include general operations.

One form of extinguishment not treated in the model is that which would result from the merger of the easement with the underlying fee in the event the grantee were ever to become the owner of the property. (In some states, where merger doctrine may be modified by statutes dealing with charitable uses, merger may not be automatic.) Some easement drafters go to considerable lengths to avoid merger, usually by having the grantee covenant to immediately convey a new easement to a new grantee or to reserve an easement upon subsequent transfer of the fee. Alternatively, the executory limitation of supplementary paragraph 10.1 might be enlarged to include the grantee's acquisition of the fee as a triggering event. But from the standpoint of achieving the substantive purposes of the easement, it seems odd that merger, accompanying as it does the grantee's obtaining complete control over the property, should be viewed as a result to be avoided. Nevertheless, the concern apparently is that the possibility of merger, which affects the perpetuity of the easement, might raise doubts about the deductibility of the easement under federal tax law, if not its enforceability under state laws that require that conservation easements be perpetual. Merger, however, is only one of many remote possibilities that can

---

10. For a thorough discussion of the termination issue, see Gerald Korngold, "Privately Held Conservation Servitudes: A Policy Analysis in the Context of In Gross Real Covenants and Easements," 63 *Tex L. Rev.* 433 (1984). See also Barrett and Livermore, *Conservation Easement in California*, 32-34, 117-118; Powell, *Law of Real Property*, 430.7. It should be noted that some states have addressed the economic hardship issue by statute. See, e.g., Me. Rev. Stat. Ann. tit. 33 Sec. 478 (West Supp. 1986); Iowa Code Ann. Sec. 111D.2 (West 1984).

affect an easement; to try to provide for all of them is to engage in an exercise in futility. The IRS recognizes this, stating in the regulations that where the possibility of some future act or event occurring is "so remote as to be negligible," it can safely be disregarded. (*See* Treas. Reg. § 1.170A-14(g)(3), which cites as an example the failure to rerecord the easement every 30 years as required by a state marketable title statute.) In most cases the possibility of merger, it is submitted, will fall squarely within this rubric. What effect the doctrine of merger might have on deductibility when the possibility of merger is certain or near certain (for example, where a remainder or testamentary gift to the grantee is contemplated at the time of the easement grant) is another question—one that has not been authoritatively answered to date.[11] As for state law, as long as the easement instrument expressly provides for a perpetual term, there should be no problem.

29. Proceeds

This provision meets the requirements of Section 1.170A-14(g)(6)(ii) of the tax regulations, which provides that the grantee is entitled to a share of the proceeds of a sale, exchange, or involuntary conversion of the property following extinguishment of an easement "at least equal to the proportionate value that the . . . conservation restriction at the time of the gift bears to the property as a whole at that time." It has been included in the model, along with its antecedent in paragraph 9, to err on the side of caution in the face of uncertainty as to the intent of the regulations, which can be interpreted either to require such a provision or merely to require a personal side agreement between the original donor and donee. Although at first blush the proceeds-sharing requirement seems an attractive one for grantees, it has given pause to some students of this field who are concerned that the arbitrary assignment of a "market value" to the easement could prove troublesome in practice.

The provision turns on two fictions: (1) that a conservation easement has a market value at the time of conveyance equal to the value of the deduction claimed by the original donor and (2) that the ratio of the value of the easement to the value of the property unencumbered by the easement will remain constant over the life of the easement. Properly speaking, of course, at least where substantial affirmative rights are not involved, there is no true market for conservation easements and thus no accurate measure of their monetary value. If there were a market, one would expect the value of an easement to reflect the value of the rights transferred to the donee (enforcement rights), not the value of the rights relinquished by the donor (development rights), which is what the deduction represents.

---

11. For a rare discussion of the subject in a tax planning context see Stephen J. Small, *The Federal Tax Law of Conservation Easements* (Land Trust Exchange, 1986), E-3, E-5.

But assuming for purposes of discussion that equating the value of an easement with the value of the development rights restricted by the easement is an appropriate way to assure that the public receive fair value for the deduction even if the easement should be extinguished in the future, the requirement that the proportionate value of the easement be held constant remains troubling. The value of the development rights of a property, and thus the theoretical value of the easement, could go down over time for any number of reasons, including, for example, down-zoning or a shift in local development patterns or even the conveyance of other easements in the area. Where the value of the development rights did go down, a division of proceeds according to the artificially fixed formula of this provision would be manifestly unfair. It would overcompensate the grantee and undercompensate the landowner, whose equity in the property (assumed for purposes of discussion to be equivalent to the restricted value of the property) would have to be invaded to satisfy it. In addition, although predicting market behavior is beyond the scope of this commentary, it is at least conceivable that the provision might have a deflating effect on the market value of the property as future buyers or their lenders take it into account.

The IRS proceeds provision raises other problems as well. For example, the IRS makes no allowance for appreciation due to improvements, although an allocation similar to that in the model provision is certainly called for as a matter of basic fairness. Similarly, the possibility that senior claims might exist must be acknowledged and a mechanism for deducting the amount of such claims provided. One approach would be to apply the ratio to the owner's "net proceeds," but the model stops short of that, providing only that senior claims must be satisfied before the grantee's. There is also the problem of verifying the correct ratio, which may not be known at the time of the gift and, technically, is not final until the statute of limitations for the gift (three years) has run. One way to deal with this is to require the parties to amend the easement to set forth the ratio when known. It should be noted, though, that in order to determine the correct ratio the grantee must have information about the value of the property that has not customarily been provided to it. Finally, the mechanics of enforcing this provision may prove complicated, perhaps requiring the imposition, following extinguishment, of a lien for the stipulated proportionate value of the easement, which presumably would be due on sale. If the event subsequent to extinguishment is an "exchange" rather than a sale or involuntary conversion, an expectation of "cashing out" may not be realistic.

One further note. Although the apparent purpose of the IRS proceeds requirement is to perpetuate the conservation gift, it is fair to ask whether the provision might not create a certain pressure for extinguishment of otherwise viable easements. A cash-poor conservation organization may find it difficult to resist agreeing to extinguishment under circumstances where, absent this provision, it might otherwise have fought to preserve an easement. For conservation policy generally, of course, this would be an unwelcome side effect. Coupled with the fairness issue raised earlier, this concern, if founded, suggests that the conservation community—and the IRS—might do well to give some further study to the relative merits of this requirement.

30. Condemnation

The IRS requirement for the allocation of proceeds is triggered by extinguishment under the "impossibility" or "changed conditions" doctrine, whichever is applicable to easements in a given jurisdiction. Condemnation is an entirely separate method of extinguishment. Nevertheless, some drafters have been treating it as a triggering event. One problem with doing so is that, far from being bound by the parties' fictional valuation of the grantee's interest, condemning agencies and the courts will apply settled valuation rules that may or may not attribute any compensable value to the easement (or the rights restricted by the easement). If, because of the easement, a property were adjudged to have no development value, application of the mechanical proceeds formula of paragraph 9.1 would be grossly unfair. On the other hand, in order to prevent properties under easement from becoming easy targets for condemnation, statutes in some states provide that the landowner is entitled to be compensated for the full value of the property without regard to the easement—a circumstance the IRS expressly excepts from its requirement. Although the parties are always free to bargain for an allocation between themselves, there is no compulsion to do so, and the model reflects this fact.

31. Assignment

The model restriction on transfer complies with a requirement of the IRS regulations. *See* Treas. Reg. § 1.170A-14(c)(2). This provision is also important for assuring continuing qualification under any applicable state law. Some easements require the grantor's consent to an assignment, but circumstances might arise that could make such a requirement sticky, if not with the grantor then with subsequent owners. In any case, unless carefully limited, the enforceability of such a restraint could be questioned. The grantor's retention, through a consent clause, of some degree of control over the ultimate disposition of the easement might also raise a question about the completeness of an easement gift for gift tax purposes. To avoid problems the model allows the grantee to assign freely to any qualified organization. If a grantor has particular concerns on the subject (for example, a preference for certain organizations or reservations about others), this provision could be linked to an executory limitation, such as paragraph 10.1 of the supplementary provisions, and the list of designated back-up grantees could be lengthened. However, the grantor's concerns are likely to be different from a subsequent owner's, so it seems pointless to go too far in the easement document itself to satisfy them. A side agreement might be a better place to allay the grantor's concerns. The IRS regulations state that the grantee must, as a "condition" of transfer, require that a transferee continue to carry out the conservation purposes of the grant. Whether the intent of the regulations is to require that the easement revert to the original grantee if the subsequent grantee fails to enforce it properly is not entirely clear, though that is the implication. If the grantor endows a monitoring fund at the time of the grant, it may be appropriate to provide for its transfer along with the easement.

32. Subsequent Transfers

Recording the easement is sufficient in virtually all jurisdictions to put any subsequent transferees of the fee or other interests in the property on constructive notice of the easement and to bind them to its terms. Paragraph 14 is included in the easement not because it is strictly necessary but as a practical means of increasing the likelihood that future purchasers, encumbrancers, or lessees will have actual notice of the easement ahead of any transfer. Some easements include a right of first refusal in favor of the grantee, providing it a preemptive right to buy the property in the event the grantor decides to sell. Whether such a right can run with the land in perpetuity, however, is doubtful.

33. Estoppel Certificates

Potential lenders and buyers are likely to require proof of the landowner's compliance with the easement, and this provision requires the grantee to certify the landowner's good standing upon request.

34. Notices

Although the model does not require it, if delivery cannot be made in person, certified mail (return receipt requested) is recommended whenever proof of receipt is necessary to determine the relevant dates for the running of any time period triggered by notice.

35. Recordation

Recordation is the only way to put the world at large on constructive notice of a conservation easement. It is required by many state easement enabling statutes and, for all practical purposes, by the IRS. *See* Treas. Reg. § 1.170A-14(g)(1).[12] Rerecording an easement may be required after a prescribed period of years under the marketable title acts that have been passed in some states to clear land titles of dormant interests.

36. General Provisions

To a limited extent the parties can guide the courts in the interpretation of the easement, particularly with respect to the application of general rules of

---

12. An IRS requirement for submitting suitable evidence of recordation is, apparently, in the works. See Department of the Treasury, *A Report to the Congress on the Use of Tax Deductions for Donations of Conservation Easements* (December 18, 1987), 13.

construction, and these general provisions, by and large, are included for that purpose. Many of them are standard terms, routinely included in substantial written agreements. State easement statutes might provide independent support for liberal construction of an easement, and if so, these provisions should be keyed to them (paragraph 15(b)).

In some easements one finds provision for more esoteric legal doctrines such as the rule against perpetuities or the rule against unreasonable restraints on alienation. It would lead too far afield to attempt to explain these rules here; they are as complex as they are ancient. It may be enough to know that, although they are based on public policies of long standing in our legal tradition favoring the free use of real property, they are entirely irrelevant to the grant of a conservation easement—at least in those jurisdictions that have acknowledged the conservation easement to be a real property interest in its own right. It is possible that individual easements might contain one or more provisions that could run afoul of these rules. The inclusion of open-ended options or rights of first refusal, for example, would almost certainly raise questions. However, the "severability" provision of paragraph 15(c) should control any damage. Their invocation in the easement serves more to confuse than enlighten (not only laymen but most judges and lawyers have only the vaguest sense of what these rules mean); it is better—and probably safer—to leave them out.

The "no forfeiture" clause (paragraph 15(e)) is included to enable title insurers to provide coverage to this effect—something routinely required by mortgage lenders.

Paragraph 15(f) provides that grantors are liable under the easement both collectively and individually.

Since an easement runs with the land (paragraph 15(g)), an express provision for terminating the parties' rights and obligations upon transfer may seem superfluous. It is included here (paragraph 15(h)), however, by way of making it clear that liability for acts or omissions occurring prior to transfer does *not* terminate upon transfer.

Paragraph 15(j) is included to enable either party, as a matter of convenience, to submit its copy of the easement as the original in a judicial proceeding.

Finally, practitioners should be alert to the possibility that a grantor might propose inserting a provision for termination of the easement in the event a federal tax deduction for the donation is denied. The validity of this kind of condition is, under an established line of tax cases, problematic at best.[13] In any case, there is the danger that by calling into question the grantor's "donative intent," which is a prerequisite to deductibility, such a provision could become self-fulfilling. The proper way to resolve any substantial doubt about the deductibility of a proposed conservation easement gift is to seek a private letter ruling from the IRS before making the donation.

---

13. See *Commissioner v. Procter*, 142 F.2d 824 (1944); *Ward v. Commissioner*, 87 T.C. 78 (1986).

37. Habendum Clause

"To have and to hold . . . etc . . . . " ("*habendum et tenendum,*" in Latin) is traditional language for concluding a grant. As in the grant clause, care must be taken to choose language that complies with the conveyancing requirements of the jurisdiction in which the property is located. Among other things, a statement of delivery may be required.

38. Signatures, Acknowledgements, and Exhibits

This form conservation easement, like a lease, is not only a conveyance but also a contract, intended to bind both parties by its terms. Consequently, it is structured as a two-party deed, called an indenture, to be signed by both the grantor and grantee. Besides the grantor and grantee, additional signatories might include any state or local agency whose approval of the easement may be required by applicable law, the preparer of the easement (required in some jurisdictions), and the designated back-up grantee, if any. Corporate signatories may be required to affix their corporate seal in some states. Acknowledgment of the signatures by a notary is a prerequisite to recordation of a document. Exhibits are attached immediately following the signature pages.

39. Supplementary Provisions

The designation of the provisions that follow as "supplementary" is not meant to imply that everything that has come before is essential but only that a decision to include them in an easement is likely to turn more on particular facts, or involve stronger preferences, than the provisions that have already been discussed.

40. Arbitration

It is impossible to anticipate every potential problem in an agreement intended, theoretically, to endure forever. Disputes are bound to arise, and some mechanism must be provided for their resolution. Increasingly in recent years, arbitration has been viewed as an attractive alternative to resorting to the courts. Many see it as a cheaper, faster, and somehow less threatening, even gentler, means of settling differences—a kind of soft path to reconciliation. That image may or may not square with reality in particular cases. It is important to realize that arbitration is not the equivalent of mediation or counseling. It can be every bit as adversarial as trial, and depending on the issues, it can be equally if not more consuming of the time and resources of the parties and their attorneys. It is true that, whereas access to the courts can be substantially delayed, the availability of arbitrators is almost immediate. But if the issues to be heard are complex, the relatively relaxed rules of arbitration (little or no pre-hearing discovery and few if any restrictions on the admissibility of evidence) can prolong the matter painfully, and unlike judges, arbitrators are paid by the parties.

Arbitration is absolutely inadequate in circumstances where an injunction is required; only the courts have the power to provide such relief, and in at least this one area they act with dispatch. A temporary restraining order, for example, can be issued immediately upon the application of one party even before the other party has had the opportunity to appear and oppose it. But the courts' extraordinary powers extend beyond their ability to issue injunctions and include, among other things, the authority to impose sanctions where appropriate and a broad latitude to fashion meaningful remedies. In the easement context this could be of great importance, particularly where a "creative" approach to the issue of damages, including punitive or exemplary damages, is needed. Conservation values are hard to express in monetary terms, but easement holders, encouraged in some jurisdictions by liberal state statutes, will want to establish standards of compensation for the loss of aesthetic or "quality of life" values. For this, of course, the courts are indispensible. Equally important, whereas arbitration may settle a dispute, it does not make law, and the creation of favorable precedent through the careful and selective judicial enforcement of conservation easements will be a matter of great significance for easement programs nationwide. It also should be pointed out that arbitrators have no enforcement powers; resort to the courts is still necessary to confirm and enforce an arbitrator's award against a recalcitrant loser. In short, although arbitration has its virtues, it is no panacea. For relatively simple disputes involving questions that can be easily stated and that call for straightforward answers, arbitration may be appropriate. For more complicated matters, which could benefit from either the focusing that modern litigation, for all its faults, demands or the application of a court's plenary powers, arbitration can be a poor choice.

The model sets forth a typical arbitration provision but intentionally limits its scope to the kind of dispute for which it is most suited in the easement context: prospective application of the consistency test. The parties may choose to expand its applicability to other contexts as they deem appropriate for their particular circumstances. Of course, whatever the easement provides, the parties remain free to submit any disagreement to arbitration at any time by mutual consent.

The procedure established in the model encourages the parties to agree on the selection of a single arbitrator. Both parties should recognize that this is in their best interest, not only for controlling costs but also for ensuring that the matter proceeds expeditiously (simplified scheduling) and efficiently (it is easier to educate one person than three). As for the choice of rules to govern the proceedings, the drafter has a number of sources to consult, including the various arbitration association rules and, in some jurisdictions, statutory rules.

41. Amendment

Until quite recently, most conservation easements have been silent regarding amendment. It is unrealistic to think, however, that the need to amend will never arise. Because easements are perpetual, there are bound to be changed circumstances over time that require amendment—at least in a substantial number of cases—and many consider it prudent to set the ground rules ahead of time (see chapter 10). In some states, unless amendment is expressly provided for, the supervision of a court is required to modify an easement.

To prevent the model provision from raising any question about the deductibility of a donated easement or the qualification of the grantee or the easement under any applicable law, a restriction on amendment is provided with reference to state law and Section 170(h) of the Internal Revenue Code. Absent fraud, the IRS's interest in a particular gift ends when the statute of limitations has run. However, its interest in the affairs of the tax-exempt grantee continues for as long as the grantee exists, so the requirements of the tax code and regulations remain relevant to the amendment issue long after the grant. It is possible, of course, that an amendment could affect the valuations of an easement for tax purposes, in which case it would be the donor's responsibility, if still the landowner, to report the recovery of any amount previously deducted.[14]

Most practitioners would counsel that the right to amend be used sparingly and, especially where an areawide easement program is in effect, equitably (like properties should be treated alike). The impact of an amendment goes beyond the easement at hand; it can affect an organization's entire program, as well as the attitude of the courts, the IRS, and state and local legislatures toward conservation easements. Great care should be taken to see that the consistency requirement of this paragraph is not allowed to become an empty one. If an amendment is inconsistent with the purpose of the easement, its validity—or worse, the validity of the easement as a whole—may be questioned.

42. Executory Limitation

"Executory limitation" is the legal term used to describe the creation of a future interest in real property in favor of a third party. Although under normal circumstances an open-ended executory interest would violate the common law rule against perpetuities, which prohibits the creation of interests that may not become vested until the remote future, a grant to a charitable organization followed by a limitation to another charitable organization constitutes, in most jurisdictions, an exception to the rule.[15] Some easements provide a detailed list of potential future grantees stated in order of preference. The model indicates the basic approach. An alternative would be simply to provide that the grantee will choose a successor if any of the events specified occurs. Of the triggering events, qualification under section 170(h) of the Internal Revenue Code is the

---

14. This is the so-called "tax benefit rule." See *Alice Phelan Sullivan Corporation v. United States*, 381 F. 2d 399 (1967); Rev.-Rul. 76-150, 1976-1 C.B. 38.

15. For a discussion of executory limitations and defeasible grants in general see Barrett and Livermore, *The Conservation Easement in California*, 95-101.

least important over the long term since the adverse consequences of a failure to qualify disappear after the statute of limitations has run with respect to the gift. Some easements add that the grantee's failure to enforce the easement will trigger the limitation. What constitutes a failure to enforce is open to interpretation, however, and for obvious reasons a limitation of this type works better if there is no room for doubt that the triggering event has occurred. In any case, it should be remembered that the attorney general of the state where the property is located has authority to assure that the easement is enforced. Although, theoretically, the transfer effected by an executory limitation is automatic upon occurrence of the triggering event, in practice a quiet title action may be necessary to confirm the back-up grantee's interest. The ultimate back-up to the easement, as the model illustrates, is provided by the courts. If a back-up grantee is to be designated, its consent to the designation should be obtained beforehand. As with an assignment, provision for transfer of any monitoring fund may be appropriate.

43. Subordination

Foreclosure of a prior mortgage or deed of trust would extinguish an easement. Consequently, for a qualified conservation contribution, the IRS requires existing mortgage holders to subordinate their rights to "the right of the qualified organization to enforce the conservation purposes of the gift in perpetuity." *See* Treas. Reg. § 1.170A-14(g)(2). A limited subordination on the terms described in this supplementary paragraph should meet this requirement.

Because a conservation easement represents a significant portion of a property's value, it may be difficult to get a mortgagee to enter into a subordination agreement. Recognizing this fact, the model attempts to the extent possible to reconcile the mortgagee's need for economic protection with the grantee's need to assure the perpetuity of the easement. Neutralizing the effect of paragraph 9, which governs the division of proceeds subsequent to extinguishment, is likely to be particularly important. A lender may have other concerns in addition to those set forth in the model (for example, it may request notice and an opportunity to cure a grantor's default under the easement), and the parties should make every effort to satisfy them in the subordination agreement itself. In addition to providing for an existing mortgage, the model seeks to prevent the easement from interfering unnecessarily with the grantor's or the grantor's successors' opportunities to obtain mortgage financing in the future by providing for partial subordination of the easement to future mortgages. The assumption, untested to date, is that as long as the IRS standard for existing mortgages is met and the easement cannot be wiped out by foreclosure, this accommodation is appropriate.

Where deductibility is not an issue and the parties choose not to seek subordination of an existing mortgage or deed of trust, the parties should, nevertheless, review the financing documents and if necessary consult with the lender or legal counsel to determine whether creation of the easement might trigger any due-on-sale or due-on-encumbrance clause in the mortgage or deed of trust. If so, a waiver should be sought from the mortgage holder.

A Note on Transferable Development Rights

The model is silent on an emerging issue that drafters may wish to address: the relationship of the conservation easement to transferable development rights created by state or local law. Transferable development rights programs, which create a market mechanism for the transfer of development rights from low to high density areas, are being used with increasing frequency across the country to moderate the inequities inherent in zoning decisions. Although related by their subject matter, easements and transferable development rights are not necessarily mutually exclusive. An easement is not, properly speaking, a conveyance of development rights but rather a conveyance of, among other things, the right to prevent or restrict development on a particular parcel of land. Created by statute or ordinance, transferable development rights constitute an additional, entirely distinct property interest. How entitlements are apportioned under a transferable development rights program is likely to be a highly-charged political issue. Theoretically, the jurisdiction instituting a transferable development rights program could, if it chose, create an entitlement to such rights without in any way impinging on an easement over the same property. From a property law perspective, an easement holder should have no claim on such rights merely as a consequence of its easement interest. Presumably, though, the parties would be free to agree otherwise. In any case, provisions clarifying the parties' interests are beginning to find their way into easements in jurisdictions where transferable development rights programs are under way or anticipated. One consideration involved is assuring that a transfer of development rights not adversely affect the conservation values of the property under easement, as it might if made to an adjacent or nearby parcel. How an entitlement is handled may affect the valuation of an easement for tax purposes.

CHAPTER 14

Model Historic Preservation Easement and Commentary

*Richard J. Roddewig and
Cheryl A. Inghram*

(Stefan Nagel, editor)

Introduction

The following model easement and commentary, edited and adapted by Stefan Nagel, Assistant General Counsel, National Trust for Historic Preservation, are based on drafts prepared by Richard J. Roddewig and Associates, Chicago, Illinois. The drafts were prepared for a project jointly sponsored by the South Carolina Department of Archives and History and the South Carolina Department of Parks, Recreation, and Tourism, which was assisted by a historic preservation fund grant from the National Park Service, U.S. Department of the Interior.

The easement model is based on approximately 25 easement documents involved in donations to a wide variety of private and governmental easement recipients. Provisions of the Internal Revenue Code and 1986 IRS regulations concerning required content of preservation and conservation documents were also reviewed.

No one model easement document can be universally used in every potential easement donation situation. Each document must be custom tailored to fit the particular characteristics of the historic property and circumstances of the donation transaction. For example, an easement donated on a historically important natural area will be quite different from one donated on a historically important building on a narrow lot in an urban setting. An easement imposed on a property undergoing rehabilitation may have the renovation plans attached as an exhibit, while one donated on an already renovated property may simply contain photos of the restored facade.

The model easement has been prepared to meet a particular set of circumstances: a historically or architecturally significant building or group of buildings on a fairly large site. In such a situation, the relationship between the buildings and the setting is as important as the facades. The terms "the Premises," "the Buildings," and "the Facades" have been carefully defined for the purposes of this model and assumed set of circumstances. In a different, urban context, there may be only one building on the premises, and the easement may be simplified. But even in that situation, there may be a coach house or other accessory buildings on the premises with some architectural or historic significance important enough to protect through the easement donation.

Checklists

Checklist I
Model Historic Preservation Easement
Complete Outline

CAPTION

RECITALS

- Qualifications of Grantee
- Authorizing State Law
- Property Description
- Affirmative Recital of Historic Certification or Significance
- Mutual Recognition of Significance
- Easement to Assist Preservation of Features (Purpose)
- Easement to Maintain Historic Significance (Purpose)
- Statement of Intent to Grant and Accept

GRANT

- Legal Description of Property

PROVISIONS

1. Description of Facades (Baseline Documentation)

2. Grantor's Covenants
   (a) No Demolition
   (b) No Modifications without Prior Authorization
   (c) Covenant to Repair and Maintain
   (d) No New Structures
   (e) No Signs, Billboards, or Advertisements
   (f) No Topographical Changes
   (g) No Landscape Changes Except Compatible Changes with Approval
   (h) No Trash
   (i) Covenant to Use Consistent with Easement
   (j) No Subdivision
   (k) No New Transmission Lines

3. Public View or Access

4. Standards for Review

5. Casualty Damage or Destruction

6. Grantee's Remedies Following Casualty Damage
   (a) Reconstruction
   (b) Salvage

7. Review after Casualty Loss

8. Grantee's Covenants
   (a) Grantee to Remain a Qualified Organization
   (b) Merger without Novation is Prohibited

HABENDUM
SIGNATURES AND ACKNOWLEDGEMENTS
SCHEDULE OF EXHIBITS

Checklist II
Provisions Relating to IRS Requirements
(Treas. Reg. Sec. 1.170A-14)

RECITALS

- Qualifications of Grantee
- Affirmative Recital of Historic Certification or Significance
- Purpose

GRANT (Perpetual)

PROVISIONS

1.	Baseline Documentation
2.	Grantor's Covenants (Prohibited Uses)
3.	Public View or Access
4.	Standards for Review of Permitted Alterations
8(a)	Grantee's Covenant to Remain a Qualified Organization
10.	Grantee's Remedies (Including Restoration)
10(b)	Right of Entry for Inspection
14.	Recording
16.	Subordination of Mortgages*
24.	Stipulated Value of Grantee's Interest in Extinguishment
26(a)	Extinguishment by Judicial Proceeding
(c)	Use of Proceeds in Extinguishment**
27(b)	Successors and Assigns

---

*Mandatory if property is encumbered with a preexisting mortgage or lien.

**Donor must agree "at the time of the gift;" unclear if agreement must appear in easement instrument.

Model Historic Preservation Easement

Note: The boxed numbers inserted in the text of the easement correspond with the subheading numbers in the commentary that follows.

THIS PRESERVATION AND CONSERVATION EASEMENT, made this _____ day of _____ 19 _____ , by and between _____ ("Grantor") and the _____ ("Grantee"), a nonprofit corporation of _[state of incorporation]_ .

WITNESSETH:

WHEREAS, the Grantee is organized as _____ under the laws of the State of _____ and is a qualifying recipient of qualified conservation contributions under Sections 170(b), (f), and (h) of the Internal Revenue Code of 1986 as amended (hereinafter the "Code");

WHEREAS, the Grantee is authorized to accept preservation and conservation easements to protect property significant in __[state]__ history and culture under the provisions of Section _____ of the __[state law]__ Act (hereinafter the "Act");

WHEREAS, the Grantor is owner in fee simple of certain real property in _____ County, __[state]__ , which property is hereinafter sometimes referred to as the _____ (hereinafter "the Premises"), said Premises including _[number of]_ structure(s) commonly known as _____ _____ (hereinafter "the Buildings"), and is more particularly described below;

WHEREAS, the _____ was listed in the National Register of Historic Places on _____ , 19 ____ and is a certified historic structure [or historically important land area—if historically important land area, explain significance];

WHEREAS, the Grantor and Grantee recognize the historical, cultural, and aesthetic value and significance of the Premises, and have the common purpose of conserving and preserving the aforesaid value and significance of the Premises;

WHEREAS, the grant of a preservation and conservation easement by Grantor to Grantee on the real property referred to herein will assist in preserving and maintaining the Premises and its architectural, historical, and cultural features;

WHEREAS, the grant of a preservation and conservation easement by Grantor to Grantee on the Premises will assist in preserving and maintaining the aforesaid value and significance of the Premises;

WHEREAS, to that end, Grantor desires to grant to Grantee, and Grantee desires to accept, a preservation and conservation easement on the Premises, pursuant to ___[state law]___ ; ▢1

NOW, THEREFORE, in consideration of Ten Dollars ($10.00) and other good and valuable consideration, receipt of which is hereby acknowledged, _____ does hereby irrevocably grant and convey unto the Grantee a preservation and conservation easement in gross in perpetuity (which easement is more particularly described below and is hereinafter "the Easement") in and to that certain real property and the exterior surfaces of the Buildings located thereon, owned by the Grantor, and more particularly described as:

[legal description]▢2

The Easement, to be of the nature and character hereinafter further expressed, shall constitute a binding servitude upon said Premises of the Grantor, and to that end Grantor covenants on behalf of itself, its successors, and assigns, with Grantee, its successors, and assigns, such covenants being deemed to run as a binding servitude, in perpetuity, with the land, to do upon the Premises each of the following covenants and stipulations, which contribute to the public purpose in that they aid significantly in the preservation of the Buildings and surrounding land area, and which help maintain and assure the present and future historic integrity of the Buildings:

1. <u>Description of Facades.</u> In order to make more certain the full extent of Grantor's obligations and the restrictions on the Premises (including the Buildings), and in order to document the external nature of the Buildings as of the date hereof, attached hereto as Exhibit A and incorporated herein by this reference are a set of photographs depicting the exterior surfaces of the Buildings and the surrounding property and an affidavit specifying certain technical and locational information relative to said photographs satisfactory to Grantee, attached hereto as Exhibit B. It is stipulated by and between Grantor and Grantee that the external nature of the Buildings as shown in Exhibit A is deemed to be the external nature of the Buildings as of the date hereof and as of the date this instrument is first recorded in the land records of _____ County, ___[state]___ . The external nature of the Buildings as shown in Exhibit A is hereinafter referred to as the "Facades."▢3

2. <u>Grantor's Covenants.</u> In furtherance of the easement herein granted, Grantor undertakes, of itself, to do (and to refrain from doing as the case may be) upon the Premises each of the following covenants, which contribute to the public purpose of significantly protecting and preserving the Premises:

(a) Grantor shall not demolish, remove, or raze the Buildings or the Facades except as provided in Paragraphs 6 and 7.

(b) Without the prior express written permission of the Grantee, signed by a duly authorized representative thereof, Grantor shall not undertake any of the following actions:

(i) increase or decrease the height of the Facades or the Buildings;

(ii) adversely affect the structural soundness of the Facades;

(iii) make any changes in the Facades including the alteration, partial removal, construction, remodeling, or other physical or structural change including any change in color or surfacing, with respect to the appearance or construction of the Facades, with the exception of ordinary maintenance pursuant to Paragraph 2(c) below;

(iv) erect anything on the Premises or on the Facades which would prohibit them from being visible from street level, except for a temporary structure during any period of approved alteration or restoration;

(v) permit any significant reconstruction, repair, repainting, or refinishing of the Facades that alters their state from the existing condition. This subsection (v) shall not include ordinary maintenance pursuant to Paragraph 2(c) below;

(vi) erect, construct, or move anything on the Premises that would encroach on the open land area surrounding the Buildings and interfere with a view of the Facades or be incompatible with the historic or architectural character of the Buildings or the Facades. [4]

(c) Grantor agrees at all times to maintain the Buildings in a good and sound state of repair and to maintain the Facades and the structural soundness and safety of the Buildings and to undertake the minimum maintenance program attached as Exhibit C so as to prevent deterioration of the Facades. Subject to the casualty provisions of Paragraphs 5 through 7, this obligation to maintain shall require replacement, rebuilding, repair, and reconstruction whenever necessary to have the external nature of the Buildings at all times appear to be and actually be the same as the Facades. [5]

(d) No buildings or structures, including satellite receiving dishes, camping accommodations, or mobile homes not presently on the Premises shall be erected or placed on the Premises hereafter, except for temporary structures required for the maintenance or rehabilitation of the property, such as construction trailers.

(e) No signs, billboards, awnings, or advertisements shall be displayed or placed on the Premises or Buildings; provided, however, that Grantor may, with prior written approval from and in the sole discretion of Grantee, erect such signs or awnings as are compatible with the preservation and conservation purposes of this easement and appropriate to identify the Premises and Buildings and any activities on the Premises or in the Buildings. Such approval from Grantee shall not be unreasonably withheld. [6]

(f) No topographical changes, including but not limited to excavation, shall occur on the Premises; provided, however, that Grantor may, with prior written approval from and in the sole discretion of Grantee, make such topographical changes as are consistent with and reasonably necessary to promote the preservation and conservation purposes of this easement.

(g) There shall be no removal, destruction, or cutting down of trees, shrubs, or other vegetation on the Premises; provided, however, that Grantor may with prior written approval from and in the sole discretion of Grantee, undertake such landscaping of the Premises as is compatible with the preservation and conservation purposes of this easement and which may involve removal or alteration of present landscaping, including trees, shrubs, or other vegetation. In all events, Grantor shall maintain trees, shrubs, and lawn in good manner and appearance in conformity with good forestry practices.

(h) No dumping of ashes, trash, rubbish, or any other unsightly or offensive materials shall be permitted on the Premises. [7]

(i) The Premises shall be used only for purposes consistent with the preservation and conservation purposes of this easement.

(j) The Premises shall not be subdivided and the Premises shall not be devised or conveyed except as a unit; provided, however, that the Grantor shall be permitted to convert the Buildings into cooperatives or condominiums and to convey interests in the resulting cooperatives or condominium units, provided that the Grantor shall form or cause to be formed, in connection with such conveyance, a single entity for the purposes of performing all obligations of the Grantor and its successors under this easement.

(k) No utility transmission lines, except those reasonably necessary for the existing Buildings, may be created on said land, subject to utility easements already recorded.

3(a) <u>Public View.</u> Grantor agrees not to obstruct the substantial and regular opportunity of the public to view the exterior architectural features of any building, structure, or improvements of the Premises from adjacent publicly accessible areas such as public streets.

-or-

3(b) <u>Public Access.</u> Grantor shall make the premises accessible to the public on a minimum of two (2) days per year from 10:00 a.m. to 4:00 p.m., and at other times by appointment, to permit persons affiliated with educational organizations, professional architectural associations, and historical societies to study the property. Any such public admission may be subject to restrictions mutually agreed upon as reasonably designed for the protection and maintenance of the property, and the Grantee on request of the Grantor shall furnish such guides and/or guardians as may reasonably be necessary or desirable for such restrictions. Such admission may also be subject to a reasonable fee, if any, as may be approved by the Grantee. The Grantee may make photographs, drawings, or other representations documenting the significant historical, cultural, or architectural character and features of the property and distribute them to magazines, newsletters, or other publicly available publications, or use them in any of its efforts or activities for the preservation and conservation of _____[state's]_____ heritage. [8]

4. <u>Standards for Review.</u> In exercising any authority created by the Easement to inspect the Premises, the Buildings, or the Facades; to review any construction, alteration, repair, or maintenance; or to review casualty damage or to reconstruct or approve reconstruction of the Buildings following casualty damage, Grantee shall apply the Standards for Rehabilitation and Guidelines for Rehabilitating Historic Buildings, issued and as may be amended from time to time by the Secretary of the United States Department of the Interior

(hereinafter the "Standards") and/or state or local standards considered appropriate by Grantee for review of work affecting historically or architecturally significant structures or for construction of new structures within historically, architecturally, or culturally significant areas. A copy of the Standards is attached as Exhibit D in the Addenda, and whenever Grantee receives notice that the Standards have been amended, it shall notify Grantor of the amendment. Grantor agrees to abide by the Standards in performing all ordinary repair and maintenance work and the minimum maintenance program described in Paragraph 2(c) and contained in Exhibit C in the Addenda. In the event the Standards are abandoned or materially altered or otherwise become, in the sole judgment of the Grantee, inappropriate for the purposes set forth above, the Grantee may apply reasonable alternative standards and notify Grantor of the substituted standards. ⑨

5. <u>Casualty Damage or Destruction.</u> In the event that the Premises or any part thereof shall be damaged or destroyed by casualty, the Grantor shall notify the Grantee in writing within one (1) day of the damage or destruction, such notification including what, if any, emergency work has already been completed. For purposes of this instrument, the term "casualty" is defined as such sudden damage or loss as would qualify for a loss deduction pursuant to Section 165(c)(3) of the Code (construed without regard to the legal status, trade, or business of the Grantor or any applicable dollar limitation). No repairs or reconstruction of any type, other than temporary emergency work to prevent further damage to the Property and to protect public safety, shall be undertaken by Grantor without the Grantee's prior written approval of the work. Within four (4) weeks of the date of damage or destruction, the Grantor shall submit to the Grantee a written report prepared by a qualified restoration architect and an engineer, if required, acceptable to the Grantor and the Grantee which shall include the following:

(a) an assessment of the nature and extent of the damage;

(b) a determination of the feasibility of the restoration of the Facades and/or reconstruction of damaged or destroyed portions of the Premises; and

(c) a report of such restoration/reconstruction work necessary to return the Premises to the condition existing at the date [hereof or of the completion of any required work as set forth in the Easement]. If in the opinion of the Grantee, after reviewing such report, the purpose and intent of the Easement will be served by such restoration/reconstruction, the Grantor shall within eighteen (18) months after the date of such change or destruction complete the restoration/construction of the premises in accordance with plans and specifications consented to by the Grantee up to at least the total of the casualty insurance proceeds. Grantee has the right to raise funds toward the costs of restoration of partially destroyed premises above and beyond the total of the casualty insurance proceeds as may be necessary to restore the appearance of the Facades, and such additional costs shall constitute a lien on the Premises until repaid by Grantor.

6. <u>Grantee's Remedies Following Casualty Damage.</u> The foregoing notwithstanding, in the event of damage resulting from casualty, as defined at

Paragraph 5, which is of such magnitude and extent as to render repairs or reconstruction of the Buildings impossible using all applicable insurance proceeds, as determined by Grantee by reference to bona fide cost estimates, then

(a) Grantee may elect to reconstruct the Building using insurance proceeds, donations, or other funds received by Grantor or Grantee on account of such casualty, but otherwise at its own expense (such expense of Grantee to constitute a lien on the premises until repaid in full); or

(b) Grantee may elect to choose any salvageable portion of the Facades and remove them from the premises, extinguish the easement pursuant to Paragraph 26, and this instrument shall thereupon lapse and be of no further force and effect, and Grantee shall execute and deliver to Grantor acknowledged evidence of such fact suitable for recording in the land records of _____ County, ___[state]___ , and Grantor shall deliver to Grantee a good and sufficient Bill of Sale for such salvaged portions of the Facade.

7. Review After Casualty Loss. If in the opinion of the Grantee, restoration/reconstruction would not serve the purpose and intent of the Easement, then the Grantor shall continue to comply with the provisions of the Easement and obtain the prior written consent of the Grantee in the event the Grantor wishes to alter, demolish, remove, or raze the Buildings, and/or construct new improvements on the Premises. [10]

8. Grantee's Covenants. The Grantee hereby warrants and covenants that:

(a) Grantee is and will remain a Qualified Organization for purposes of Section 170(h) of the Internal Revenue Code. In the event that the Grantee's status as a Qualified Organization is successfully challenged by the Internal Revenue Service, then the Grantee shall promptly select another Qualified Organization and transfer all of its rights and obligations under the Easement to it.

(b) In the event that the Grantee shall at any time in the future become the fee simple owner of the Premises, Grantee for itself, its successors, and assigns, covenants and agrees, in the event of a subsequent conveyance of the same to another, to create a new preservation and conservation easement containing the same restrictions and provisions as are contained herein, and either to retain such easement in itself or to convey such easement to a similar unit of federal, state, or local government or local, state, or national organization whose purposes, inter alia, are to promote preservation or conservation of historical, cultural, or architectural resources, and which is a qualified organization under Section 170(h)(3) of the Internal Revenue Code.

(c) Grantee may, at its discretion and without prior notice to Grantor, convey, assign, or transfer this easement to a unit of federal, state, or local government or to a similar local, state, or national organization whose purposes, inter alia, are to promote preservation or conservation of historical, cultural, or architectural resources, and which at the time of the conveyance, assignment, or transfer is a qualified organization under Section 170(h)(3) of the Internal

Revenue Code, provided that any such conveyance, assignment, or transfer requires that the preservation and conservation purposes for which the Easement was granted will continue to be carried out.

(d) Grantee shall exercise reasonable judgment and care in performing its obligations and exercising its rights under the terms of the Easement. [11]

9. <u>Inspection.</u> Grantor hereby agrees that representatives of Grantee shall be permitted at all reasonable times to inspect the Premises, including the Facades and the Buildings. Grantor agrees that representatives of Grantee shall be permitted to enter and inspect the interior of the Buildings to ensure maintenance of structural soundness and safety; inspection of the interior will not, in the absence of evidence of deterioration, take place more often than annually, and may involve reasonable testing of interior structural condition. Inspection of the interior will be made at a time mutually agreed upon by Grantor and Grantee, and Grantor covenants not to withhold unreasonably its consent in determining a date and time for such inspection. [12]

10. <u>Grantee's Remedies.</u> Grantee has the following legal remedies to correct any violation of any covenant, stipulation, or restriction herein, in addition to any remedies now or hereafter provided by law:

(a) Grantee may, following reasonable written notice to Grantor, institute suit(s) to enjoin such violation by ex parte, temporary, preliminary, and/or permanent injunction, including prohibitory and/or mandatory injunctive relief, and to require the restoration of the Premises to the condition and appearance required under this instrument.

(b) Representatives of the Grantee may, following reasonable notice to Grantor, enter upon the Premises, correct any such violation, and hold Grantor, its successors, and assigns, responsible for the cost thereof.

(i) Such cost until repaid shall constitute a lien on the Premises.

(ii) Grantee shall exercise reasonable care in selecting independent contractors if it chooses to retain such contractors to correct any such violations, including making reasonable inquiry as to whether any such contractor is properly licensed and has adequate liability insurance and workman's compensation coverage.

(c) Grantee shall also have available all legal and equitable remedies to enforce Grantor's obligations hereunder.

(d) In the event Grantor is found to have violated any of its obligations, Grantor shall reimburse Grantee for any costs or expenses incurred in connection therewith, including all reasonable court costs, and attorney's, architectural, engineering, and expert witness fees.

(e) Exercise by Grantee of one remedy hereunder shall not have the effect of waiving or limiting any other remedy, and the failure to exercise any remedy shall not have the effect of waiving or limiting the use of any other remedy or the use of such remedy at any other time. [13]

11. <u>Notice from Government Authorities.</u> Grantor shall deliver to Grantee copies of any notice, demand, letter, or bill received by Grantor from any government authority within five (5) days of receipt by Grantor. Upon request

by Grantee, Grantor shall promptly furnish Grantee with evidence of Grantor's compliance with such notice, demand, letter, or bill, where compliance is required by law.

12. <u>Notice of Proposed Sale.</u> Grantor shall promptly notify Grantee in writing of any proposed sale of the Premises and provide the opportunity for Grantee to explain the terms of the Easement to potential new owners prior to sale closing. ⒁

13. <u>Runs with the Land.</u> The obligations imposed by this Easement shall be effective in perpetuity and shall be deemed to run as a binding servitude with the premises. This Easement shall extend to and be binding upon Grantor and Grantee, their respective successors in interest, and all persons hereafter claiming under or through Grantor and Grantee, and the words "Grantor" and "Grantee" when used herein shall include all such persons. Anything contained herein to the contrary notwithstanding, a person shall have no obligation pursuant to this instrument where such person shall cease to have any interest in the premises by reason of a bona fide transfer. Restrictions, stipulations, and covenants contained in this instrument shall be inserted by Grantor, verbatim or by express reference, in any subsequent deed or other legal instrument by which Grantor divests itself of either the fee simple title to or any lesser estate in the premises or any part thereof, including, by way of example and not limitation, a lease of office space. ⒂

14. <u>Recording.</u> Grantee shall do and perform at its own cost all acts necessary to the prompt recording of this instrument in the land records of _____ County, ___[state]___ . This instrument is effective only upon recording in the land records of _____ County, ___[state]___ . ⒃

15. <u>Existing Liens.</u> Except for those matters shown in Exhibit E hereto, Grantor warrants to Grantee that no lien or encumbrance exists on the premises as of the date hereof. Grantor shall immediately cause to be satisfied or release any lien or claim of lien that may hereafter come to exist against the premises which would have priority over any of the rights, title, or interest hereunder of Grantee.

16. <u>Subordination of Mortgages.</u> Grantor and Grantee agree that all mortgages and rights in the property of all Mortgagees are subject and subordinate at all times to the rights of the Grantee to enforce the purposes of the preservation and conservation easement. Grantor has provided a copy of the Easement to all Mortgagees of the Premises as of the date of this agreement, and the agreement of each Mortgagee to subordinate the mortgage to the Easement is contained in the Addenda as Exhibit F. The following provisions apply to all Mortgagees now existing or hereafter holding a mortgage on the Premises:

(a) If a mortgage grants to a Mortgagee the right to receive the proceeds of condemnation proceedings arising from any exercise of the power of eminent domain as to all or any part of the Premises or the right to receive insurance proceeds as a result of any casualty, hazard, or accident occurring to or about the Premises, the Mortgagee shall have a prior claim to the insurance and condemnation proceeds and shall be entitled to same in preference to Grantee until the mortgage is paid off and discharged, notwithstanding that the mortgage is subordinate in priority to the Easement.

(b) If a Mortgagee has received an assignment of the leases, rents, and profits of the Premises as security or additional security for a loan, then the Mortgagee shall have a prior claim to the leases, rents, and profits of the Premises and shall be entitled to receive same in preference to Grantee until said Mortgagee's debt is paid off, notwithstanding that the Mortgage is subordinate to the Easement.

(c) Until a Mortgagee or purchaser at foreclosure obtains ownership of the Premises following foreclosure of its Mortgage or deed in lieu of foreclosure, the Mortgagee or purchaser shall have no obligation, debt, or liability under the Easement.

(d) Before exercising any right or remedy due to breach of the Easement except the right to enjoin a violation hereof, Grantee shall give all Mortgagees of record written notice describing the default, and the Mortgagees shall have sixty (60) days thereafter to cure or cause a cure of the default.

(e) Nothing contained in the above paragraphs or in the Easement shall be construed to give any Mortgagee the right to extinguish this Easement by taking title to the Premises by foreclosure or otherwise. [17]

17. <u>Plaques.</u> Grantor agrees that Grantee may provide and maintain a plaque on the Facades of the Buildings, which plaque shall not exceed ___ by _____ inches in size, giving notice of the significance of the Buildings or the Premises and the existence of this perpetual preservation and conservation easement. [18]

18. <u>Indemnification.</u> The Grantor hereby agrees to pay, protect, indemnify, hold harmless, and defend at its own cost and expense, the Grantee, its agents, director, and employees, or independent contractors from and against any and all claims, liabilities, expenses, costs, damages, losses, and expenditures (including reasonable attorneys' fees and disbursements hereafter incurred) arising out of or in any way relating to the administration, performed in good faith, of this preservation and conservation easement, including, but not limited to, the granting or denial of consents hereunder, the reporting on or advising as to any condition on the Premises, and the execution of work on the Premises. In the event that the Grantor is required to indemnify the Grantee pursuant to the terms of the Easement, the amount of such indemnity, until discharged, shall constitute a lien on the Premises. [19]

19. <u>Taxes.</u> Grantor shall pay immediately, when first due and owing, all general taxes, special taxes, special assessments, water charges, sewer service charges, and other charges which may become a lien on the premises. Grantee is hereby authorized, but in no event required or expected, to make or advance, upon three (3) days prior written notice to Grantor, in the place of Grantor, any payment relating to taxes, assessments, water rates, sewer rentals, and other governmental or municipality charge, fine, imposition, or lien asserted against the premises and may do so according to any bill, statement, or estimate

procured from the appropriate public office without inquiry into the accuracy of such bill, statement, or assessment or into the validity of such tax, assessment, sale, or forfeiture. Such payment, if made by Grantee, shall become a lien on the premises of the same priority as the item if not paid would have had and shall bear interest until paid by Grantor at two (2) percentage points over the prime rate of interest from time to time charged by _____ [bank] _____ .

20. <u>Insurance.</u> The Grantor shall keep the premises insured by an insurance company rated "A+" or better by Best's for the full replacement value against loss from the perils commonly insured under standard fire and extended coverage policies and comprehensive general liability insurance against claims for personal injury, death, and property damage of a type and in such amounts as would, in the opinion of Grantee, normally be carried on a property such as the Premises protected by a preservation and conservation easement. Such insurance shall include Grantee's interest and name Grantee as an additional insured and shall provide for at least thirty (30) days' notice to Grantee before cancellation and that the act or omission of one insured will not invalidate the policy as to the other insured party. Furthermore, the Grantor shall deliver to the Grantee fully executed copies of such insurance policies evidencing the aforesaid insurance coverage at the commencement of this grant and copies of new or renewed policies at least ten (10) days prior to the expiration of such policy. The Grantee shall have the right to provide insurance at the Grantor's cost and expense, should the Grantor fail to obtain same. In the event the Grantee obtains such insurance, the cost of such insurance shall be a lien on the Premises until repaid by the Grantor. [10]

21. <u>Liens.</u> Any lien on the Premises created pursuant to any Paragraph of the Easement may be confirmed by judgment and foreclosed by Grantee in the same manner as a mechanic's lien.

22. <u>Written Notice.</u> Any notice which either Grantor or Grantee may desire or be required to give to the other party shall be in writing and shall be mailed postage prepaid by registered or certified mail with return receipt requested, or hand delivered; if to Grantor, then at _____ [address] _____ , and if to Grantee, then to _____ [address] _____ . Each party may change its address set forth herein by a notice to such effect to the other party. Any notice, consent, approval, agreement, or amendment permitted or required of Grantee under the Easement may be given by the _____ [title] _____ of the Grantee or by any duly authorized representative of the Grantee. [14]

23. <u>Evidence of Compliance.</u> Upon request by Grantee, Grantor shall promptly furnish Grantee with evidence of Grantor's compliance with any obligation of Grantor contained herein.

24. <u>Stipulated Value of Grantee's Interest.</u> Grantor acknowledges that upon execution and recording of the Easement, Grantee shall be immediately vested with a real property interest in the Premises and that such interest of Grantee shall have a stipulated fair market value, for purposes of allocating net proceeds in an extinguishment pursuant to Paragraph 26, equal to the ratio

between the fair market value of the Easement and the fair market value of the Premises prior to considering the impact of the Easement (hereinafter the "Easement Percentage") as determined in the Qualified Appraisal provided to the Grantee pursuant to Paragraph 25. Upon submission of the Qualified Appraisal, the Grantor and Grantee shall sign an affidavit verifying the Easement Percentage and record it as an amendment to the Easement. In the event Grantor does not claim a charitable gift deduction for purposes of calculating federal income taxes and submit a Qualified Appraisal, the Easement Percentage shall be ___ percent. [20]

25. Qualified Appraisal. In the event Grantor claims a federal income tax deduction for donation of a "qualified real property interest" as that term is defined in Section 170(h) of the Internal Revenue Code, Grantor shall provide Grantee with a copy of all appraisals (hereinafter, the "Qualified Appraisal" as that term is defined in P.L. 98-369, 155(a), 98 Stat. 691 (1984), and by reference therein Section 170(a)(1) of the Internal Revenue Code) of the fair market value of the Easement. Upon receipt of the Qualified Appraisal, this fully executed easement, and any endowment requested hereunder by Grantee, Grantee shall sign any appraisal summary form prepared by the Internal Revenue Service and submitted to the Grantee by Grantor. [21]

26. Extinguishment. Grantor and Grantee hereby recognize that an unexpected change in the conditions surrounding the Premises may make impossible the continued ownership or use of the Premises for the preservation and conservation purposes and necessitate extinguishment of the Easement. Such a change in conditions includes, but is not limited to, partial or total destruction of the Buildings or the Facades resulting from a casualty of such magnitude that Grantee approves demolition as explained in Paragraphs 5 and 7, or condemnation or loss of title of all or a portion of the Premises, the Buildings, or the Facades. Such an extinguishment must comply with the following requirements:

(a) The extinguishment must be the result of a final judicial proceeding;

(b) Grantee shall be entitled to share in the net proceeds resulting from the extinguishment in an amount equal to the Easement Percentage determined pursuant to Paragraph 24 multiplied by the net proceeds.

(c) Grantee agrees to apply all of the portion of the net proceeds it receives to the preservation and conservation of other buildings, structures, or sites having historical, architectural, cultural, or aesthetic value and significance to the people of the State of _____ .

(d) Net proceeds shall include, without limitation, insurance proceeds, condemnation proceeds or awards, proceeds from a sale in lieu of condemnation, and proceeds from the sale or exchange by Grantor of any portion of the Premises after the extinguishment, but shall specifically exclude any preferential claim of a Mortgagee under Paragraph 16. [20]

27. Interpretation and Enforcement. The following provisions shall govern the effectiveness, interpretation, and duration of the Easement.

(a) Any rule of strict construction designed to limit the breadth of restrictions on alienation or use of property shall not apply in the construction or interpretation of this instrument, and this instrument shall be interpreted broadly to effect its preservation and conservation purposes and the transfer of rights and the restrictions on use herein contained as provided in the Act.

(b) This instrument shall extend to and be binding upon Grantor and all persons hereafter claiming under or through Grantor, and the word "Grantor" when used herein shall include all such persons, whether or not such persons have signed this instrument or then have an interest in the premises. Anything contained herein to the contrary notwithstanding, a person shall have no obligation pursuant to this instrument where such person shall cease to have any interest (present, partial, contingent, collateral, or future) in the premises by reason of a bona fide transfer for full value. Any right, title, or interest herein granted to Grantee also shall be deemed granted to each successor and assign of Grantee and each such following successor and assign thereof, and the word "Grantee" shall include all such successors and assigns.

(c) This instrument is executed in counterparts, each page of which (including exhibits) has been initialed by Grantor and Grantee for purposes of identification. In the event of any disparity between the counterparts produced, the recorded counterpart shall in all cases govern. Except as provided above, each counterpart shall constitute the agreement of the parties. Immediately after execution hereof, one counterpart shall be held by each of Grantor, Grantee, and the preparer of this instrument, _____ , one counterpart shall be recorded as provided above and may be returned to Grantee, and one counterpart shall be stored as a matter of public record at ___[appropriate town, county, or state office, museum, or library]___ . [16]

(d) Except as expressly provided herein, nothing contained in this instrument grants, nor shall be interpreted to grant, to the public any right to enter on the Premises or into the Buildings.

(e) To the extent that Grantor owns or is entitled to development rights which may exist now or at some time hereafter by reason of the fact that under any applicable zoning or similar ordinance the Premises may be developed to use more intensive (in terms of height, bulk, or other objective criteria regulated by such ordinances) than the Premises are devoted as of the date hereof, such development rights shall not be exercisable on, above, or below the Premises during the term of the Easement, nor shall they be transferred to any adjacent parcel and exercised in a manner that would interfere with the preservation and conservation purposes of the Easement.

(f) For purposes of furthering the preservation of the Premises and Buildings and of furthering the other purposes of this instrument, and to meet changing conditions, Grantor and Grantee are free to amend jointly the terms of this instrument in writing without notice to any party; provided, however, that no such amendment shall limit the perpetual duration or interfere with the preservation and conservation purposes of the donation. Such amendment shall become effective upon recording among the land records of _____ County, _____[state]_____ .

(g) The terms and conditions of this easement shall be referenced in any transfer of the property by the Grantor, his heirs, successors, and assigns.

(h) This instrument is made pursuant to Article _____ of Title _____ , Code of Laws of _____ [state] _____ , but the invalidity of such statute or any part thereof shall not affect the validity and enforceability of this instrument according to its terms, it being the intent of the parties to agree and to bind themselves, their successors, and their assigns in perpetuity to each term of this instrument whether this instrument be enforceable by reason of any statute, common law, or private agreement either in existence now or at any time subsequent hereto. This instrument may be re-recorded at any time by any person if the effect of such re-recording is to make more certain the enforcement of this instrument or any part thereof. The invalidity or unenforceability of any provision of this instrument shall not affect the validity or enforceability of any other provision of this instrument or any ancillary or supplementary agreement relating to the subject matter hereof.

(i) Nothing contained herein shall be interpreted to authorize or permit Grantor to violate any ordinance or regulation relating to building materials, construction methods, or use. In the event of any conflict between any such ordinance or regulation and the terms hereof, Grantor promptly shall notify Grantee of such conflict and shall cooperate with Grantee and the applicable governmental entity to accommodate the purposes of both this instrument and such ordinance or regulation.

(j) This instrument reflects the entire agreement of Grantor and Grantee. Any prior or simultaneous correspondence, understandings, agreements, and representations are null and void upon execution hereof, unless set out in this instrument. [22]

IN WITNESS WHEREOF, on the date first shown above, Grantor has caused this preservation and conservation easement to be executed, sealed, and delivered; and Grantee has caused this instrument to be accepted, sealed, and executed in its corporate name by its _____ and attested by its Secretary.

GRANTOR:

_____

_____   By: _____
Witness   [Title]

ATTEST: GRANTEE:

_____   By: _____
Secretary   [Title]

SCHEDULE OF EXHIBITS

A. Photographs of Protected Property (Baseline Documentation)

B. Verification Affidavit

C. Minimum Maintenance Program

D. Standards for Rehabilitation and Guidelines for Rehabilitating Historic Buildings

E. Affidavit of Existing Liens or Encumbrances

F. Mortgage Subordination Agreement(s)

Commentary

Note: The numbers at the beginning of the subheads in this section correspond with the boxed numbers inserted in the text of the model historic preservation easement preceding this commentary.

1. The "Whereas" Clauses

The model document opens with the naming of the grantor and grantee. The name of the property owner making the donation will need to be provided in each transaction.

A series of introductory paragraphs, each beginning with the word "whereas," explains the purposes of the easement donation. These paragraphs also explain the legal basis for the donation and give some information about the significance of the property. If the property is listed in the National Register of Historic Places, that fact should be mentioned. Indeed, it might be helpful to add a few pertinent facts from the National Register nomination or from other documentation that explains the historic significance of the property. The introductory paragraphs also make the legal basis of the donation quite clear and include a reference to the applicable sections of the Internal Revenue Code and the state legislation authorizing easement donations.

2. Legal Description

A precise legal description of each property on which a donation is made should be included in the easement document. This may be obtained from a survey, a title report, or other documentation provided by the owner of the property.

3. Description of Facades

Photographs of the character and conditions of the facades on the date of the donation are required to be attached as an exhibit to the easement. This photographic record should be made and recorded as a permanent reference against which all future changes can be measured. Also to be attached as an exhibit is a written statement of the location of the photographer when each photograph was taken. This will help in future interpretation of the photos.

If other portions of the property are to be protected—for example, important natural features—these too should be photographed and included in the photographic record attached as an exhibit. The same is true if any interior features of the building are to be protected.

If the property is one proposed for rehabilitation (or is actually undergoing rehabilitation), plans should be attached. The easement text should require that all work be completed in accordance with the plans and should specify a deadline for completion.

4. Grantor's Covenants

Paragraph 2 of the model easement document is one of the most important. It carefully sets out the principal responsibilities imposed upon current and future owners of the property. Actions that must receive the prior written consent of the grantee are carefully set out. In addition to alterations of exterior changes, any increase or decrease in the height of the facades or the buildings is also subject to review. Construction of additional floors on a building may affect its architectural character and must be carefully reviewed by the easement holder. Interior work that affects the structural soundness of the building also should be reviewed. This model easement also includes a provision requiring prior review and approval of any construction of new improvements on the premises that might interfere with a view of the facades or be incompatible with the historic or architectural character of the protected property.

5. Minimum Maintenance Program

While not required by the 1986 Internal Revenue Service regulations, referencing minimum maintenance requirements can be useful. Paragraph 2(c) requires present and future owners to maintain the buildings in a good and sound state of repair. This creates an affirmative obligation on the owner. A maintenance schedule is not included with the model easement as an exhibit. One should be developed according to the requirements and characteristics of each protected property.

Attaching a minimum maintenance schedule to each easement donation is important. The schedule should include a timing requirement—that is, the frequency of the inspections and the actual maintenance or repair itself. This shifts some of the burden of administering an easement to the owner of the property. The owner must perform the inspections according to the schedule in the minimum maintenance program. It is not a substitute, however, for regularly scheduled inspections by the easement holder.

6. Signs, Billboards, and Advertisements

Paragraph 2(e) of the model document also carefully states that installation of any signs or construction of billboards must be reviewed and approved by the grantee. This should include temporary signs placed in windows or doors.

7. Topographical and Landscaping Changes

Paragraphs 2(f) through (h) require review before any topographical or landscaping changes are made to the site on which the historic buildings are located. These paragraphs may be important to include when the protected property is in a rural setting, but may be less important to include in easements in an urban context.

8. Public View or Access

Regulations issued by the Internal Revenue Service in January 1986 contain a strict requirement that some form of public access or public view be available on easement-protected properties for the grantor to obtain a charitable gift deduction. The regulations state the following:

> [S]ome visual public access to the donated property is required. In the case of an historically important land area, the entire property need not be visible to the public for a donation to qualify under this section. However, the public benefit from the donation may be insufficient to qualify for a deduction if only a small portion of the property is so visible. Where the historic land area or certified historic structure which is the subject of the donation is not visible from a public way (e.g., the structure is hidden from view by a wall or shrubbery, the structure is too far from the public way, or interior characteristics and features of the structure are the subject of the easement), the terms of the easement must be such that the general public is given the opportunity on a regular basis to view the characteristics and features of the property which are preserved by the easement to the extent consistent with the nature and condition of the property. *See* Treas. Reg. § 1.170A-14(d)(5)(iv).

Among the factors listed by the Internal Revenue Service in determining the type and amount of public access are the following:

☐ Historical significance of the donated property;

☐ Nature of the protected features;

☐ Remoteness or accessibility of the site;

☐ Possibility of physical hazards to visiting public (e.g., an unoccupied structure in a dilapidated condition);

☐ Extent to which public access would be an unreasonable intrusion on owner's privacy;

☐ Impact of public access upon the preservation interest for which the donation was made; and

☐ Availability of opportunities for public view by means other than site visits.

The 1986 regulations provide two examples to illustrate the public access requirements. The first example involves an exterior and interior easement on a house surrounded by a high stone wall that obscures the view from the street. Terms of the easement state that the house may be open to the public from 10 a.m. to 4 p.m. on one Sunday in May and one Sunday in November each year. Tours are to be conducted by the recipient organization and visitors must pay a small fee. The easement recipient may also photograph the interior and exterior of the house and distribute the photographs. Special appointments may be made to study the property by persons affiliated with educational, professional, or historical societies. The Internal Revenue Service states: "The two opportunities for public visits per year, when combined with the ability of the general public to view the architectural characteristics and features that are the subject of the easement through photographs, the opportunity for scholarly study of the property, and the fact that the house is used as an occupied residence, will enable the donation to satisfy the requirement of public access." *See* Treas. Reg. § 1.170A-14(d)(5)(v).

The second IRS example involves an unoccupied farmhouse built in the 1840s and located next to a Civil War battlefield. The farmhouse was used during the historic battle but is not visible from the battlefield or any public road. The battlefield is open to the general public year-round, and the condition of the house is safe for the general public to visit it. The owner of the property donates an easement and provides that the house may be open to the general public on four weekends each year from 8:30 a.m. to 4:00 p.m. The regulations state: "The donation does not meet the public access requirement because the farmhouse is safe, unoccupied, and easily accessible to the general public who have come to the site to visit Civil War historic land areas (and related resources), but will only be open to the public on four weekends each year." *See* Treas. Reg. § 1.170A-14(d)(5)(v). The regulations explain that if the farmhouse were open every other weekend during the year, then it might qualify.

Alternative language has been provided in the model to meet the public view or public access requirement. Paragraph 3(a) would be sufficient if the easement protects only the exterior facades and if the structure is readily visible from an adjacent public street. If there are significant interior portions of the structure that are protected by the easement, or the property is not readily visible from a public street, then the language of paragraph 3(b) is recommended to be included in the easement document. Hours of visitation may have to be expanded, however, if the protected property is one, such as the farmhouse in the Internal Revenue Service example, that is adjacent to a heavily visited historic site and is not occupied.

9. Standards for Review of Alterations

It is important to include precise standards for review of alterations and changes. The model easement document refers to the *Standards for Rehabilitation and Guidelines for Rehabilitating Historic Buildings* issued by the Secretary of the Interior.

This language, too, is inserted to comply with the 1986 federal tax regulations. The regulations contain the following requirement:

> When restrictions to preserve a building or land area within a registered historic district permit future development on the site, a deduction will be allowed under this section only if the terms of the restrictions require that such development conform with appropriate local, state, or Federal standards for construction or rehabilitation within the district. *See* Treas. Reg. § 1.170A-14(d)(5)(i).

10. Casualty Damage or Destruction and Insurance

Some of the most important paragraphs in a preservation and conservation easement document concern the rights of each party when the protected property is damaged or destroyed by fire, earthquake, flood, or other casualty. Good easement documents give the recipient the right to review and approve the amount and type of insurance coverage maintained by the owner of the property, and to be notified of changes in coverage.

Paragraph 20 carefully sets out the insurance requirements. The grantee must be named as an additional insured party and must be given notice at least 30 days before any cancellation. Casualty and liability insurance coverage must be kept on the property in amounts that the easement recipient believes would normally be carried on properties protected by preservation and conservation easements. The grantee should carefully review each insurance policy on the property to make sure that it provides enough protection for the property and for the position of the grantee.

When casualty damage does occur, the grantee must be given written notice. As a holder of the easement, it then has the right to get involved in the repair and reconstruction work. Written approval of the easement grantee is required before any reconstruction work begins, and a report prepared by a qualified restoration architect and an engineer may be required by the grantee. If the damage is minor, but there are insufficient insurance proceeds to restore the protected features, the easement holder may make the repairs and impose a lien to collect the cost from the property owner.

In some cases, damage may be so significant that repair or reconstruction is impossible. The grantee then has the right to decide whether repair or reconstruction is possible. The grantee must look to the available insurance proceeds and cost estimates of reconstruction. If there are not sufficient insurance proceeds for the reconstruction, then the easement holder may launch a fund campaign to raise the additional cost of the reconstruction. It may impose this cost as a lien on the property. Or the easement holder may remove any salvageable portions of the facades or other protected features and extinguish the easement. Even then, however, prior written approval from the grantee must be received by the owner before he or she may demolish the damaged structure or construct a new structure on the property.

11. Responsibilities of Easement Recipient

A preservation and conservation easement is a contract between the grantor and the grantee. While most of the burden of the easement falls on the property owner, there are some duties and responsibilities imposed on the easement recipients as well. Paragraph 8 sets out the responsibilities of the grantee, which include taking all necessary steps to maintain its status as a qualified easement recipient and finding another qualified recipient if for any reason the grantee has its tax-exempt status challenged or for any other reason decides to transfer the easement to another holder. The grantor also must reasonably exercise its responsibilities and judgment in all matters relating to the easement.

12. Inspection

The easement holder has the right to inspect both the exterior and the interior of the protected property. Reasonable notice of the proposed interior inspection must be given to the property owner, and inspection may involve testing of interior structural conditions.

Interior inspection is an important right that should be provided by every easement document. Such problems as termite infestation, dry rot, flooding or seepage, or foundation settling can eventually threaten the structural integrity of a protected facade.

13. Grantee's Remedies

A variety of legal remedies is provided to the grantee to enforce the terms of the model easement. The grantee retains all legal and equitable remedies provided in law and has some specifically mentioned authority as well. Suits to enjoin violation of any term or provision of the easement may be filed, and restoration of the altered or damaged feature to the condition prior to the violation can be sought.

Significant "self-help" authority is also given the easement holder. If the property owner fails to respond to a notice of a violation, the grantee may enter the premises, correct the violation itself, and hold the owner responsible for the cost. That cost will be a lien on the premises that can be enforced by judicial action in the same manner that a mechanic's lien is foreclosed.

The easement holder is entitled to be reimbursed for all its legal costs in enforcing the terms of the easement if a court finds that the property owner has violated its terms. These costs include attorney's fees, architectural and engineering fees, and even expert witness fees.

14. Notices

The property owner must give the grantee written notice, including a copy, of any communication from a government authority about the protected property, and also notice of any proposed sale of the property. The property owner must comply with any demand in a notice from a government authority and must give the grantee an opportunity to explain the terms of the easement to potential new owners of the property.

Paragraph 22 requires that notice be provided by registered or certified mail. Notice of a change in address must be given.

15. Runs with the Land: Easement in Perpetuity

The Internal Revenue Code requires that a preservation easement donation be made in perpetuity if a charitable gift deduction is claimed by the owner.

Paragraph 13 of the model easement document clearly states that the easement agreement "runs with the land" as a binding servitude in perpetuity. However, obligations of any full or partial owner of the property terminate when that person sells or otherwise disposes of the interest in it. Every subsequent owner of the property is bound by the easement terms, and every time the property is sold or leased, a reference to the easement must be provided to the new party in interest.

16. Recording

The easement document must be recorded by the grantee to be effective. The recording takes place in the county (in New England, in the town) in which the property is located. Paragraph 27(c) also requires that a copy of the document be kept at some office of the grantee. For those jurisdictions in which referenced photographs, diagrams, and sketches cannot be recorded and must be publicly stored, a provision should be included requiring a copy of the document to be maintained as public record in an appropriate public depository, such as a museum, library, or agency office.

Recording is important to assure that all future owners or potential buyers are given notice of the easement agreement. Once recorded, the existence of the easement will be picked up in any title report.

17. Existing Liens and Mortgage Subordination

A preservation and conservation easement must carefully set out the rights of mortgagees and other lienholders in the property on the date of the donation. The 1986 regulations require that existing mortgagees subordinate their rights in the property to the right of the easement recipient. *See* Treas. Reg. § 1.170A-14(g)(6)(i).

However, paragraph 16 of the easement document attempts to reconcile the interests of mortgage lenders and those of the easement holder so that the requirement of subordination will not unreasonably interfere with the ability of the property owner to obtain mortgage loans or to obtain the consent of an existing mortgage lender to subordinate. The interest of the mortgage lender is protected in any condemnation proceeding or under any provision of the mortgage loan documents giving the lender the right to receive insurance proceeds as a result of a casualty. The mortgage lender's prior rights to receive leases, rents, or profits from the property as security for a loan are also protected. Mortgage lenders of record must be notified before the grantee exercises any of its legal remedies for a violation of the easement, except the right to seek an injunction. The mortgage lender has 60 days to work with the property owner to cure the default.

The right of a mortgage lender to foreclose on its loan and extinguish the easement is eliminated. The easement survives the mortgage foreclosure, but the responsibilities of the mortgage lender to comply with all easement terms and conditions do not begin until the mortgagee actually becomes the owner of the property following a foreclosure.

18. Plaques and Signs

The grantee has the right to install and maintain a small plaque on the protected facades. The size of the plaque is left open and can vary from one easement to another.

This paragraph may be modified depending upon the circumstances of the gift. For example, it may be important for the grantee to install a small sign or a series of posted signs at strategic points on the boundaries of a large estate or rural tract.

19. Indemnification

Paragraph 18 of the model easement document is a clear-cut requirement that the owner of the property indemnify and hold the grantee harmless from any and all costs and expenses arising out of or in any way related to the preservation and conservation easement. This is intended to provide additional protection to the grantee over and above the requirement that adequate liability and casualty insurance be maintained that names the grantee as an insured party. If the owner of the property fails to indemnify the easement holder, the amount owed can become a lien on the property. The grantee can also make sure that all taxes are paid when due, and if they are not, can make the payment and impose a lien on the property.

20. Extinguishment and the Stipulated Value of the Easement

Paragraphs 24 and 26 of the model easement document are written to comply with the new requirements published by the Internal Revenue Service in January of 1986. To assure that easement donations are truly made in perpetuity, tax code regulations now specify that proceeds resulting from a subsequent sale or exchange of the protected property after extinguishment of the easement must be shared between the owner and the easement holder. There are a number or circumstances in which extinguishment of the easement may make sense. For example, if casualty damage to the protected property is so severe that reconstruction of the protected facades is physically or economically impossible, both parties to the easement agreement may want to extinguish it and allow demolition. An eminent domain proceeding by federal, state, or local government may also condemn the easement restriction for an overriding public project such as road construction or downtown urban redevelopment.

The tax code allows a preservation easement to be extinguished, but only if the following requirements are met:

☐ An unexpected change in the conditions surrounding the property makes it impossible or impractical to continue to use it for the conservation or preservation purposes;

☐ The easement is extinguished by judicial proceedings; and

☐ Any proceeds received by the easement holder from a subsequent sale or exchange of the property are used by it in a manner consistent with the conservation of preservation purposes of the original easement donation. *See* Treas. Reg. § 1.170A-14(g)(6)(i) and (ii).

The regulations also specify the manner in which the easement holder's participation in the proceeds of sale are to be measured. The value of the charitable gift deduction taken by the owner at the date of donation is compared to the market value of the property as a whole at that date. The ratio becomes the fixed constant that must later be used in allocating the proceeds of an extinguishment between the property owner and the easement holder.

Paragraph 26 of the model easement document recognizes the circumstances in which an extinguishment may be possible. The language follows the wording of the new regulations and recognizes partial or total destruction of the property as the result of a casualty, condemnation, or loss of title as one of the "changes in conditions" that may result in extinguishment. The paragraph also makes it clear that the easement holder participates in any net proceeds remaining after payment of costs of the sale and preferential claims of mortgage lenders.

Paragraph 24 of the model easement document outlines the method for determining the respective interest of property owner and easement holder in an extinguishment. If the original donor took a charitable gift deduction for the value of the easement, a copy of the qualified appraisal must be provided to the easement grantee. The indicated ratio between the fair market value of the easement and the fair market value of the entire property before the impact of the easement is called the "easement percentage," which thereafter fixes the respective interest of each party in an extinguishment. If the easement donor is not seeking a charitable gift deduction, paragraph 24 allows the parties to the easement agreement to insert a minimum percentage as the "easement percentage" that will apply in the event of an extinguishment.

Fixing some minimum "easement percentage," even if no charitable gift deduction has been taken, should be done. An amount as low as 5 percent should be enough to discourage an easement donor from considering arson or some other illegal action to destroy the easement-protected property.

The "easement percentage" must be recorded in an affidavit signed by both parties and attached to the recorded easement as an amendment. In some donation situations, the owner of the property may have a qualified appraisal in hand prior to the date on which negotiations concerning the terms of the easement are completed and the document is recorded. However, federal income tax regulations do not require that the qualified appraisal be obtained by the donor until the date on which a federal income tax return is filed for the year in which the donation was made. Donations are typically made in December, and income tax returns are usually not due until April of the following year. The donor may not have the completed appraisal report in hand until a few months after the donation date. At that time, the easement document would be amended by filing of the affidavit. If the qualified appraisal was obtained before the date of the donation—tax regulations allow it to be completed as early as 60 days before donation—paragraph 24 could be modified so that the easement percentage is written directly into the easement document rather than attached later as an amendment.

21. Qualified Appraisal

Federal tax regulations also require that the grantee sign an "appraisal summary" acknowledging receipt of the easement donation. *See* Temp. Reg. § 1.170A-13T(c)(3). Although it is not good policy for an easement recipient to become involved in the process whereby the easement is appraised (other than to give potential donors a list of appraisers known to be skilled in easement assignments), the grantee should obtain a copy of the appraisal from the donor and keep a copy of it in its files. Paragraph 25 of the model easement document imposes this condition.

22. Miscellaneous Provisions

The last section of the model easement document is a series of subparagraphs explaining how the wording of the easement document is to be interpreted and its legal effectiveness. It carefully states that if any portion of the easement document is held to be unconstitutional or otherwise illegal, only that portion is affected and not any other portion of the document. It carefully states also that language in the easement document should be interpreted to affect broadly the preservation and conservation purpose of the donation. This is, in effect, an instruction to the courts to try to uphold the easement document against challenge to the extent possible.

The final paragraph also discusses the effectiveness of any future transfer of development rights from the protected property to another parcel. An easement that prohibits demolition often results in a reduction of the development potential of a piece of property. Land value may be seriously affected by the donation. Subparagraph (e) of paragraph 27 recognizes that development potential may be affected by the gift, and states that such development potential cannot be exercised on the property during the term of the easement, nor can it be shifted to an adjacent parcel and exercised if the result of that development would interfere with the preservation and conservation purposes of the easement. For example, a property owner donating an easement that prohibits demolition of a small historic building on a downtown site quite valuable for new construction might otherwise be able to acquire an adjacent site, demolish the improvements on that adjacent site, combine it with the easement-protected property into one zoning lot, and develop a new high-rise office building or high-density retail structure adjacent to the smaller historic building. This could adversely affect the historic or architectural character of the easement-protected building, and the easement document would allow this only after review and approval by the easement holder.

Sometimes there may be a conflict between the local building or zoning code and the standards used by an easement holder in enforcing an easement.

For example, a particular type of exterior cleaning method or replacement material may be prohibited by a local building code. Subparagraph (i) of paragraph 27 requires the owner of the property to notify the easement holder of any such conflict, and the two parties to the easement agreement are required to cooperate with each other and with the local government unit to find a compromise solution to the impasse.

Sec. 170(h) Qualified conservation contribution.—

(1) **In general.**—For purposes of subsection (f)(3)(B)(iii), the term "qualified conservation contribution" means a contribution—

    (A) of a qualified real property interest,

    (B) to a qualified organization,

    (C) exclusively for conservation purposes.

(2) **Qualified real property interest.**—For purposes of this subsection, the term "qualified real property interest" means any of the following interests in real property:

    (A) the entire interest of the donor other than a qualified mineral interest,

    (B) a remainder interest, and

    (C) a restriction (granted in perpetuity) on the use which may be made of the real property.

(3) **Qualified organization.**—For purposes of paragraph (1), the term "qualified organization" means an organization which—

    (A) is described in clause (v) or (vi) of subsection (b)(1)(A), or

    (B) is described in section 501(c)(3) and—

        (i) meets the requirements of section 509(a)(2), or

        (ii) meets the requirements of section 509(a)(3) and is controlled by an organization described in subparagraph (A) or in clause (i) of this subparagraph.

(4) **Conservation purpose defined.—**

    (A) **In general.**—For purposes of this subsection, the term "conservation purpose" means—

        (i) the preservation of land areas for outdoor recreation by, or the education of, the general public,

        (ii) the protection of a relatively natural habitat of fish, wildlife, or plants, or similar ecosystem,

        (iii) the preservation of open space (including farmland and forest land) where such preservation is—

            (I) for the scenic enjoyment of the general public, or

            (II) pursuant to a clearly delineated Federal, State, or local governmental conservation policy,

and will yield a significant public benefit, or

        (iv) the preservation of an historically important land area or a certified historic structure.

    (B) **Certified historic structure.**—For purposes of subparagraph (A)(iv), the term "certified historic structure" means any building, structure, or land area which—

        (i) is listed in the National Register, or

        (ii) is located in a registered historic district (as defined in section 48(g)(3)(B)) and is certified by the Secretary of the Interior to the Secretary as being of historic significance to the district.

A building, structure, or land area satisfies the preceding sentence if it satisfies such sentence either at the time of the transfer or on the due date (including extensions) for filing the transferor's return under this chapter for the taxable year in which the transfer is made.

(5) Exclusively for conservation purposes.—For purposes of this subsection—

(A) Conservation purpose must be protected.—A contribution shall not be treated as exclusively for conservation purposes unless the conservation purpose is protected in perpetuity.

(B) No surface mining permitted.—

(i) In general.—Except as provided in clause (ii), in the case of a contribution of any interest where there is a retention of a qualified mineral interest, subparagraph (A) shall not be treated as met if at any time there may be extraction or removal of minerals by any surface mining method.

(ii) Special rule.—With respect to any contribution of property in which the ownership of the surface estate and mineral interests were separated before June 13, 1976, and remain so separated, subparagraph (A) shall be treated as met if the probability of surface mining occurring on such property is so remote as to be negligible.

(6) Qualified mineral interest.—For purposes of this subsection, the term "qualified mineral interest" means—

(A) subsurface oil, gas, or other minerals, and

(B) the right to access to such minerals.

meaning of section 165(g)(2) of the Code) which are not publicly traded securities as defined in paragraph (c)(7)(iv) of this section.

(vi) *Nonpublicly traded stock.* The term "nonpublicly traded stock "means any stock of a corporation (evidence by a stock certificate) which is not a publicly traded security. The term stock does not include a debenture or any other evidence of indebtedness.

(68A Stat. 58, 26 U.S.C. 170(a)(1); 96 Stat. 693, 26 U.S.C. 6050L; 68A Stat. 917, 26 U.S.C. 7805; sec. 155 of the Tax Reform Act of 1984, Pub. L. 98-369, 96 Stat. 691)

[T.D. 8003, 49 FR 50659, Dec. 31, 1984]

§ 1.170A-14 **Qualified conservation contributions.**

(a) *Qualified conservation contributions.* A deduction under section 170 is generally not allowed for a charitable contribution of any interest in property that consists of less than the donor's entire interest in the property other than certain transfers in trust (see § 1.170A-6 relating to charitable contributions in trust and § 1.170A-7 relating to contributions not in trust of partial interests in property). However, a deduction may be allowed under section 170(f)(3)(B)(iii) for the value of a qualified conservation contribution if the requirements of this section are met. A qualified conservation contribution is the contribution of a qualified real property interest to a qualified organization exclusively for conservation purposes. To be eligible for a deduction under this section, the conservation purpose must be protected in perpetuity.

(b) *Qualified real property interest*— (1) *Entire interest of donor other than qualified mineral interest.* (i) The entire interest of the donor other than a qualified mineral interest is a qualified real property interest. A qualified mineral interest is the donor's interest in subsurface oil, gas, or other minerals and the right of access to such minerals.

(ii) A real property interest shall not be treated as an entire interest other than a qualified mineral interest by reason of section 170(h)(2)(A) and this paragraph (b)(1) if the property in which the donor's interest exists was divided prior to the contribution in order to enable the donor to retain control of more than a qualified mineral interest or to reduce the real property interest donated. See Treasury regulations § 1.170A-7(a)(2)(i). An entire interest in real property may consist of an undivided interest in the property. But see section 170(h)(5)(A) and the regulations thereunder (relating to the requirement that the conservation purpose which is the subject of the donation must be protected in perpetuity). Minor interests, such as rights-of-way, that will not interfere with the conservation purposes of the donation, may be transferred prior to the conservation contribution without affecting the treatment of a property interest as a qualified real property interest under this paragraph (b)(1).

(2) *Perpetual conservation restriction.* A perpetual conservation restriction is a qualified real property interest. A "perpetual conservation restriction" is a restriction granted in perpetuity on the use which may be made of real property—including, an easement or other interest in real property that under state law has attributes similar to an easement (e.g., a restrictive covenant or equitable servitude). For purposes of this section, the terms "easement", "conservation restriction", and "perpetual conservation restriction" have the same meaning. The definition of "perpetual conservation restriction" under this paragraph (b)(2) is not intended to preclude the deductibility of a donation of affirmative rights to use a land or water area under § 1.170A-13(d)(2). Any rights reserved by the donor in the donation of a perpetual conservation restriction must conform to the requirements of this section. See *e.g.,* paragraph (d)(4)(ii), (d)(5)(i), (e)(3), and (g)(4) of this section.

(c) *Qualified organization*—(1) *Eligible donee.* To be considered an eligible donee under this section, an organization must be a qualified organization, have a commitment to protect the conservation purposes of the donation, and have the resources to enforce the restrictions. A conservation group organized or operated primarily or substantially for one of the conservation purposes   specified   in   section

170(h)(4)(A) will be considered to have the commitment required by the preceding sentence. A qualified organization need not set aside funds to enforce the restrictions that are the subject of the contribution. For purposes of this section, the term "qualified organization" means:

(i) A governmental unit described in section 170(b)(1)(A)(v);

(ii) An organization described in section 170(b)(1)(A)(vi);

(iii) A charitable organization described in section 501(c)(3) that meets the public support test of section 509(a)(2);

(iv) A charitable organization described in section 501(c)(3) that meets the requirements of section 509(a)(3) and is controlled by an organization described in paragraphs (c)(1) (i), (ii), or (iii) of this section.

(2) *Transfers by donee.* A deduction shall be allowed for a contribution under this section only if in the instrument of conveyance the donor prohibits the donee from subsequently transferring the easement (or, in the case of a remainder interest or the reservation of a qualified mineral interest, the property), whether or not for consideration, unless the donee organization, as a condition of the subsequent transfer, requires that the conservation purposes which the contribution was originally intended to advance continue to be carried out. Moreover, subsequent transfers must be restricted to organizations qualifying, at the time of the subsequent transfer, as an eligible donee under paragraph (c)(1) of this section. When a later unexpected change in the conditions surrounding the property that is the subject of a donation under paragraph (b)(1), (2), or (3) of this section makes impossible or impractical the continued use of the property for conservation purposes, the requirement of this paragraph will be met if the property is sold or exchanged and any proceeds are used by the donee organization in a manner consistent with the conservation purposes of the original contribution. In the case of a donation under paragraph (b)(3) of this section to which the preceding sentence applies, see also paragraph (g)(5)(ii) of this section.

(d) *Conservation purposes*—(1) *In general.* For purposes of section 170(h) and this section, the term "conservation purposes" means—

(i) The preservation of land areas for outdoor recreation by, or the education of, the general public, within the meaning of paragraph (d)(2) of this section,

(ii) The protection of a relatively natural habitat of fish, wildlife, or plants, or similar ecosystem, within the meaning of paragraph (d)(3) of this section,

(iii) The preservation of certain open space (including farmland and forest land) within the meaning of paragraph (d)(4) of this section, or

(iv) The preservation of a historically important land area or a certified historic structure, within the meaning of paragraph (d)(5) of this section.

(2) *Recreation or education*—(i) *In general.* The donation of a qualified real property interest to preserve land areas for the outdoor recreation of the general public or for the education of the general public will meet the conservation purposes test of this section. Thus, conservation purposes would include, for example, the preservation of a water area for the use of the public for boating or fishing, or a nature or hiking trail for the use of the public.

(ii) *Access.* The preservation of land areas for recreation or education will not meet the test of this section unless the recreation or education is for the substantial and regular use of the general public.

(3) *Protection of environmental system*—(i) *In general.* The donation of a qualified real property interest to protect a significant relatively natural habitat in which a fish, wildlife, or plant community, or similar ecosystem normally lives will meet the conservation purposes test of this section. The fact that the habitat or environment has been altered to some extent by human activity will not result in a deduction being denied under this section if the fish, wildlife, or plants continue to exist there in a relatively natural state. For example, the preservation of a lake formed by a man-made dam or a salt pond formed by a man-made dike would meet the conservation purposes test if the lake or pond

were a nature feeding area for a wildlife community that included rare, endangered, or threatened native species.

(ii) *Significant habitat or ecosystem.* Significant habitats and ecosystems include, but are not limited to, habitats for rare, endangered, or threatened species of animal, fish, or plants; natural areas that represent high quality examples of a terrestrial community or aquatic community, such as islands that are undeveloped or not intensely developed where the coastal ecosystem is relatively intact; and natural areas which are included in, or which contribute to, the ecological viability of a local, state, or national park, nature preserve, wildlife refuge, wilderness area, or other similar conservation area.

(iii) *Access.* Limitations on public access to property that is the subject of a donation under this paragraph (d)(3) shall not render the donation nondeductible. For example, a restriction on all public access to the habitat of a threatened native animal species protected by a donation under this paragraph (d)(3) would not cause the donation to be nondeductible.

(4) *Preservation of open space*—(i) *In general.* The donation of a qualified real property interest to preserve open space (including farmland and forest land) will meet the conservation purposes test of this section if such preservation is—

(A) Pursuant to a clearly delineated Federal, state, or local governmental conservation policy and will yield a significant public benefit, or

(B) For the scenic enjoyment of the general public and will yield a significant public benefit.

An open space easement donated on or after December 18, 1980, must meet the requirements of section 170(h) in order to be deductible.

(ii) *Scenic enjoyment*—(A) *Factors.* A contribution made for the preservation of open space may be for the scenic enjoyment of the general public. Preservation of land may be for the scenic enjoyment of the general public if development of the property would impair the scenic character of the local rural or urban landscape or would interfere with a scenic panorama that can be enjoyed from a park,

nature preserve, road, waterbody, trail, or historic structure or land area, and such area or transportation way is open to, or utilized by, the public. "Scenic enjoyment" will be evaluated by considering all pertinent facts and circumstances germane to the contribution. Regional variations in topography, geology, biology, and cultural and economic conditions require flexibility in the application of this test, but do not lessen the burden on the taxpayer to demonstrate the scenic characteristics of a donation under this paragraph. The application of a particular objective factor to help define a view as "scenic" in one setting may in fact be entirely inappropriate in another setting. Among the factors to be considered are:

(1) The compatibility of the land use with other land in the vicinity;

(2) The degree of contrast and variety provided by the visual scene;

(3) The openness of the land (which would be a more significant factor in an urban or densely populated setting or in a heavily wooded area);

(4) Relief from urban closeness;

(5) The harmonious variety of shapes and textures;

(6) The degree to which the land use maintains the scale and character of the urban landscape to preserve open space, visual enjoyment, and sunlight for the surrounding area;

(7) The consistency of the proposed scenic view with a methodical state scenic identification program, such as a state landscape inventory; and

(8) The consistency of the proposed scenic view with a regional or local landscape inventory made pursuant to a sufficiently rigorous review process, especially if the donation is endorsed by an appropriate state or local governmental agency.

(B) *Access.* To satisfy the requirement of scenic enjoyment by the general public, visual (rather than physical) access to or across the property by the general public is sufficient. Under the terms of an open space easement on scenic property, the entire property need not be visible to the public for a donation to qualify under this section, although the public benefit from the donation may be insufficient to qualify for a deduction if only a small portion of the property is visible to the public.

(iii) *Governmental conservation policy*—(A) *In general.* The requirement that the preservation of open space be pursuant to a clearly delineated Federal, state, or local governmental policy is intended to protect the types of property identified by representatives of the general public as worthy of preservation or conservation. A general declaration of conservation goals by a single official or legislative body is not sufficient. However, a governmental conservation policy need not be a certification program that identifies particular lots or small parcels of individually owned property. This requirement will be met by donations that further a specific, identified conservation project, such as the preservation of land within a state or local landmark district that is locally recognized as being significant to that district; the preservation of a wild or scenic river, the preservation of farmland pursuant to a state program for flood prevention and control; or the protection of the scenic, ecological, or historic character of land that is contiguous to, or an integral part of, the surroundings of existing recreation or conservation sites. For example, the donation of a perpetual conservation restriction to a qualified organization pursuant to a formal resolution or certification by a local governmental agency established under state law specifically identifying the subject property as worthy of protection for conservation purposes will meet the requirement of this paragraph. A program need not be funded to satisfy this requirement, but the program must involve a significant commitment by the government with respect to the conservation project. For example, a governmental program according preferential tax assessment or preferential zoning for certain property deemed worthy of protection for conservation purposes would constitute a significant commitment by the government.

(B) *Effect of acceptance by governmental agency.* Acceptance of an easement by an agency of the Federal Government or by an agency of a state or local government (or by a commission, authority, or similar body duly constituted by the state or local government and acting on behalf of the state or local government) tends to establish the requisite clearly delineated governmental policy, although such acceptance, without more, is not sufficient. The more rigorous the review process by the governmental agency, the more the acceptance of the easement tends to establish the requisite clearly delineated governmental policy. For example, in a state where the legislature has established an Environmental Trust to accept gifts to the state which meet certain conservation purposes and to submit the gifts to a review that requires the approval of the state's highest officials, acceptance of a gift by the Trust tends to establish the requisite clearly delineated governmental policy. However, if the Trust merely accepts such gifts without a review process, the requisite clearly delineated governmental policy is not established.

(C) *Access.* A limitation on public access to property subject to a donation under this paragraph (d)(4)(iii) shall not render the deduction nondeductible unless the conservation purpose of the donation would be undermined or frustrated without public access. For example, a donation pursuant to a governmental policy to protect the scenic character of land near a river requires visual access to the same extent as would a donation under paragraph (d)(4)(ii) of this section.

(iv) *Significant public benefit*—(A) Factors. All contributions made for the preservation of open space must yield a significant public benefit. Public benefit will be evaluated by considering all pertinent facts and circumstances germane to the contribution. Factors germane to the evaluation of public benefit from one contribution may be irrelevant in determining public benefit from another contribution. No single factor will necessarily be determinative. Among the factors to be considered are:

(*1*) The uniqueness of the property to the area;

(*2*) The intensity of land development in the vicinity of the property (both existing development and foreseeable trends of development);

(3) The consistency of the proposed open space use with public programs (whether Federal, state or local) for conservation in the region, including programs for outdoor recreation, irrigation or water supply protection, water quality maintenance or enhancement, flood prevention and control, erosion control, shoreline protection, and protection of land areas included in, or related to, a government approved master plan or land management area;

(4) The consistency of the proposed open space use with existing private conservation programs in the area, as evidenced by other land, protected by easement or fee ownership by organizations referred to in § 1.170A-14(c)(1), in close proximity to the property;

(5) The likelihood that development of the property would lead to or contribute to degradation of the scenic, natural, or historic character of the area;

(6) The opportunity for the general public to use the property or to appreciate its scenic values;

(7) The importance of the property in preserving a local or regional landscape or resource that attracts tourism or commerce to the area;

(8) The likelihood that the donee will acquire equally desirable and valuable substitute property or property rights;

(9) The cost to the donee of enforcing the terms of the conservation restriction;

(10) The population density in the area of the property; and

(11) The consistency of the proposed open space use with a legislatively mandated program identifying particular parcels of land for future protection.

(B) *Illustrations.* The preservation of an ordinary tract of land would not in and of itself yield a significant public benefit, but the preservation of ordinary land areas in conjunction with other factors that demonstrate significant public benefit or the preservation of a unique land area for public employment would yield a significant public benefit. For example, the preservation of a vacant downtown lot would not by itself yield a significant public benefit, but the preserva-

tion of the downtown lot as a public garden would, absent countervailing factors, yield a significant public benefit. The following are other examples of contributions which would, absent countervailing factors, yield a significant public benefit: The preservation of farmland pursuant to a state program for flood prevention and control; the preservation of a unique natural land formation for the enjoyment of the general public; the preservation of woodland along a public highway pursuant to a government program to preserve the appearance of the area so as to maintain the scenic view from the highway; and the preservation of a stretch of undeveloped property located between a public highway and the ocean in order to maintain the scenic ocean view from the highway.

(v) *Limitation.* A deduction will not be allowed for the preservation of open space under section 170(h)(4)(A)(iii), if the terms of the easement permit a degree of intrusion or future development that would interfere with the essential scenic quality of the land or with the governmental conservation policy that is being furthered by the donation. See § 1.170A-14(e)(2) for rules relating to inconsistent use.

(vi) *Relationship of requirements—* (A) *Clearly delineated governmental policy and significant public benefit.* Although the requirements of "clearly delineated governmental policy" and "significant public benefit" must be met independently, for purposes of this section the two requirements may also be related. The more specific the governmental policy with respect to the particular site to be protected, the more likely the governmental decision, by itself, will tend to establish the significant public benefit associated with the donation. For example, while a statute in State X permitting preferential assessment for farmland is, by definition, governmental policy, it is distinguishable from a state statute, accompanied by appropriations, naming the X River as a valuable resource and articulating the legislative policy that the X River and the relatively natural quality of its surrounding be protected. On these facts, an open space easement on farmland in

State X would have to demonstrate additional factors to establish "significant public benefit." The specificity of the legislative mandate to protect the X River, however, would by itself tend to establish the significant public benefit associated with an open space easement on land fronting the X River.

(B) *Scenic enjoyment and significant public benefit.* With respect to the relationship between the requirements of "scenic enjoyment" and "significant public benefit," since the degrees of scenic enjoyment offered by a variety of open space easements are subjective and not as easily delineated as are increasingly specific levels of governmental policy, the significant public benefit of preserving a scenic view must be independently established in all cases.

(C) *Donations may satisfy more than one test.* In some cases, open space easements may be both for scenic enjoyment and pursuant to a clearly delineated governmental policy. For example, the preservation of a particular scenic view identified as part of a scenic landscape inventory by a rigorous governmental review process will meet the tests of both paragraphs (d)(4)(i)(A) and (d)(4)(i)(B) of this section.

(5) *Historic preservation—*(i) *In general.* The donation of a qualified real property interest to preserve an historically important land area or a certified historic structure will meet the conservation purposes test of this section. When restrictions to preserve a building or land area within a registered historic district permit future development on the site, a deduction will be allowed under this section only if the terms of the restrictions require that such development conform with appropriate local, state, or Federal standards for construction or rehabilitation within the district. See also, § 1.170A-14(h)(3)(ii).

(ii) *Historically important land area.* The term "historically important land area" includes:

(A) An independently significant land area including any related historic resources (for example, an archaeological site or a Civil War battlefield with related monuments, bridges, cannons, or houses) that meets the National Register Criteria for Evaluation in 36 CFR 60.4 (Pub. L. 89-665, 80 Stat. 915);

(B) Any land area within a registered historic district including any buildings on the land area that can reasonably be considered as contributing to the significance of the district; and

(C) Any land area (including related historic resources) adjacent to a property listed individually in the National Register of Historic Places (but not within a registered historic district) in a case where the physical or environmental features of the land area contribute to the historic or cultural integrity of the property.

(iii) *Certified historic structure.* The term "certified historic structure," for purposes of this section, means any building, structure or land area which is—

(A) Listed in the National Register, or

(B) Located in a registered historic district (as defined in section 48(g)(3)(B)) and is certified by the Secretary of the Interior (pursuant to 36 CFR 67.4) to the Secretary of the Treasury as being of historic significance to the district.

A "structure" for purposes of this section means any structure, whether or not it is depreciable. Accordingly easements on private residences may qualify under this section. In addition, a structure would be considered to be a certified historic structure if it were certified either at the time the transfer was made or at the due date (including extensions) for filing the donor's return for the taxable year in which the contribution was made.

(iv) *Access.* (A) In order for a conservation contribution described in section 170(h)(4)(A)(iv) and this paragraph (d)(5) to be deductible, some visual public access to the donated property is required. In the case of an historically important land area, the entire property need not be visible to the public for a donation to qualify under this section. However, the public benefit from the donation may be insufficient to qualify for a deduction if only a small portion of the property is so visible. Where the historic land area or certified historic structure which is the subject of the donation is not visible from a public way (*e.g.*, the structure is hidden from view by a wall or shrubbery, the structure is too far from the public way, or interior characteristics and features of the structure are the subject of the easement), the terms of the easement must be such that the general public is given the opportunity on a regular basis to view the characteristics and features of the property which are preserved by the easement to the extent consistent with the nature and condition of the property.

(B) Factors to be considered in determining the type and amount of public access required under paragraph (d)(5)(iv)(A) of this section include the historical significance of the donated property, the nature of the features that are the subject of the easement, the remoteness or accessibility of the site of the donated property, the possibility of physical hazards to the public visiting the property (for example, an unoccupied structure in a dilapidated condition), the extent to which public access would be an unreasonable intrusion on any privacy interests of individuals living on the property, the degree to which public access would impair the preservation interests which are the subject of the donation, and the availability of opportunities for the public to view the property by means other than visits to the site.

(C) The amount of access afforded the public by the donation of an easement shall be determined with reference to the amount of access permitted by the terms of the easement which are established by the donor, rather than the amount of access actually provided by the donee organization. However, if the donor is aware of any facts indicating that the amount of access that the donee organization will provide is significantly less than the amount of access permitted under the terms of the easement, then the amount of access afforded the public shall be determined with reference to this lesser amount.

(v) *Examples.* The provisions of paragraph (d)(5)(iv) of this section may be illustrated by the following examples:

Example (1). A and his family live in a house in a certified historic district in the State of X. The entire house, including its interior, has architectural features representing classic Victorian period architecture. A donates an exterior and interior easement on the property to a qualified organization but continues to live in the house with his family. A's house is surrounded by a high stone wall which obscures the public's view of it from the street. Pursuant to the terms of the easement, the house may be opened to the public from 10:00 a.m. to 4:00 p.m. on one Sunday in May and one Sunday in November each year for house and garden tours. These tours are to be under the supervision of the donee and open to members of the general public upon payment of a small fee. In addition, under the terms of the easement, the donee organization is given the right to photograph the interior and exterior of the house and distribute such photographs to magazines, newsletters, or other publicly available publications. The terms of the easement also permit persons affiliated with educational organizations, professional architectural associations, and historical societies to make an appointment through the donee organization to study the property. The donor is not aware of any facts indicating that the public access to be provided by the donee organization will be significantly less than that permitted by the terms of the easement. The 2 opportunities for public visits per year, when combined with the ability of the general public to view the architectural characteristics and features that are the subject of the easement through photographs, the opportunity for scholarly study of the property, and the fact that the house is used as an occupied residence, will enable the donation to satisfy the requirement of public access.

Example (2). B owns an unoccupied farmhouse built in the 1840's and located on a property that is adjacent to a Civil War battlefield. During the Civil War the farmhouse was used as quarters for Union troops. The battlefield is visited year round by the general public. The condition of the farmhouse is such that the safety of visitors will not be jeopardized and opening it to the public will not result in significant deterioration. The farmhouse is not visible from the battlefield or any public way. It is accessible only by way of a private road owned by B. B donates a conservation easement on the farmhouse to a qualified organization. The terms of the easement provide that the donee organization may open the property (via B's road) to the general public on four weekends each year from 8:30 a.m. to 4:00

p.m. The donation does not meet the public access requirement because the farmhouse is safe, unoccupied, and easily accessible to the general public who have come to the site to visit Civil War historic land areas (and related resources), but will only be open to the public on four weekends each year. However, the donation would meet the public access requirement if the terms of the easement permitted the donee organization to open the property to the public every other weekend during the year and the donor is not aware of any facts indicating that the donee organization will provide significantly less access than that permitted.

(e) *Exclusively for conservation purposes.* (1) *In general.* To meet the requirements of this section, a donation must be exclusively for conservation purposes. See paragraphs (c)(1) and (g)(1) through (g)(6)(ii) of this section. A deduction will not be denied under this section when incidental benefit inures to the donor merely as a result of conservation restrictions limiting the uses to which the donor's property may be put.

(2) *Inconsistent use.* Except as provided in paragraph (e)(4) of this section, a deduction will not be allowed if the contribution would accomplish one of the enumerated conservation purposes but would permit destruction of other significant conservation interests. For example, the preservation of farmland pursuant to a State program for flood prevention and control would not qualify under paragraph (d)(4) of this section if under the terms of the contribution a significant naturally occurring ecosystem could be injured or destroyed by the use of pesticides in the operation of the farm. However, this requirement is not intended to prohibit uses of the property, such as selective timber harvesting or selective farming if, under the circumstances, those uses do not impair significant conservation interests.

(3) *Inconsistent use permitted.* A use that is destructive of conservation interests will be permitted only if such use is necessary for the protection of the conservation interests that are the subject of the contribution. For example, a deduction for the donation of an easement to preserve an archaeological site that is listed on the National Register of Historic Places will not be disallowed if site excavation consistent

with sound archaeological practices may impair a scenic view of which the land is a part. A donor may continue a pre-existing use of the property that does not conflict with the conservation purposes of the gift.

(f) *Examples.* The provisions of this section relating to conservation purposes may be illustrated by the following examples.

Example (1). State S contains many large tract forests that are desirable recreation and scenic areas for the general public. The forests' scenic values attract millions of people to the State. However, due to the increasing intensity of land development in State S, the continued existence of forestland parcels greater than 45 acres is threatened. J grants a perpetual easement on a 100-acre parcel of forestland that is part of one of the State's scenic areas to a qualifying organization. The easement imposes restrictions on the use of the parcel for the purpose of maintaining its scenic values. The restrictions include a requirement that the parcel be maintained forever as open space devoted exclusively to conservation purposes and wildlife protection, and that there be no commercial, industrial, residential, or other development use of such parcel. The law of State S recognizes a limited public right to enter private land, particularly for recreational pursuits, unless such land is posted or the landowner objects. The easement specifically restricts the landowner from posting the parcel, or from objecting, thereby maintaining public access to the parcel according to the custom of the State. J's parcel provides the opportunity for the public to enjoy the use of the property and appreciate its scenic values. Accordingly, J's donation qualifies for a deduction under this section.

Example (2). A qualified conservation organization owns Greenacre in fee as a nature preserve. Greenacre contains a high quality example of a tall grass prairie ecosystem. Farmacre, an operating farm, adjoins Greenacre and is a compatible buffer to the nature preserve. Conversion of Farmacre to a more intense use, such as a housing development, would adversely affect the continued use of Greenacre as a nature preserve because of human traffic generated by the development. The owner of Farmacre donates an easement preventing any future development on Farmacre to the qualified conservation organization for conservation purposes. Normal agricultural uses will be allowed on Farmacre. Accordingly, the donation qualifies for a deduction under this section.

Example (3). H owns Greenacre, a 900-acre parcel of woodland, rolling pasture, and orchards on the crest of a mountain. All of Greenacre is clearly visible from a nearby national park. Because of the strict enforcement of an applicable zoning plan, the highest and best use of Greenacre is as a subdivision of 40-acre tracts. H wishes to donate a scenic easement on Greenacre to a qualifying conservation organization, but H would like to reserve the right to subdivide Greenacre into 90-acre parcels with no more than one single-family home allowable on each parcel. Random building on the property, even as little as one home for each 90 acres, would destroy the scenic character of the view. Accordingly, no deduction would be allowable under this section.

Example (4). Assume the same facts as in *example (3),* except that not all of Greenacre is visible from the park and the deed of easement allows for limited cluster development of no more than five nine-acre clusters (with four houses on each cluster) located in areas generally not visible from the national park and subject to site and building plan approval by the donee organization in order to preserve the scenic view from the park. The donor and the donee have already identified sites where limited cluster development would not be visible from the park or would not impair the view. Owners of homes in the clusters will not have any rights with respect to the surrounding Greenacre property that are not also available to the general public. Accordingly, the donation qualifies for a deduction under this section.

Example (5). In order to protect State S's declining open space that is suited for agricultural use from increasing development pressure that has led to a marked decline in such open space, the Legislature of State S passed a statute authorizing the purchase of "agricultural land development rights" on open acreage. Agricultural land development rights allow the State to place agricultural preservation restrictions on land designated as worthy of protection in order to preserve open space and farm resources. Agricultural preservation restrictions prohibit or limit construction or placement of buildings except those used for agricultural purposes or dwellings used for family living by the farmer and his family and employees; removal of mineral substances in any manner that adversely affects the land's agricultural potential; or other uses detrimental to retention of the land for agricultural use. Money has been appropriated for this program and some landowners have in fact sold their "agricultural land development rights" to State S. K owns and operates a small dairy farm in State S located in an area designated by the Legislature as worthy of protection. K desires to preserve his farm for agricultural purposes in perpetuity. Rather than selling the development rights to State S, K grants to a qualified or-

ganization an agricultural preservation restriction on his property in the form of a conservation easement. K reserves to himself, his heirs and assigns the right to manage the farm consistent with sound agricultural and management practices. The preservation of K's land is pursuant to a clearly delineated governmental policy of preserving open space available for agricultural use, and will yield a significant public benefi⁺ by preserving open space against increasing development pressures.

(g) *Enforceable in perpetuity.*—(1) *In general.* In the case of any donation under this section, any interest in the property retained by the donor (and the donor's successors in interest) must be subject to legally enforceable restrictions (for example, by recordation in the land records of the jurisdiction in which the property is located) that will prevent uses of the retained interest inconsistent with the conservation purposes of the donation. In the case of a contribution of a remainder interest, the contribution will not qualify if the tenants, whether they are tenants for life or a term of years, can use the property in a manner that diminishes the conservation values which are intended to be protected by the contribution.

(2) *Protection of a conservation purpose in case of donation of property subject to a mortgage.* In the case of conservation contributions made after February 13, 1986, no deducion will be permitted under this section for an interest in property which is subject to a mortgage unless the mortgagee subordinates its rights in the property to the right of the qualified organization to enforce the conservation purposes of the gift in perpetuity. For conservation contributions made prior to February 14, 1986, the requirement of section 170 (h)(5)(A) is satisfied in the case of mortgaged property (with respect to which the mortgagee has not subordinated its rights) only if the donor can demonstrate that the conservation purpose is protected in perpetuity without subordination of the mortgagee's rights.

(3) *Remote future event.* A deduction shall not be disallowed under section 170(f)(3)(B)(iii) and this section merely because the interest which passes to, or is vested in, the donee or-

ganization may be defeated by the performance of some act or the happening of some event, if on the date of the gift it appears that the possibility that such act or event will occur is so remote as to be negligible. See paragraph (e) of § 1.170A-1. For example, a state's statutory requirement that use restrictions must be rerecorded every 30 years to remain enforceable shall not, by itself, render an easement nonperpetual.

(4) *Retention of qualified mineral interest*—(i) *In general.* Except as otherwise provided in paragraph (g)(4)(ii) of this section, the requirements of this section are not met and no deduction shall be allowed in the case of a contribution of any interest when there is a retention by any person of a qualified mineral interest (as defined in paragraph (b)(1)(i) of this section) if at any time there may be extractions or removal of minerals by any surface mining method. Moreover, in the case of a qualified mineral interest gift, the requirement that the conservation purposes be protected in perpetuity is not satisfied if any method of mining that is inconsistent with the particular conservation purposes of a contribution is permitted at any time. See also § 1.170A-14(e)(2). However, a deduction under this section will not be denied in the case of certain methods of mining that may have limited, localized impact on the real property but that are not irremediably destructive of significant conservation interests. For example, a deduction will not be denied in a case where production facilities are concealed or compatible with existing topography and landscape and when surface alteration is to be restored to its original state.

(ii) *Exception for qualified conservation contributions after July 1984.* (A) A contribution made after July 18, 1984, of a qualified real property interest described in section 170(h)(2)(A) shall not be disqualified under the first sentence of paragraph (g)(4)(i) of this section if the following requirements are satisfied.

(1) The ownership of the surface estate and mineral interest were separated before June 13, 1976, and remain so separated up to and including the time of the contribution.

(2) The present owner of the mineral interest is not a person whose relationship to the owner of the surface estate is described at the time of the contribution in section 267(b) or section 707(b), and

(3) The probability of extraction or removal of minerals by any surface mining method is so remote as to be negligible.

Whether the probability of extraction or removal of minerals by surface mining is so remote as to be negligible is a question of fact and is to be made on a case by case basis. Relevant factors to be considered in determining if the probability of extraction or removal of minerals by surface mining is so remote as to be negligible include: Geological, geophysical or economic data showing the absence of mineral reserves on the property, or the lack of commercial feasibility at the time of the contribution of surface mining the mineral interest.

(B) If the ownership of the surface estate and mineral interest first became separated after June 12, 1976, no deduction is permitted for a contribution under this section unless surface mining on the property is completely prohibited.

(iii) *Examples.* The provisions of paragraph (g)(4)(i) and (ii) of this section may be illustrated by the following examples:

Example. (1) K owns 5,000 acres of bottomland hardwood property along a major watershed system in the southern part of the United States. Agencies within the Department of the Interior have determined that southern bottomland hardwoods are a rapidly diminishing resource and a critical ecosystem in the south because of the intense pressure to cut the trees and convert the land to agricultural use. These agencies have further determined (and have indicated in correspondence with K) that bottomland hardwoods provide a superb habitat for numerous species and play an important role in controlling floods and purifying rivers. K donates to a qualified organization his entire interest in this property other than his interest in the gas and oil deposits that have been identified under K's property. K covenants and can ensure that, although drilling for gas and oil on the property may have some temporary localized impact on the real property, the drilling will not interfere with the overall conservation purpose of the gift, which is to protect the unique bottomland hardwood ecosystem. Accordingly, the donation qualifies for a deduction under this section.

Example (*2*). Assume the same facts as in example (1), except that in 1979, K sells the mineral interest to A, an unrelated person, in an arm's-length transaction, subject to a recorded prohibition on the removal of any minerals by any surface mining method and a recorded prohibition against any mining technique that will harm the bottomland hardwood ecosystem. After the sale to A, K donates a qualified real property interest to a qualified organization to protect the bottomland hardwood ecosystem. Since at the time of the transfer, surface mining and any mining technique that will harm the bottomland hardwood ecosystem are completely prohibited, the donation qualifies for a deduction under this section.

(5) *Protection of conservation purpose where taxpayer reserves certain rights.* (i) *Documentation.* In the case of a donation made after February 13, 1986, of any qualified real property interest when the donor reserves rights the exercise of which may impair the conservation interests associated with the property, for a deduction to be allowable under this section the donor must make available to the donee, prior to the time the donation is made, documentation sufficient to establish the condition of the property at the time of the gift. Such documentation is designed to protect the conservation interests associated with the property, which although protected in perpetuity by the easement, could be adversely affected by the exercise of the reserved rights. Such documentation may include:

(A) The appropriate survey maps from the United States Geological Survey, showing the property line and other contiguous or nearby protected areas;

(B) A map of the area drawn to scale showing all existing man-made improvements or incursions (such as roads, buildings, fences, or gravel pits), vegetation and identification of flora and fauna (including, for example, rare species locations, animal breeding and roosting areas, and migration routes), land use history (including present uses and recent past disturbances), and distinct natural features (such as large trees and aquatic areas);

(C) An aerial photograph of the property at an appropriate scale taken as close as possible to the date the donation is made; and

(D) On-site photographs taken at appropriate locations on the property. If the terms of the donation contain restrictions with regard to a particular natural resource to be protected, such as water quality or air quality, the condition of the resource at or near the time of the gift must be established. The documentation, including the maps and photographs, must be accompanied by a statement signed by the donor and a representative of the donee clearly referencing the documentation and in substance saying "This natural resources inventory is an accurate representation of [the protected property] at the time of the transfer.".

(ii) *Donee's right to inspection and legal remedies.* In the case of any donation referred to in paragraph (g)(5)(i) of this section, the donor must agree to notify the donee, in writing, before exercising any reserved right, *e.g.* the right to extract certain minerals which may have an adverse impact on the conservation interests associated with the qualified real property interest. The terms of the donation must provide a right of the donee to enter the property at reasonable times for the purpose of inspecting the property to determine if there is compliance with the terms of the donation. Additionally, the terms of the donation must provide a right of the donee to enforce the conservation restrictions by appropriate legal proceedings, including but not limited to, the right to require the restoration of the property to its condition at the time of the donation.

(6) *Extinguishment.* (i) In general. If a subsequent unexpected change in the conditions surrounding the property that is the subject of a donation under this paragraph can make impossible or impractical the continued use of the property for conservation purposes, the conservation purpose can nonetheless be treated as protected in perpetuity if the restrictions are extinguished by judicial proceeding and all of the donee's proceeds (determined under paragraph (g)(6)(ii) of this section) from a subsequent sale or exchange of the property are used by

the donee organization in a manner consistent with the conservation purposes of the original contribution.

(ii) *Proceeds.* In case of a donation made after February 13, 1986, for a deduction to be allowed under this section, at the time of the gift the donor must agree that the donation of the perpetual conservation restriction gives rise to a property right, immediately vested in the donee organization, with a fair market value that is at least equal to the proportionate value that the perpetual conservation restriction at the time of the gift, bears to the value of the property as a whole at that time. See § 1.170A-14(h)(3)(iii) relating to the allocation of basis. For purposes of this paragraph (g)(6)(ii), that proportionate value of the donee's property rights shall remain constant. Accordingly, when a change in conditions give rise to the extinguishment of a perpetual conservation restriction under paragraph (g)(6)(i) of this section, the donee organization, on a subsequent sale, exchange, or involuntary conversion of the subject property, must be entitled to a portion of the proceeds at least equal to that proportionate value of the perpetual conservation restriction, unless state law provides that the donor is entitled to the full proceeds from the conversion without regard to the terms of the prior perpetual conservation restriction.

(h) *Valuation*—(1) *Entire interest of donor other than qualified mineral interest.* The value of the contribution under section 170 in the case of a contribution of a taxpayer's entire interest in property other than a qualified mineral interest is the fair market value of the surface rights in the property contributed. The value of the contribution shall be computed without regard to the mineral rights. See paragraph (h)(4), *example (1)*, of this section.

(2) *Remainder interest in real property.* In the case of a contribution of any remainder interest in real property, section 170(f)(4) provides that in determining the value of such interest for purposes of section 170, depreciation and depletion of such property shall be taken into account. See § 1.170A-12. In the case of the contri-

bution of a remainder interest for conservation purposes, the current fair market value of the property (against which the limitations of § 1.170A-12 are applied) must take into account any pre-existing or contemporaneously recorded rights limiting, for conservation purposes, the use to which the subject property may be put.

(3) *Perpetual conservation restriction*—(i) *In general.* The value of the contribution under section 170 in the case of a charitable contribution of a perpetual conservation restriction is the fair market value of the perpetual conservation restriction at the time of the contribution. See § 1.170A-7(c). If there is a substantial record of sales of easements comparable to the donated easement (such as purchases pursuant to a governmental program), the fair market value of the donated easement is based on the sales prices of such comparable easements. If no substantial record of market-place sales is available to use as a meaningful or valid comparison, as a general rule (but not necessarily in all cases) the fair market value of a perpetual conservation restriction is equal to the difference between the fair market value of the property it encumbers before the granting of the restriction and the fair market value of the encumbered property after the granting of the restriction. The amount of the deduction in the case of a charitable contribution of a perpetual conservation restriction covering a portion of the contiguous property owned by a donor and the donor's family (as defined in section 267(c)(4)) is the difference between the fair market value of the entire contiguous parcel of property before and after the granting of the restriction. If the granting of a perpetual conservation restriction after January 14, 1986, has the effect of increasing the value of any other property owned by the donor or a related person, the amount of the deduction for the conservation contribution shall be reduced by the amount of the increase in the value of the other property, whether or not such property is contiguous. If, as a result of the donation of a perpetual conservation restriction, the donor or a related person receives, or can reasonably expect to

receive, financial or economic benefits that are greater than those that will inure to the general public from the transfer, no deduction is allowable under this section. However, if the donor or a related person receives, or can reasonably expect to receive, a financial or economic benefit that is substantial, but it is clearly shown that the benefit is less than the amount of the transfer, then a deduction under this section is allowable for the excess of the amount transferred over the amount of the financial or economic benefit received or reasonably expected to be received by the donor or the related person. For purposes of this paragraph (h)(3)((i), related person shall have the same meaning as in either section 267(b) or section 707(b). (See example (10) of paragraph (h)(4) of this section.)

(ii) *Fair market value of property before and after restriction.* If before and after valuation is used, the fair market value of the property before contribution of the conservation restriction must take into account not only the current use of the property but also an objective assessment of how immediate or remote the likelihood is that the property, absent the restriction, would in fact be developed, as well as any effect from zoning, conservation, or historic preservation laws that already restrict the property's potential highest and best use. Further, there may be instances where the grant of a conservation restriction may have no material effect on the value of the property or may in fact serve to enhance, rather than reduce, the value of property. In such instances no deduction would be allowable. In the case of a conservation restriction that allows for any development, however limited, on the property to be protected, the fair maket value of the property after contribution of the restriction must take into account the effect of the development. In the case of a conservation easement such as an easement on a certified historic structure, the fair market value of the property after contribution of the restriction must take into account the amount of access permitted by the terms of the easement. Additionally, if before and after valuation is used, an appraisal of the property after contribution of the restriction must take into account the effect of restrictions that will result in a reduction of the potential fair market value represented by highest and best use but will, nevertheless, permit uses of the property that will increase its fair market value above that represented by the property's current use. The value of a perpetual conservation restriction shall not be reduced by reason of the existence of restrictions on transfer designed solely to ensure that the conservation restriction will be dedicated to conservation purposes. See § 1.170A-14 (c)(3).

(iii) *Allocation of basis.* In the case of the donation of a qualified real property interest for conservation purposes, the basis of the property retained by the donor must be adjusted by the elimination of that part of the total basis of the property that is properly allocable to the qualified real property interest granted. The amount of the basis that is allocable to the qualified real property interest shall bear the same ratio to the total basis of the property as the fair market value of the qualified real property interest bears to the fair market value of the property before the granting of the qualified real property interest. When a taxpayer donates to a qualifying conservation organization an easement on a structure with respect to which deductions are taken for depreciation, the reduction required by this paragraph (h)(3)(ii) in the basis of the property retained by the taxpayer must be allocated between the structure and the underlying land.

(4) *Examples.* The provisions of this section may be illustrated by the following examples. In examples illustrating the value or deductibility of donations, the applicable restrictions and limitations of § 1.170A-4, with respect to reduction in amount of charitable contributions of certain appreciated property, and § 1.170A-8, with respect to limitations on charitable deductions by individuals. must also be taken into account.

Example (1). A owns Goldacre, a property adjacent to a state park. A wants to donate Goldacre to the state to be used as part of the park, but A wants to reserve a qualified mineral interest in the property, to exploit currently and to devise at death. The fair market value of the surface rights in Goldacre is $200,000 and the fair market value of the mineral rights in $100.000. In order to ensure that the quality of the park will not be degraded, restrictions must be imposed on the right to extract the minerals that reduce the fair market value of the mineral rights to $80,000. Under this section, the value of the contribution is $200,000 (the value of the surface rights).

Example (2). In 1984 B, who is 62, donates a remainder interest in Greenacre to a qualifying organization for conservation purposes. Greenacre is a tract of 200 acres of undeveloped woodland that is valued at $200,000 at its highest and best use. Under § 1.170A-12(b), the value of a remainder interest in real property following one life is determined under § 25.2512-5 of the Gift Tax Regulations. (See § 25.2512-9 with respect to the valuation of annuities, life estates, terms for years, remainders, and reversions transferred after December 31, 1970 and before December 1, 1983. With respect to the valuation of annuities, life estates, terms for years, remainders, and reversions transferred before January 1, 1971, see T.D. 6334, 23 FR 8904, November 15, 1958, as amended by T.D. 7077, 35 FR 18464, December 4, 1970). Accordingly, the value of the remainder interest, and thus the amount eligible for an income tax deduction under section 170(f), is $55,996 ($200,000 × .27998).

Example (3). Assume the same facts as in example (2), except that Greenacre is B's 200-acre estate with a home built during the colonial period. Some of the acreage around the home is cleared; the balance of Greenacre, except for access roads, is wooded and undeveloped. See section 170(f)(3)(B)(i). However, B would like Greenacre to be maintained in its current state after his death, so he donates a remainder interest in Greenacre to a qualifying organization for conservation purposes pursuant to section 170 (f)(3)(B)(iii) and (h)(2)(B). At the time of the gift the land has a value of $200,000 and the house has a value of $100,000. The value of the remainder interest, and thus the amount eligible for an income tax deduction under section 170(f), is computed pursuant to § 1.170A-12. See § 1.170A-12(b)(3).

Example (4). Assume the same facts as in example (2), except that at age 62 instead of donating a remainder interest B donates an easement in Greenacre to a qualifying organization for conservation purposes. The fair market value of Greenacre after the donation is reduced to $110,000. Accordingly, the value of the easement, and thus the amount eligible for a deduction under section 170(f), is $90,000 ($200,000 less $110,000).

Example (5). Assume the same facts as in example (4), and assume that three years later, at age 65, B decides to donate a remainder interest in Greenacre to a qualifying organization for conservation purposes. Increasing real estate values in the area have raised the fair market value of Greenacre (subject to the easement) to $130,000. Accordingly, the value of the remainder interest, and thus the amount eligible for a deduction under section 170(f), is $41,639 ($130,000 × .32030).

Example (6). Assume the same facts as in example (2), except that at the time of the donation of a remainder interest in Greenacre, B also donates an easement to a different qualifying organization for conservation purposes. Based on all the facts and circumstances, the value of the easement is determined to be $100,000. Therefore, the value of the property after the easement is $100,000 and the value of the remainder interest, and thus the amount eligible for deduction under section 170(f), is $27,998 ($100,000 × .27998).

Example (7). C owns Greenacre, a 200-acre estate containing a house built during the colonial period. At its highest and best use, for home development, the fair market value of Greenacre is $300,000. C donates an easement (to maintain the house and Green acre in their current state) to a qualifying organization for conservation purposes. The fair market value of Greenacre after the donation is reduced to $125,000. Accordingly, the value of the easement and the amount eligible for a deduction under section 170(f) is $175.000 ($300,000 less $125,000).

Example (8). Assume the same facts as in example (7) and assume that three years later, C decides to donate a remainder interest in Greenacre to a qualifying organization for conservation purposes. Increasing real estate values in the area have raised the fair market value of Greenacre to $180.000. Assume that because of the perpetual easement prohibiting any development of the land, the value of the house is $120,000 and the value of the land is $60,000. The value of the remainder interest, and thus the amount eligible for an income tax deduction under section 170(f), is computed pursuant to § 1.170A-12. See § 1.170A-12(b)(3).

Example (9). D owns property with a basis of $20,000 and a fair market value of $80,000. D donates to a qualifying organization an easement for conservation purposes that is determined under this section to have a fair market value of $60,000. The amount of basis allocable to the easement is $15,000 ($60,000/$80,000=$15,000/$20,000). Accordingly, the basis of the property is reduced to $5,000 ($20,000 minus $15,000).

Example (10). E owns 10 one-acre lots that are currently woods and parkland. The fair market value of each of E's lots is $15,000 and the basis of each lot is $3,000. E grants to the county a perpetual easement for conservation purposes to use and maintain eight of the acres as a public park and to restrict any future development on those eight acres. As a result of the restrictions, the value of the eight acres is reduced to $1,000 an acre. However, by perpetually restricting development on this portion of the land, E has ensured that the two remaining acres will always be bordered by parkland, thus increasing their fair market value to $22,500 each. If the eight acres represented all of E's land, the fair market value of the easement would be $112,000, an amount equal to the fair market value of the land before the granting of the easement ($8 \times $15,000 = $120,000$) minus the fair market value of the encumbered land after the granting of the easement ($8 \times $1,000 = $8,000$). However, because the easement only covered a portion of the taxpayer's contiguous land, the amount of the deduction under section 170 is reduced to $97,000 ($150,000–$53,000), that is, the difference between the fair market value of the entire tract of land before ($150,000) and after (($8 \times $1,000$)+($2 \times $22,500$)) the granting of the easement.

Example (11). Assume the same facts as in *example (10).* Since the easement covers a portion of E's land, only the basis of that portion is adjusted. Therefore, the amount of basis allocable to the easement is $22,400 (($8 \times $3,000$) \times ($112,000/$120,000$)). Accordingly, the basis of the eight acres encumbered by the easement is reduced to $1,600 ($24,000–$22,400), or $200 for each acre. The basis of the two remaining acres is not affected by the donation.

Example (12). F owns and uses as professional offices a two-story building that lies within a registered historic district. F's building is an outstanding example of period architecture with a fair market value of $125,000. Restricted to its current use, which is the highest and best use of the property without making changes to the facade, the building and lot would have a fair market value of $100,000, of which $80,000 would be allocable to the building and $20,000 woud be allocable to the lot. F's basis in the property is $50,000, of which $40,000 is allocable to the building and $10,000 is allocable to the lot. F's neighborhood is a mix of residential and commercial uses, and it is possible that F (or another owner) could enlarge the building for more extensive commercial use, which is its highest and best use. However, this would require changes to the facade. F would like to donate to a qualifying preservation organization an easement restricting any changes to the facade and promising to maintain the facade in perpetuity. The donation would qualify for a deduction under this section.

The fair market value of the easement is $25,000 (the fair market value of the property before the easement, $125,000, minus the fair market value of the property after the easement, $100,000). Pursuant to § 1.170A–14(h)(3)(iii), the basis allocable to the easement is $10,000 and the basis of the underlying property (building and lot) is reduced to $40,000.

(i) *Substantiation requirement.* If a taxpayer makes a qualified conservation contribution and claims a deduction, the taxpayer must maintain written records of the fair market value of the underlying property before and after the donation and the conservation purpose furthered by the donation and such information shall be stated in the taxpayer's income tax return if required by the return or its instructions. See also § 1.170A–13T(c) (relating to substantiation requirements for deductions in excess of $5,000 for charitable contributions made after 1984), and section 6659 (relating to additions to tax in the case of valuation overstatements).

(j) *Effective date.* Except as otherwise provided in § 1.170A–14(g)(4)(ii), this section applies only to contributions made on or after December 18, 1980.

[T.D. 8069, 51 FR 1499, Jan. 14, 1986; 51 FR 5322, Feb. 13, 1986; 51 FR 6219, Feb. 21, 1986]

§ 1.171–1   Amortizable bond premium.

(a) *In general.* Under section 171, bond premium is amortizable by the owner of the bond (as defined in § 1.171–4) in accordance with subparagraph (1) or (2) of this paragraph as follows:

(1) Amortization of bond premium is mandatory with respect to:

(i) Fully tax-exempt bonds (the interest on which is excludable from gross income), whether the owner is a corporation, individual, or other taxpayer; and

(ii) Partially tax-exempt bonds owned by a corporation.

(2) Amortization of bond premium is optional, at the election of the taxpayer, with respect to:

(i) Fully taxable bonds, whether the owner is a corporation, individual, or other taxpayer; and

Further Suggested Reading

American Law Institute. *Historic Preservation Law and Tax Planning for Old and Historic Buildings.* Study materials for American Law Institute-American Bar Association/National Trust for Historic Preservation co-sponsored conferences. Philadelphia, Pa.: American Law Institute, 1985, 1986, 1987.

Barrett, Thomas S. and Putnam Livermore for the Trust for Public Land. *The Conservation Easement in California.* Covelo, Calif.: Island Press, 1983.

Bates, Sarah M. and Russell L. Brenneman, eds. *Land Saving Action.* Covelo, Calif.: Island Press, 1984.

Boasberg, Tersh, Thomas A. Coughlin, and Julia H. Miller. *Historic Preservation Law and Taxation.* 3 vols. New York: Matthew Bender and Co., 1986.

Brenneman, Russell L. *Private Approaches to the Preservation of Open Land.* New London, Conn.: Conservation and Research Foundation, 1967.

Coughlin, Robert E. and John C. Keene, *et al. The Protection of Agricultural Land: A Reference Guidebook for State and Local Governments.* Washington, D.C.: National Agricultural Lands Study, 1981.

Duerksen, Christopher, ed. *A Handbook on Historic Preservation Law.* Washington, D.C.: The Conservation Foundation and the National Center for Preservation Law, 1983.

Fisher, Charles E., William G. MacRostie, and Christopher E. Sowick, compilers. *Directory of Historic Preservation Easement Organizations.* Washington, D.C.: Technical Preservation Services Division, National Park Service, 1981.

Hoose, Phillip M. *Building an Ark: Tools for the Preservation of Natural Diversity through Land Protection.* Covelo, Calif.: Island Press, 1981.

Land Trust Exchange. *Directory of Local and Regional Land Conservation Organizations.* Alexandria, Va.: Land Trust Exchange, 1985.

Lemire, Robert A. *Creative Land Development: Bridge to the Future.* Boston: Houghton Mifflin Company, 1979.

Listokin, David. *Landmarks Preservation and the Property Tax.* New York: Center for Urban Policy Research, Rutgers University, and the New York Landmarks Conservancy, 1982.

Meder-Montgomery, Marilyn. *Preservation Easements: A Legal Mechanism for Protecting Cultural Resources*. Denver: The Colorado Historical Society, 1984.

Montana Land Reliance and Land Trust Exchange. *Private Options: Tools and Concepts for Land Conservation*. Covelo, Calif.: Island Press, 1982.

National Trust for Historic Preservation and Land Trust Exchange. *Appraising Easements: Guidelines for the Valuation of Historic Preservation and Land Conservation Easements*. Washington, D.C.: National Trust for Historic Preservation, 1984.

Reynolds, Judith. *Historic Properties: Preservation and the Valuation Process*. Chicago: American Institute of Real Estate Appraisers, 1982.

Roddewig, Richard J. and Jeffrey Jahns. *Preservation Easements in Illinois*. Chicago, Ill.: Landmarks Preservation Council of Illinois and The Nature Conservancy, 1981.

Small, Stephen J. *The Federal Tax Law of Conservation Easements*. Alexandria, Va.: Land Trust Exchange, 1986.

Whyte, William H. *The Last Landscape*. Garden City, N.Y.: Doubleday and Company, Inc., 1968.

_____ . *Securing Open Space for Urban America: Conservation Easements*. Washington, D.C.: Urban Land Institute, 1959.

Useful Contacts

NONPROFIT LAND CONSERVATION ORGANIZATIONS

American Farmland Trust
1920 N St., NW, Suite 400
Washington, DC 20036
(202) 659-5170

American Rivers
801 Pennsylvania Ave., SE, Suite 303
Washington, DC 20003
(202) 547-6900

Land Trust Exchange
1017 Duke St.
Alexandria, VA 22314
(703) 683-7778

National Audubon Society
950 Third Ave.
New York, NY 10022
(212) 832-3200
(call for field office or chapter near you)

National Trust for Historic Preservation
1785 Massachusetts Ave., NW
Washington, DC 20036
(202) 673-4000
(call for regional office near you)

Rails-to-Trails Conservancy
1325 Massachusetts Ave., NW, Suite 400
Washington, DC 20005
(202) 783-0980

The Nature Conservancy
1800 N. Kent St., Suite 800
Arlington, VA 22209
(703) 841-5300
(call for regional or field office near you)

Trust for Public Land
116 New Montgomery St., 4th floor
San Francisco, CA 94105
(415) 495-4014

Southeast Office
Trust for Public Land
322 Beard St.
Tallahassee, FL 32303
(904) 222-9280

New England Office
Trust for Public Land
33 Harrison Ave.
Boston, MA 02111
(617) 451-7208

Southwest Office
Trust for Public Land
P.O. Box 2383
Santa Fe, NM 87504
(505) 988-5922

Northeast Office
Trust for Public Land
666 Broadway
New York, NY 10012
(212) 677-7171

Midwest Office
Trust for Public Land
The Old Arcade
401 Euclid, Room 608
Cleveland, OH 44114
(216) 241-7630

Northwest Office
Trust for Public Land
Smith Tower, Suite 2123
506 2nd Ave.
Seattle, WA 98104
(206) 587-2447

FEDERAL CONTACTS

Bureau of Land Management
U.S. Department of the Interior
Washington, DC 20240
(202) 343-5717

Forest Service
P.O. Box 2417
Washington, DC 20013
(202) 447-3957

National Fish and Wildlife Foundation
18th and C Sts., NW, Room 2626
Washington, DC 20240
(202) 343-1040

National Park Service
Interior Building
P.O. Box 37127
Washington, DC 20013-7127
(202) 343-6843

Soil Conservation Service
P.O. Box 2890
Washington, DC 20013
(202) 447-4543

U.S. Fish and Wildlife Service
U.S. Department of the Interior
Washington, DC 20240
(202) 343-4717

U.S. Geological Survey
National Center
Reston, VA 22092
(703) 860-7000

Contributors

Thomas S. Barrett, a lawyer, is secretary of the Public Resource Foundation in Washington, D.C. His legal writings include *The Conservation Easement in California* (coauthored with Putnam Livermore for the Trust for Public Land) and *Self-Initiation: The Hardrock Miner's Right*, an essay on the 1872 mining law.

Russell Brenneman is a partner in the Hartford, Connecticut, law firm of Murtha, Cullina, Richter & Pinney, where he chairs the Environmental Practice Group. He is the author of *Private Approaches to the Preservation of Open Land* and articles on land conservation, conservation easements, and historic preservation and was coeditor of *Land Saving Action*.

Kingsbury Browne is a partner in the Boston law firm of Hill & Barlow and a tax specialist by training and practice. His specialty is estate planning for family lands. Mr. Browne is general counsel of the Land Trust Exchange and chairman and editor of the *Conservation Tax Program,* a subscription service covering federal tax developments in land conservation, offered through the Exchange. He also serves as a member of the Advisory Council of the Trust for Public Land.

Janet Diehl is a project manager with the Trust for Public Land, where she has worked for five years setting up new land trusts and conducting joint land protection ventures with established land trusts in the Pacific states. She previously worked as a newspaper reporter.

William R. Ginsberg is a professor at Hofstra University School of Law in Hempstead, New York, and counsel to the New York law firm of Sive, Paget & Riesel. He serves as legal advisor to the northeast regional office of the Trust for Public Land and is author of "Conservation Easements" in *Powell on Real Property*, published by Matthew Bender and Co., Inc.

William T. Hutton is a professor of law at the University of California Hastings School of Law and a member of the San Francisco law firm of Howard, Rice, Nemerovski, Canady, Robertson & Falk. He has served as counsel to numerous conservation organizations over the past 15 years and is a trustee of the Land Trust Exchange's *Conservation Tax Program*.

Cheryl A. Inghram is a real estate analyst with Pannell Kerr Forster in Chicago. Ms. Inghram has more than three years experience working on preservation and conservation easement assignments. She previously worked as a field representative with the National Trust for Historic Preservation.

Stefan Nagel is assistant general counsel for the National Trust for Historic Preservation, where he provides legal services for the Trust's commercial and historic property real estate transactions. Mr. Nagel has extensive experience in real estate and nonprofit law in the United States and Europe. Prior to joining the National Trust, he was national staff attorney for The Nature Conservancy.

Richard J. Roddewig is a real estate consultant and attorney in the Chicago office of Pannell Kerr Forster. Mr. Roddewig also serves as vice-chairman of the Land Use, Planning, and Zoning Committee of the American Bar Association.

Edward Thompson, Jr., is general counsel for the American Farmland Trust. Prior to his association with AFT, Mr. Thompson served as director of the Agricultural Lands Project of the National Association of Counties Research Foundation and as Washington, D.C., counsel for the Environmental Defense Fund.

Participating Organizations

The Trust for Public Land is a national nonprofit conservation organization renowned for its innovative approaches to land protection. Since its founding in 1973, TPL has used the conservation easement and other techniques to arrange for the permanent protection of hundreds of thousands of acres of open space, ranging from thousand-acre ranches in California to inner-city vacant lots in New York City. In addition to its work with government agencies to protect land, TPL has shown more than 500 communities how to form local land trusts and protect important natural resources on their own.

The Land Trust Exchange is a national network and service center for local and regional nonprofit land conservation organizations, often called land trusts. Its sole purpose is to help the nation's nearly 600 land trusts do the best possible job of conserving land resources. The Exchange provides a variety of technical and educational materials related to voluntary land conservation, including the use of conservation easements, educates the public about the accomplishments of land trusts, and represents the interests of land trusts in public policy issues.

The Public Resource Foundation is an independent nonprofit organization dedicated to the wise use, renewal, and conservation of natural resources. The Public Resource Foundation actively engages in research and public education on issues relating to the land and its natural resources, with particular emphasis on promoting the development and use of innovative legal techniques designed to achieve balanced resources management.

The National Trust for Historic Preservation is the only national nonprofit organization dedicated to stimulating and leading public participation in preserving districts, sites, structures, and objects significant in American history and culture. The National Trust, with membership exceeding 200,000, maintains 17 museum properties and 76 easements nationwide. It also provides technical and financial assistance to qualified preservation groups, issues a variety of publications, initiates demonstration projects and model programs, and advocates preservation policies in public and private forums.

Index

ORDERING EASEMENT MATERIALS FROM THE LAND TRUST EXCHANGE

The following materials, mentioned in the handbook, are available from the Land Trust Exchange.

The Federal Tax Law of Conservation Easements, by Stephen J. Small. The most comprehensive treatment of federal tax law, regulations, and court rulings regarding conservation easements, written by a former IRS tax attorney. Cost: $39.95 plus $3.00 postage and handling.

Appraising Easements: Guidelines for the Valuation of Historic Preservation and Land Conservation Easements, by the National Trust for Historic Preservation and the Land Trust Exchange. A detailed treatment of current law and practices relating to easement appraisals. Out of print, photocopy available for $4.00 plus $1.00 postage.

Conservation Tax Program, edited by Kingsbury Browne and Stephen J. Small. This subscription service covers conservation tax developments including national legislation and policy, Tax Court rulings, IRS letter rulings, and a variety of other developments. An indispensible service for active conservation easement programs. Regular subscriptions are $250; $125 for sponsors of the Land Trust Exchange. Six-month trial subscriptions also available.

"For the Common Good: Preserving Private Lands with Conservation Easements," produced by the Land Trust Exchange. This 16-minute color documentary film provides an introduction to the easement concept through case studies in Maine, Montana, and the Chesapeake Bay region. Excellent for introducing government officials, landowners, or the general community to the easement concept. Video and film formats available for rental or purchase. Contact LTE for prices.

"Conservation Easements: Protecting Legacies Forever," by the Land Trust Exchange. This attractive four-page, four-color, 8 ½" x 11" brochure is a good promotional and educational piece for the general public or local officials. Can be used as a cover for fact sheets on easements and adapted to a variety of uses. Quantities of 1 - 50, $.10 each; 50 - 100, $.07 each.

1985-1986 National Directory of Local and Regional Land Conservation Organizations, by the Land Trust Exchange. Available at reduced price of $5.00 plus $2.00 postage and handling. Update in progress, contact the Land Trust Exchange for availability and current price.

Green Umbrella Insurance Program. Low-cost insurance available for private nonprofit land conservation organizations. Currently serves dozens of land trusts and trails organizations. Organizations must be members of the Land Trust Exchange at the $100 level to apply; membership refundable if insurance coverage is denied.

Land Trusts' Exchange, a quarterly professional journal of information about land protection law and policy, tax treatment, land protection techniques, and land trust management. Cost: $30 per year, includes membership in the Land Trust Exchange.

...p in the Land Trust Exchange is available to all interested individuals organizations. Associate memberships, which include a subscription to *Land Trusts' Exchange,* are $30 a year. Supporting Associate memberships, which include eligibility for the Green Umbrella insurance program, are $100 a year. Sponsors of the Land Trust Exchange are nonprofit land conservation organizations that contribute 1 percent of their annual land conservation operating budgets, with a minimum of $100 for organizations with budgets of less than $10,000 and a maximum of $1,000 for organizations with budgets greater than $100,000. Sponsors receive reduced rates on publications, are eligible for Green Umbrella insurance, and qualify for a variety of other benefits.

ORDER FORM

Name: _____

Organization: _____

Address: _____

_____

I/we would like to join the Land Trust Exchange (check appropriate level)

☐ Associate ($30)   ☐ Supporting Associate ($100)

☐ Sponsor (Our annual budget is _____ . Our dues (1%) are
_____ .)

We would like to order the following items (list):

Item	Qty.	Price
_____	_____	_____
_____	_____	_____
_____	_____	_____
_____	_____	_____
_____	_____	_____
_____	_____	_____
_____	_____	_____

Subtotal: _____

Add Postage and Handling: _____

TOTAL AMOUNT ENCLOSED: _____

Please send information on:
  ☐ Green Umbrella Insurance
  ☐ The Conservation Tax Program
  ☐ Sponsor Membership Benefits
  ☐ Other: _____